Becoming and Consumption

Becoming and Consumption

The Contemporary Spanish Novel

Candice L. Bosse

LEXINGTON BOOKS

A DIVISION OF
ROWMAN & LITTLEFIELD PUBLISHERS, INC.
Lanham • Boulder • New York • Toronto • Plymouth, UK

LEXINGTON BOOKS

A division of Rowman & Littlefield Publishers, Inc.
A wholly owned subsidiary of The Rowman & Littlefield Publishing Group, Inc.
4501 Forbes Boulevard, Suite 200
Lanham, MD 20706

Estover Road
Plymouth PL6 7PY
United Kingdom

Copyright © 2007 by Lexington Books

All rights reserved. No part of this publication may be reproduced,
stored in a retrieval system, or transmitted in any form or by any
means, electronic, mechanical, photocopying, recording, or otherwise,
without the prior permission of the publisher.

British Library Cataloguing in Publication Information Available

Library of Congress Cataloging-in-Publication Data

Bosse, Candice L., 1975–
  Becoming and consumption : the contemporary Spanish novel / Candice L. Bosse.
    p. cm.
  Includes bibliographical references.
  ISBN-13: 978-0-7391-1630-2 (cloth : alk. paper)
  ISBN-10: 0-7391-1630-4 (cloth : alk. paper)
  ISBN-13: 978-0-7391-1631-9 (pbk. : alk. paper)
  ISBN-10: 0-7391-1631-2 (pbk. : alk. paper)
 1. Spanish fiction—Women authors—History and criticism. 2. Spanish fiction—20th century—History and criticism. 3. Women and literature—Spain. 4. Women in literature. I. Title.
  PQ6055.B67 2007
  863'.3099287—dc22   2007009264

Printed in the United States of America

∞™ The paper used in this publication meets the minimum requirements of
American National Standard for Information Sciences—Permanence of Paper
for Printed Library Materials, ANSI/NISO Z39.48-1992.

3950
algo más que un número

Contents

Chapter 1	Introduction	1
Chapter 2	Critical Framework	23
Chapter 3	*Amor, curiosidad, prozac y dudas:* The Raver, the Cyborg, and the Housewife	67
Chapter 4	*Veo, veo:* Consumption and the Dazzling Diva of Image	115
Chapter 5	*Alivio rápido:* Traversing the Techno Terrain to the Multinational	153
Chapter 6	*Los placeres de Anastasia:* Sexing It Up!	197
Chapter 7	Interconnections	235
	Bibliography	245
	Index	253
	About the Author	257

CHAPTER ONE

Introduction

Becoming and Consumption: The Contemporary Spanish Novel is organized into six chapters that address issues of becoming—the creation of female subjectivity—across the spectrum of diverse cultures of consumption. This study takes into consideration the type of selfhood encouraged and cultivated in various spaces by way of multifarious practices and the consumption of distinct goods both tangible and abstract. In this vein, this investigation examines how commodities are appropriated and the meaning created by the protagonists through their consumption of goods; at the same time it explores how each woman effectually embodies the commodities she elects to consume. Overall, by way of the aforementioned, this research inquires about the embodiment of new types of creativity and the unveiling of spaces for the potential nourishment of female subjectivity, as well as the acknowledgement of the potential for toxic subjectivity rooted in the slippery paradox of consumption.

The novels of the contemporary Spanish women writers who are the object of study—Lucía Etxebarria, Gabriela Bustelo, Silvia Grijalba, and Susana Plané—provide a fertile ground to examine culture and identity vis-à-vis consumption practices during postmodern times as it has only been two and half decades since the fall of the Franco dictatorship. This particular corpus was chosen as the narratives illustrate dynamic and intimate relationships among cultures of consumption and female subjectivity. Their novels—pop culture genre—reflect tendencies reverberating throughout the Spanish society, and as such, the reader may potentially relate. Furthermore, this body of women writers indeed is diverse; from famous authors who have won literary prizes to emerging novelists, they vary in age from early forties to mid-twenties. Likewise, the narrative corpus does not merely reflect the center—Madrid—but also the periphery and the space of the international. Some of these female authors represent the first generation of women writers born into the regime of Francoism yet spent their formative years—that is, their youth—in transition between two opposing worlds. Their passage from one state (dictatorship) to another (democracy) infuses their writing with transnational dimensions as they portray culture and female identity as products of a globally integrated economy. The perspectives offered through the narratives may give us a measure of cultural, political, and social change in Spanish society mediated by the world of commodities. Other authors, such as Susana Plané, were born into the Information Age and raised amidst the radical and rampant changes that emerged from the political transition and mass consumerism. Consequently, her writing manifests the fundamental role technology has played in her life.

The inclusion of these four women writers is not casual or gratuitous. These particular authors were selected because they navigate and probe themes such as cultures of consumption and economies of experiences, dialoguing with the international, while questioning representations of female subjectivity within Spain.[1] The novels of Etxebarria, Bustelo, Grijalba, and Plané—albeit in distinct manners—may portray the effects and reverberations that the globalization of cultures has had on contemporary Spanish society, in particular the mode in which female subjectivity is intimately linked to consumption practices. Furthermore, these women writers, by way of the creation of their own narratives, demonstrate "the process of becoming woman" (Braidotti) buttressed by various contingencies. Their narratives illustrate the potential for agency accessible to women through economies of consumption, as via this outlet each individual is able to negotiate and articulate her subjectivity, conscious of her self-creation. The writers' novels examine the authority given to women through the popularization of cultures of consumption, as each woman has the power to present her identity as she conceives it, despite the preconceptions of Spanish society at large. This self-governance rooted in the sphere of consumption, which manifests in the various protagonists, recalls Braidotti's notion of the nomad, essential to the "process of becoming woman." Braidotti contends:

> Como una figuración de la subjetividad contemporánea, el nómade es pues una entidad posmetafísica, intensiva, múltiple, que se desenvuelve en una red de interconexiones. El/la nómade no puede reducirse a una forma lineal, teleológica, de subjetividad sino que más bien constituye el sitio de conexiones

múltiples. Está corporizado/a, y por ello es cultural; como artefacto, es un componente tecnológico de lo humano y posthumano; es un complejo dotado de capacidades múltiples para la interconectividad en el modo impersonal. El/la nómade es un *cyborg* de Haraway, pero que cuenta además con un inconsciente. Es lo "mucoso" o "divino" de Irigary, pero dotado de perspectiva multicultural. Es abstracto/a y perfecta, operativamente real. (*Sujetos nómades* 78)

In light of this, I analyze the novels of these contemporary Spanish women authors focusing on the various cultures of consumption—drugs, music, fashion, sex, dancing, pornography, the Internet, and technology—that each protagonist embraces and also explore the resulting embodiment of the feminist subject.

Within Spain this investigation is of particular significance as evidenced in a recent worldwide survey of social values and changes undertaken by Ronald Inglehart.[2] According to the results of the research, Inglehart affirms:

> Ni previsibles ni caóticos, pero sí "muy fuertes." Así definen los científicos sociales los cambios políticos y de mentalidad producidos en España en los últimos años del siglo pasado y primeros del actual. En ningún otro país las diferencias y cortes generacionales fueron tan radicales en materias como la religión o las conductas sexuales. . . . La encuesta mundial de valores . . . dibuja una sociedad española secularizada y tolerante, muy por encima de la media mundial. (Bedoya, *El País* 6/30/04)

Not only does this survey signal the massive transformations, on a political level as well as a psychological one, that have occurred within the contemporary Spanish society within the last decade, but it also hints at something more profound. Implied in the results of Inglehart's study is the shift from a society steeped in materialist values, one that placed emphasis on securing basic economic needs, to one delving into postmaterialism, in which importance is bestowed to the potential freedom of election and self-expression. Inglehart's investigation contends:

> La primera conclusión del monumental informe sobre la sociedad actual es que todo resulta 'previsible' y que rara vez las cosas se vuelven 'caóticas'. Más: lo que ahora se sabe preguntándole a la gente en todo el mundo ya lo intuyeron científicos sociales como Carlos Marx (1818-1883) o Max Weber (1864-1920). Es decir, que una vez alcanzados 'niveles adecuados' de desarrollo se registra en las sociedades un paso desde los valores materialistas (que ponen el énfasis en la seguridad física y económica), hacia valores postmaterialistas que se fijan sobre todo en la libertad de elección o de expresión. (Bedoya, *El País* 6/30/04)

Taking into consideration the conclusions of Inglehart's research, this study looks into consumption practices from a perspective that seeks to cover an array of issues such as subjectivity formation, embodiment, and the contradictory reality of both nourishing and toxic results stemming from consumption on the erection of selfhood. By way of the analysis of the literary production of contemporary Spanish women authors, this book delves into the slippery relationships that are forged between consumption and identity construction to illustrate a plethora of modes of becoming via the consumption of tangible and intangible goods.[3]

In an era of increasingly accessible and fluid borders, as well as geographical and cultural mobility, globalization in general, and global consumer culture in particular, affect and alter the everyday lives of consumers, and in so doing, reframe notions of becoming or identity construction. Globalization may be thought of as an operation (or series of operations) that embodies a transformation in the *spatial* organization of social relations and transactions, expressed in transcontinental flows and networks of activity, interaction and power (Held and McGrew, etc.).[4] In this context, globalization may be considered a chain of motions that amplifies, intensifies, and accelerates the impact of worldwide interconnectedness. The consequences of the effectuation of these processes have been significant and prolific. Global communications media, advances in technology, and the ease of global travel have reduced the costs and augmented the potential for cross-cultural connections of all kinds, concurrently boosting the use of electronic media, tourism and emigration to higher levels. The integration of global economies journeys in a state of furious activity, while the exchanges of commodities multiplies, and countries become increasingly interdependent on each other for basic, as well as luxury, commodities. The globe is in the midst of unprecedented social and cultural changes, as world trade in consumer goods has inaugurated a new phase of expansion, which does not merely translate into an exchange of goods. Rather, beneath the activity of these global economies, more profound and significant interactions are occurring, namely in the conception and construction of identity, as a result of these transformations in cultural systems.

In the 1950s and 1960s, a Western breach in political and economic ideology occurred, which unfolded in the emergence of distinct configurations of identity. This discontinuity in ideology comprises what is frequently, yet problematically, termed postmodernism. As indicated in the prefix of the concept, postmodernism subsumes and moves beyond tendencies of modernism, a century old aesthetic movement grounded in master narratives, fixed identities, and firm core values. There exists a wide range of debates as to what postmodernism is. This investigation departs from Ihab Hassan's contributions to an inquiry and elaboration of the term: indeterminacy and immanence.[5] He declares: "The play of indeterminacy and immanence is crucial to the episteme of postmodernism" (qtd. Bertens 44). The slippery notion of postmodernism, then, denotes eclecticism, hybridization, and the absence of grand narratives. Moreover, the dissolution of unilateral history has eroded due to rivaling perceptions of culture and tradition. These expressions of difference reflected in the mutation of culture are illustrated by way of the re-contextualization and hybridization of styles. Concurrently, distinctions between high and low culture have conflated, resulting in innovative combinations. According to Jameson, manifest in postmodernism is the "effacement . . . of the older (essentially high-modernist) frontier between high culture and so-called mass or commercial culture, and the emergence of new kinds of texts infused with the forms, categories, and contents of that very culture industry so passionately denounced by all the dialogues of the modern" (2). As opposed to modernism, postmodernism is curious of and enchanted by forms of art that manifest in everyday life. The apotheosis of this new tendency was to erase the difference between the realm of fine arts and the commercial arts. From Andy Warhol to *Reader's Digest* to the genre of kitsch: "materials they no longer simply 'quote', as a Joyce or a Mahler might have done, but incorporate in their very substance" (3).

The shift in courses that appeared in the middle of the twentieth century, indeed, made itself visible with respect to aesthetics. Nevertheless, this transformation in cultural processes (as manifest in art) should be considered a reflection of the movements occurring within the economic and political scope. During the decade of the 1950s, numerous changes were set into motion by the arrival of "postindustrial society" (Daniel Bell), a term making reference to a society of consumerism, constantly in evolution due to advancements in technological media. The structure of the "postindustrial society," its political ideologies and economic motives, was not in accord with traditional capitalism. As Jameson contends, "the new social formation in question no longer obeys the laws of classical capitalism, namely, the primacy of industrial production and the omnipresence of class struggle" (3). Whereas the Marxist model of capitalism centered on the production and struggle of the subject, the ideologies and practices of "postindustrial" society ruptured and rendered void his unilateral focus on capitalism. Marx pondered the system of traditional capitalism, deconstructing its components to demonstrate the manner in which the exchange of goods evolved throughout history. His analysis elaborated upon transformations that have transpired within the past centuries, the overall focus being the transition from a symbiotic barter system to capitalism. His investigation highlights that within capitalism the production of commodity is primordial. Moreover, he argued this system exploits the subject and renders the laborer raw material, as the profit gained in capitalism is value supplied by the worker, yet not remunerated.

Perhaps anticipating the emergence of globalization and a multinational economy, Ernest Mandel in *Late Capitalism*, centers on economic developments that have made possible the acceleration in accumulation. In specific, he elaborates upon the reduction of turnover time of fixed capital, the increase in the rate of surplus value, the entry of capital into service and circulation industries, and economic programming so as "to bridge over, at least partially, the contradiction between the anarchy of capitalist production inherent in the private ownership of the means of production and the growing objective pressure to plan amortization and investments" (231). Hence, late capitalism points toward universal industrialization that saturates multitudinal aspects of daily life. According to Mandel: "for the first time in history, mechanization, standardization, overspecialization and parcellization of labor which in the past determined only the realm of commodity production in actual industry, now penetrate into all sectors of social life" (387). The proliferation and absorption of industrial diversity, and hence, competition placed emphasis on the creation of manners in which to sustain and augment capital. Expounding on an apropos circumstance to elucidate the centrality of capitalism in everyday existence, he states: "The 'profitability' of universities, music academies and museums starts to be calculated in the same way as that of brick works or screw factories" (387). According to Mandel, the "long-term protection and expanded reproduction" (231) of capital was facilitated through finance capital, a liquid medium that represents wealth. The creation of money through credit stood out as an important stable source of value that induced additional production, demand, and surplus value. As Mandel states, the accessibility and growth of credit potentially may incite economic flourishing "up to the point beyond which it risks jeopardizing the share of the world market controlled by the country in question" (455). Moreover, the "long-term diminution of the industrial reserve army, which was the corollary of the substantial growth in the accumulation of capital, enabled the working class periodically to chip away at the rate of surplus-value somewhat" (457). Thus, the spread of capital sustained and empowered by credit forged new relationships among countries due to the ever-expanding world market economy. This notion recalls Jameson's theory; he contends postmodernity and globalization are interwoven by the rise and expansion of capitalism. That is, shifts in cultural aesthetics as well as its commodification did not occur in a vacuum. Rather, these changes are steeped in profound alterations within the economic and political systems. While production remains an important aspect to late capitalism, its primary focus shifts to consumption. Likewise, the spatial dissemination of the capitalist system permits a conjoining among the global and local through consumption. The assimilation of the global into the local may further provide for the production of innovative expression (identity, art, politics, etc.), hybridization, and new cultures.

The proliferation of globalization has created profound cultural, economic, and political changes, transpiring from the level of the individual to the collectivity; engagement and identity are articulated through various economies of consumption. Of particular significance is the inquiry into links, via the effects of globalization, which compose identity and create various cultures. These cultures or groups are based not upon traditional criteria of geographical or political borders and bloodline, but rather are "imagined communities" (Anderson) formed and constituted by the consumption of a similar good or experience. It would be insightful and revealing to investigate the manner in which these dynamics have altered the conception of identity in countries around the globe. This investigation, however, centers on the particular case of Spain, a fruitful locus to embark upon this quest considering the vast and radical changes that have materialized in the past three decades on a myriad of planes. The power and dynamism of the institutions that previously served to mobilize collective power and identity—Franco's ideology and Catholic doctrines—deteriorated with the gradual absorption of consumerism into Spanish society. Following the collapse of Franco's dictatorship, capitalism indeed has become more pervasive in Spain, consumption has risen, and individual and social identity have been questioned and subsequently transformed in accord with these changes.

The object of this study is to examine the concept of becoming or constructing identity, accomplished through an examination of how relationships between globalization, consumption and economies of experience produce new understandings and practices of culture, and as result new ways of becoming or constructing identity. Although the focus of this investigation is the relationship between consumption and female subjectivity, it must be noted that consumption and economies of experience undoubtedly configure and construct masculine identity as well. The massive global flows of people, capital products, texts, images, and signs create new premises for the concept of culture in the contemporary world. A main argument that this inquiry presents is that the concept of consumption is crucial to an understanding of culture and individual identity in global mass societies. As Twitchell affirms, after nourishing and clothing the self, "needs are cultural" (11). Therefore, consumption can be seen as a primal condition of life and a way of being in the world that stresses the emotional and sensational characteristics and social dimensions of perceiving and experiencing life; it offers new ways of imagining the self (Twitchell). His argument contends that these aspects very often are neglected in the discussion of cultural studies and globalization; however, they play a central role in the reconfiguration of culture and identity, yielding new global cultures and communities through the sensual, imaginative and virtual consumption of products, locales, and narratives. The meaning of consumable goods is in large part open to interpretation. The consumer extracts a special meaning from a specific good and assembles a montage of elements such as sounds and images to construct subjectivity. Therefore, one cannot state that a particular brand or product retains a universal meaning, as meaning is not inherent in the good itself. Rather, there exists fragmentation among the lived social realities of consumers. This acknowledgement places at the forefront the plurality of the individual and the resulting diversity in her interpretation and re-appropriation of meaning. As Frank contends:

> Consumerism is no longer about 'conformity' but about 'difference'. Advertising teaches not in the ways of puritanical self-denial (a bizarre notion on the face of it), but in the orgiastic, never ending self-fulfillment. It counsels not rigid adherence to the tastes of the herd but vigilant and constantly updated individualism. We consume not to fit in, but to prove, on the surface at least, that we are rock 'n' roll rebels, each one of us as rule breaking and hierarchy defying as our heroes of the '60s. . . . This imperative of endless difference is today the genius at the heart of American capitalism, and eternal fleeing from 'sameness' that satiates our thirst for the new with such achievements of civilization as the infinite brands of identical cola, the myriad color and irrepressible variety of the cigarette rack. (34)

As Frank posits, contemporary society defines itself not so much by what it produces, but rather the how and why of what it consumes. This tendency roots itself in the prolific globalization of various economies, which subsequently become assimilated into the local culture, yielding hybridization. By virtue of consumerism, unimagined possibilities for the assemblage and re-assemblage of identity may emanate. The consumer manufactures and constructs herself through a conjugation of tangible and abstract goods. In doing so, she not only interprets and re-appropriates meaning, but also composes subjectivity through election and individual energy. Nevertheless, as consumption remains a slippery concept rife with paradoxes, it is worth pondering if subjectivity formation through cultures of consumption may represent a new form of freedom, albeit temporally. According to Foucault (1988), society not only must select a selfhood, but also must comprise itself as a self who makes selections. Consequently, all facets of existence are examined as potential means or tools in the negotiation and fabrication of the self. That is, subject formation manifests by way of the architecture (selection and appropriation) of the individual.

Having said this, an investigation of consumption practices and how they transpire in identity formation is complex and contradictory. As explained earlier, the act of consumption is not passive, but rather involves the active negotiation and articulation of meaning in the constitution of subjectivity. It would, however, be naïve and essentialist to perceive consumption as a universally empowering experience. Indeed, consumption practices may yield contradictory realities and an unhealthy, inert selfhood. Nevertheless, these negative aspects should not be unilaterally attributed to the act of consumption, but rather the manner in which the individual assumes the good, the meaning assigned to the commodity, and how it is embodied. The premise of this investigation is that consumption is an enigmatic phenomenon that yields both nourishing and toxic subjectivities. While this theory is not necessarily neat, it does render a more profound understanding of the complexities and paradoxes of the relationship between consumption and subject formation.

In consideration of the etymology of consumption, the term *phthisis* is first recorded in the writings of Hippocrates in the fifth century B.C. Hippocrates utilized the term in order to describe a condition that was the single most common affliction among society and also the most often fatal. Hippocrates gives a very accurate clinical description of tuberculosis:

> Most of them were affected by these diseases in the following manner: fevers accompanied with rigors, of the continual type, acute, having no complete intermissions . . . constant sweats, but not diffused over the whole body; extremities very cold, and warmed with difficulty . . . sputa small, dense, concocted, but brought up rarely and with difficulty . . . they were soon wasted and became worse, having no appetite for any kind of food throughout; no thirst; most persons delirious when near death. (http://classics.mit.edu/Hippocrates/epidemics.1.i.html)

It is within the realm of possibility that Hippocrates devised the name for the disease himself, from the verb *phthinein*, to waste away (the root *phthi-* is related to the Sanskrit *ksitih-*, meaning "destruction"). Medicinal practices during the Middle Ages, indebted to Greek and Latin scholarship, employed the term *phthisis*, and later medical traditions adopted it as well. It was, until the word *tuberculosis* came in vogue in the late nineteenth century, the primary "technical" name for consumption. It should be noted that, like many ancient terms for diseases (leprosy, in particular, comes to mind), *phthisis* has, over the ages, referred to more than one modern illness. While in general, *phthisis* represented tuberculosis, it also was applied to other diseases that maintained similar traits—that is, progressive wasting diseases, particularly if they involved a cough or trouble with the respiratory tract. A significant example is that which became denominated pneumoconiosis or "black lung."

The word consumption first emerged in Latin as *consumptionem* in approximately 1398 and carried a similar meaning to that of *phthisis*: to use up or waste. In the earliest sense, the word was attributed to an evil widespread disease that was generally fatal. From its inception, the term had a negative connotation, as it was associated with a toxic disease that attacked the body system, multiplying rapidly while destroying tissues and diminishing the bodily capacity. The subject was essentially fodder for pestilence. At a later date, approximately 1535, the word "consumption" became associated with the using up of materials, such as food. Studied from this angle, consumption is sustenance, a process that supplies the body with food, drink, and other necessities of life so as to provide for and uphold the subject. In this sense, consumption results nourishing; there is an active interchange between the goods ingested and the bodily processes that results symbiotic. This investigation posits a new understanding of the term; it looks at the reciprocal relationship between the consumption of a plethora of goods and subsequent production of female subjectivity, made possible by way of the articulation and transmission of meaning. On the one hand, consumption, as in the ingestion of alimentary goods, can be nourishing. It sustains, strengthens, and promotes. On the other hand, it may also be considered toxic, having a poisoning deleterious effect. In consideration of becoming and cultures of consumption, the protagonists and their maneuverings through the consumer realm are examined through the aforementioned paradox.

As previously noted, the term consumption remains slippery and there exists a host of critics that attack and demonize consumption as well as an assemblage of those who glorify its liberating qualities. What remains clear is that the construction of identity via cultures of consumption is a proposition seemingly self-contradictory, but in reality, this intimate negotiation between subject and good (tangible or abstract) unfolds into and expresses a multiplicity of identities. For some, becoming, realized through diverse cultures of consumption, proves to be nourishing, resulting in an active subjectivity, and potentially may be liberatory. Nevertheless, for others, the outcome differs radically; through consuming the various accoutrements of a particular community, the results prove toxic and subjectivity inert. Thus, this project investigates becoming vis-à-vis the various protagonists' interactions with cultures of consumption to explore the type of subjectivity cultivated. Through the metaphoric ingesting of multifarious goods and ideas, these women elect items (tangible and abstract) and negotiate meanings, which subsequently textualize the body. The results of these processes are varied. At times the subjectivities encouraged illustrate a nourishing, molecular female subject in flux that cultivates a space of her own. On the other hand, there exist those protagonists whom, through consuming, form static subjectivities. This pernicious relationship is not the mere culpability of consumption, but rather the manner in which the protagonists interact, confect meaning, and embody the good.

In consideration of the two poles of ideology regarding consumption and identity construction, this investigation proceeds with mention of the foundations of the arguments against consumption. Two issues are of particular concern to this camp. On the one hand, the subject is considered to be a victim of the manipulative machinations of capitalism, and on the other, floating in a vacuous state bombarded by spectacle, the subject remains a passive pawn of hegemonic processes. For instance, Sklair contends that consumerism remains at the nucleus of the global capitalist project, and as such, consumers are coerced into a perpetual cycle of satisfying desires that have been indoctrinated by capitalism. Sklair believes that the project of capitalism serves to persuade society to consume abundantly:

> Not simply to satisfy their biological and other modest needs, but in response to artificially created desires in order to perpetuate the accumulation of capital for private profit, in other words to ensure that the global capitalist system goes on forever. The culture ideology of consumerism proclaims, literally, that the meaning of life is to be found in the things that we possess. To consume, therefore, is to be fully alive, and to remain fully alive we must continuously consume, discard, consume. The notions of men and women as economic or political beings are marginalized by global capitalism, quite logically, as the system does not even pretend to satisfy everyone in the economic or political spheres. Men, women, children, even pets, are consumers. The point of economic activity for ordinary members of the system is simply to provide the resources to be consumers, and the point of political activity is to ensure, usually through political inactivity, that the conditions for consuming are maintained. This system has been evolving for centuries, first for aristocracies and members of the bourgeoisie all over the world, then spreading to the working classes in the First world, and slowly but surely penetrating to all those with disposable income everywhere. (62)

This ideology stresses the power of the capitalist market engendered by conglomerations whose sole purpose is not just to sell a product, but also a mindset. This passive process of absorption and appropriation indeed manifests itself in a few of the protagonists under consideration as they buy into the seductive packaged promises of marketing. Following Sklair's line of argumentation, Stuart and Elizabeth Ewen contend that implicit to consumerism is the never-ending quest to fulfill false desires, which ultimately results in failure. They state:

> Alongside the considerable achievements of industrial development, the logic of consumption has become increasingly universal in our way of life. It is embroiled in our intimacies; tattooed in our hopes; demanding of our energies. The "constant rapidity" with which we are encouraged to tire of consumable objects, of our elusive pleasures, is generalized as an axiom for existence. To buy is to succeed. Soon, this success becomes failure. (75)

Explicit to the condemnation of consumerism, the subject as consumer is a universal victim. Controlled by the powers of capitalism, the subject continuously quests to satisfy artificial wants and needs indoctrinated by the capitalist project. The result of this line of argumentation demonstrates the toxic nature of consumption. As will be discussed in later chapters, when one veers to the point of obsession with respect to their consumption of a good, the results are annihilative. The utter passivity is injurious to the formation of an active healthy female subjectivity.

Consumption, indeed, is a profound intricate process. As such, this investigation treats the contradictory realities that emerge as consumption may be nourishing, yet it may result toxic. The other side of consumption—that of nourishment—renders an active and dynamic means for becoming or the construction of subjectivity from which arise the possibility for innovative and personal affinities with the self and the collectivity.

> Commercialism is more a mirror than a lamp. That we demonize it, that we see ourselves as helpless and innocent victims of its overpowering force, that it has become scapegoat du jour, tells far more about our eagerness to be passive in the face of complexity than about our understanding of how it does its work. . . . The material world magnetizes us and we focus much energy on our relationship with it. (Twitchell 20–21)

Consumption is a continuous negotiation, a never-ending dialogue between the consumer and the material world. Not limited to the material realm, one may also consume experiences, memories, and the gaze. Of importance is how the consumer appropriates and negotiates the item, which results in the production of meaning. As such, consumers are not necessarily passive. "Consumers are just another interpretive community. They are readers. For them, consumer goods should be considered as 'polysemous cultural resources' that can be interpreted in a variety of ways by different groups of consumers" (Twitchell 46–47). While the principle of consumerism may have origins in the nineteenth century only to garner its full momentum in the middle of the twentieth century, it is not a new concept.[6] In previous centuries meaning was generated through rigid social conventions such as the intangible concept of social caste, however, with the advent of capitalism and consumerism, the construction of identity shifted. No longer revolving around birth and family origin, it converted to revolve around our interaction with a constellation of goods—whether tangible or abstract—and how we consume and appropriate those items. Consumerism is seen as a creative activity by which we form our identities. The results, however, are paradoxical; for some, consumption proves to be cancerous, as it debilitates their ability to actively form a healthy subjectivity, and for others, the intimate interactions with the consumer realm ameliorate the possibility for the creation of multiple female subjectivities that defy essence. Storey contends that the proliferation of consumer society signals the innovative manners in which individuals negotiate and appropriate identity, rather than the power of capitalism to create and indoctrinate desire for goods. Storey affirms, "using cultural consumption to articulate multiple and mobile identities has a history . . . but this is not the same as saying that it is something that capitalist entrepreneurs have imposed on an easily manipulated body of consumers" (147–48). According to the analysis, consumers are not manipulated, but rather in some sense negotiate their participation within consumer culture.

This investigation examines becoming through the optic of diverse cultures of consumption. Invariably citizens and consumers are engaged with commodities and are shaping them for their own purposes. It is through this process that one also produces identity by way of various economies. Through cultures of consumption, one produces selfhood while concurrently aligning the self with communities or groups who share these commonalities. As will be evidenced in the discussion of the novels, whether constructing an image in opposition to consumer culture—one of militancy—or embracing it wholeheartedly through purchasing elaborate markers of upper-class status, consumption manifests on the body and creates an identity. Through consumption, an individual establishes and maintains selfhood. Much like gender, class, and ethnicity, consumables become part of identity virtually inseparable from the self. The term virtually is employed since consumption choices are fluid and dynamic; subjectivity as well as identification with particular "imagined communities" may metamorphose in accord with the individual election. In the literary production under discussion, the protagonists are active agents, cognizant of their election; nevertheless, not all form healthy active subjectivities. To an extent, commodities mark these women; however, as subjects in the creation of selfhood, they re-appropriate goods instilling them with meaning and consequently express an identity tied to those items. Consumption is complex and contradictory. This inquiry posits that consumption may be nourishing or may be toxic, but nevertheless, there occurs the transmission and reception of meaning-making in the creation of female subjectivity that denies essence and allows for a multiplicity of beings.

Chapter 2, "Critical Framework," introduces the primary themes of the study and the critical methodologies that will be employed in this investigation. The principal concept utilized as a springboard for this inquiry, posited by theorist of sexual difference Rosi Braidotti, is that of becoming: How does the nomadic feminist female subject emerge? Following theories posited by Deleuze, Braidotti foments a discussion on female subjectivity from a position of difference, emphasizing the importance of seeing woman not as other than man, which connotes a negative difference. Rather, she charges her framework with a positive energy, by rethinking and redefining woman as subject of knowledge, contradicting the epistemological struggle that has confronted women historically and defined them as a lack. Braidotti's work is the historicization and de-mystification of the supposedly organic notion of woman. She critically analyzes and deconstructs the complex layers of woman's "natural" essence, so as to open up a space of critical resistance against the ideas of the dominant economy. In the relocation of the identity of woman, Braidotti dismantles patriarchal tendencies, permitting the potential for a new social imaginary. As nomad, woman is multiple and in transition, yet retains connection with history to accept responsibility for it. As subject of knowledge with accountability, woman is empowered, devoid of essentialism, and emancipated to become multiple subjectivities.

Utilizing theories of sexual difference, patch-worked with the knowledge of significant cultural occurrences that have affected and altered the lives and identities of women in Spain, as a platform, this chapter follows to discuss theories of modern consumption and its relationship to the stabilization of socio-economic factors (Bocock). The line of inquiry, then, focuses the argument on the potential for becoming, the construction of self, through lifestyles founded in consumption practices. This chapter also elaborates upon the contradictory reality of consumption: consuming as nourishing and consuming as toxic. It does give serious thought to theorists from both camps: those who condemn consumption and negate the possibility for individual emancipation within this scope and those who potentiate the possibility for liberation via consumption choices. Within this section, the discourse focuses on contradictory elements of consumption as presented by theorists such as Marx and Baudrillard. A discussion of their respective approximations evidence differing foci, but at the nucleus, the theories reflect the subject as a passive victim. With respect to the model posited by Marx, the subject (consumer) has no option but to relegate itself to the manipulations of capitalist machine, as no escape exists. Unlike Marx, Baudrillard does not locate stridulent fault with the production aspect of capitalism, but rather the proliferation of the spectacle, which results from commodification of culture. Following his theory, the distinction between reality and fiction blurs due to the aestheticization of everyday life. Upon consideration of the approximations of Marx and Baudrillard towards capitalism (production/consumption), the discussion turns to ponder the active meaning-making process entailed among the relationship between the consumer and the good. It is a central tenet that the subject is active while electing goods, negotiating meaning, and transmitting it; nonetheless, the manner in which the protagonist embodies the good may prove to fortify an active subjectivity, or on the other hand, cannibalize the female voice. Finally, this chapter elaborates upon the theories of "imagined communities" (Anderson) and neo-tribes (Maffesoli). These groups are social configurations that emerge and crystallize as a result of participation in cultures of consumption. These dynamic conglomerations provide a space in which the individual finds affinity, if only temporal, with a community participating in a communion of shared interests that transcends geographical, ethnic, religious, and gender borders.

Chapter 3, "*Amor, curiosidad, prozac y dudas*: The Raver, the Cyborg, and the Housewife," focuses on the first novel of Lucía Etxebarria, one of the most well known contemporary female authors in Spain. This author, herself, may be considered a hybrid product influenced by globalization tendencies. While she was born in the north of Spain, Etxebarria has spent a large portion of her life in Madrid; furthermore, she has traveled extensively abroad, and was in residency at the University of Aberdeen, Scotland. The myriad of experiences and perspectives gleaned from not only her international journeys, but also her territorial relocations within Spain during a time of intense political transition reflect in her narrative via the juxtaposition of the global and the local, the interrogation of societal conventions, and the heterogeneous representation of woman. This chapter concentrates on the construction of female subjectivity through the optic of the consumption of a plethora of goods in order to examine the distinct becomings of selfhood as manifest through the three Gaena sisters. The first section of this chapter provides cultural context that details Etxebarria's personal narrative, novelistic production, and ideas and experiences regarding female subjectivity and globalization. The next three parts are dedicated to analyzing the divergent construction of subjectivity of the sisters; there is a sub-chapter that elaborates upon each: Cristina, Rosa, and Ana. The part titled "Cristina Gaena: From the Multinational to Planeta X—The Consumption and Embodiment of Counterculture" traces the trajectory of identity of the youngest of the sisters based upon her consumption of global cultural references in two distinct spatial realms: the multinational and the underground bar scene. This particular section examines contingencies of the two locales and how they play into the construction of her identity; for instance, the closed, hierarchical organization of the multinational versus the affective structure composed of music, lights, drugs, and bodies in the bar. In tracking the evolution of her identity—as evidenced by the change in proximity—it is demonstrated that Cristina contemplates new spaces for the notion of becoming by way of resisting, to an extent, the hegemonic culture and toying with this paradigm. She could be said to incarnate the third wave of feminism through her interrogation of systems, resistance to hegemonic norms, and her free agency in the formation of her subjectivity. The next section, "Rosa Gaena: Technocolonization, the Cyborg, and Emotive Harmony," anatomizes the unfolding of the middle sister, a very successful single thirty-year-old director of finance in a large multinational. Her identity is mediated by various discourses and to an extent her rhetoric exemplifies the tenets of second wave feminism by way of her search for equality in a hegemony dominated by men. It highlights the downfalls of the second wave's ideology that searched for women's equality, negating to consider the inherent differences, which is also manifest in the character of Rosa. Distinct from Cristina, a primary condition for the construction of her becoming is the world of technology and capitalism. In light of this, this section explores the type of hybrid identity—part machine and part human—cultivated in this character. The notion of cyborg, as postulated by Donna Haraway, potentially serves as a subversive configuration.[7] According to Haraway, the notion of cyborg presents a provocative hybrid:

> A creature of social reality as well as a creature of fiction. Social reality is lived social relations, our most important political construction, a world-changing fiction. The international women's movements have constructed 'women's experience', as well as uncovered or discovered this crucial collective object. This experience is a fiction and fact of the most crucial, political kind. (1991 149)

Through the melding of the mind and the machine, consciousness, intelligence, and memory become enhanced. Cyborg, then, is a figuration for one who dismantles or surpasses traditional boundaries of the dominant economy. Notwithstanding, it must be mentioned that the theory of Haraway does not account for social nor historical background and context. According to her theory, the cyborg does not possess historical memory, which she contends, releases the subject (cyborg) from the groundings of patriarchy. This, however, results problematic because the celebratory theory of new technology negates differences in historical background such as race and gender. It may be possible that Haraway's use of the cyborg metaphor permits the inclusion of all by smoothing over the issue of finding common ground among marginal groups. Taking into account theories of the cyborg, this part explores how her body as text is coded with the tenets of technology, from her thought process to clothing choice and gait. Nevertheless, in studying the process of her becoming, required is a deconstruction of the various ambiguities that layer her life and the mode in which she works through these issues. Working through her experiences leads Rosa to incorporate a part that she has neglected to allow surface: the emotional. In fleshing through memory, this character begins her quest for becoming by establishing connections with music that infuse her life with passion. As cyborg, Rosa is textualized by the politics of the multinational yet in her becoming, she elects to explore her inner self through the power of song. Freed from a unitary, orthodox subjectivity, as cyborg Rosa exhibits a fluid identity of not one or the other: she embodies a multiplicity that interrogates the patriarchy and suggests an alternative to the totalizing structure. The last part of this chapter, "Ana Gaena: Consumption and Embodiment of the Angel del hogar," follows to investigate the identity of the oldest sister, Ana, a mother and housewife. Also dissimilar from the younger sisters, she constructs her toxic identity through the consumption of high-end goods and discourse gleaned from women's magazines. Interestingly, her narrative is peppered with the mention of luxury commodities, as this realm offers her a means of integrating the conflicting demands of her life, and indeed offers her a temporal resolution; however, she does create an unhealthy subjectivity. While her identity has been buttressed by the tenets of the hegemony, through contemplation of her selfhood and a working through of her experiences, Ana as a nomad traverses a series of realizations that yield in a becoming centered not on societal prescriptions, yet inner desires. While the three sisters illustrate dissimilar representations of femininity in contemporary Spain, the commonality among them manifests through their desire to interrogate prevalent gender roles and supposedly organic identities. Radicalizing the concept of difference, the

Gaenas commit to transgressive thinking which is evidenced in their nomadic wanderings and their respective becomings.

Chapter Four, "*Veo, veo*: Consumption and the Dazzling Diva of Image" (1996), treats concepts like globalization, identity, and consumption which have been interwoven into the life of Bustelo from a young age. This attributes itself to the fact that her family moved from Madrid to reside in Washington, D.C., in the later half of the 1960s; the family returned to Madrid shortly before the fall of the Franco regime. These international experiences compounded by the clashing political and social lived realities may have served to endow Bustelo with a keen perspective on female subjectivity within the various spaces and render her a composite. The object of this chapter is to deconstruct the various intrigues that conjoin to articulate the identity of the protagonist, Vania Barcia; at the same time, it will illustrate the manner in which she performs female identity through her consumption practices, negotiating a subjectivity that yields libidinal returns. Similar to Chapter One, this chapter initiates with a cultural context that elaborates upon the life of Gabriela Bustelo, detailing how her international experiences have affected the narrative under discussion. Likewise, there are personal reflections from the author, obtained during personal interviews, expounding upon her perspectives of consumption and its relationship to female subjectivity. Chapter Two is divided into five parts; following the "Cultural Context," the part titled "Madonna Reincarnate: A New Look, a New You" presents a discussion of the consumption of fashion, and the mode in which it textualizes the body of Vania as well as articulates her identity. Through her chameleon-like approach to body dressing, the protagonist fabricates her self as a hybrid, sporting a variety of fashions; however, all of the elections incarnate strongly sexually charged images. In this manner, Vania toys with gender conventions and the performance of female identity through the game of seeing and being seen. The second part, titled "Music, Dance, Drugs, and Female Subjectivity," affords a discussion on the libidinal return stemming from the creation of female subjectivity via the consumption of the assemblage of the club: music, lights, drugs, and material goods. The argument underlines the empowerment experienced by Vania to pursue a distinct lifestyle and develop an autonomous sense of self in the underground world of the *movida* nightlife. This is significant because in this world—a social space typically associated with amorous or even sexual overtures—she does not place extravagant attention on male spectators, rather lavishes focus on herself assisted by the world of consumer goods. Furthermore, her nomadic experiences within this territory deconstruct the notion of a unified subject, opening the possibility for the unbinding of the definition of female identity. The fourth section titled "Now You See Me, Now You Don't! Re-appropriation of the Gaze" explores the consumption of a central motif in the novel: the gaze and the power it endows. As elaborated upon in the previous section, Vania parodies conventional female stereotypes as she is the diva of the image and embraces at will a multiplicity of identities that negate the concept of a unified subject. The fluidity and playing with identity is expounded upon as it relates to the crafting of her selfhood and the gaze. Through the sexually charged image she creates, she is cognizant of the power she exerts over the male gaze, mocking the pathetic behavior of the men who gawk. Hence, this section delves into the pleasure Vania receives from the re-appropriation of the gaze intimately linked to displaying herself and interacting with the consumer realm. The final portion, "Conclusions," expounds upon the becoming of Vania; her nomadic departures stem from the creation of her own designs and grammar on subjectivity, which deviate from the conventions dictated by the masculine economy. Furthermore, it affirms that while Vania's life is not free from the constraints of the hegemonic system, she embodies innovative molds and exposes spaces for a libidinal return on female subjectivity.

Chapter 5, "*Alivio rápido*: Traversing the Techno Terrain to the Multinational" explores the first novel of Silvia Grijalba. Akin to the other authors under discussion, Grijalba's life has been mediated by global tendencies and cultures of consumption. As a music journalist for *El Mundo*, she has had the opportunity to travel internationally and report upon various types of music festivals: techno, rock, and beyond. Grijalba, herself, may represent the concept of a cyborg through the manifestation of the multitudinal contingencies of her identity: novelist, poet, journalist, bar owner, and electronic musician. She embodies a hybrid product of cultural negotiations as she has traversed the musical landscape participating both directly and indirectly, evident in the intrigues of the work under discussion. Resulting from her personal narrative, she has intimate knowledge of the types of female subjectivity cultivated in the sonic terrain. The principal objective of this chapter is to elaborate upon the type of female selfhood encouraged in the protagonist, Alba, within the techno realm; at the same time, it considers diverse experiences that lead to nomadic wanderings and the cultivation of her subjectivity within a new locale: the public relations industry. Consuming the accoutrements of the techno scene—in particular her boyfriend, the lead singer—proved to be not only calamitous but crippling to her subject formation. Following the "Cultural Context" is a section titled "Traversing the Techno Terrain: Music, Ritual, and Commodification," a discussion that elaborates upon the birth and history of techno music, a genre with roots in a counter-culture, anti-establishment thought process. An eternally transforming music style, techno is both innovative and progressive, and similar to other musical genres such as rock, has become commodified. This is taken into consideration as this section discusses the band *Asian Vibes*, in which Alba is a member and her boyfriend, Fernando, the much deified lead singer. As such, it discusses the role of celebrity and fan and their resulting commodification in popular culture. This discussion establishes the foundation for the consideration of female subjectivity in the terrain of techno, which is elaborated upon in "Proxemics of Techno and Portraits of Female Subjectivity." This part describes two distinct female becomings and resulting embodiments in the techno scene: that of Alba and that of her mother. Among a plethora of other elements, what Alba consumes most—albeit in a static mode—is the image and the celebrity of her boyfriend, Fernando. The argument turns to deconstruct the type of subjectivity encouraged via the consumption of the techno landscape as well as her unhealthy consumption of the spectacle of Fernando. These experiences are then contrasted with those of her mother, Sofia, a hippy who experiences this space in a nourishing manner. For Sofia, it represents a rebirth and is a territory that lends libidinal returns to the construction of female subjectivity. The following section, "Nomadic Journey of Alba to Active Subjectivity," analyzes the transformation in the consumption habits of the protagonist that emerge due to the unforeseen imprisonment of her boyfriend, Fernando. Setting off on a quest that leads her through diverse spaces and happenings—the band is defunct and she is employed full time at a public relations firm—Alba works through experiences to arise to a heightened awareness of self exhibiting the nomadic subject. No longer passively consuming the spectacle of Fernando, she reconstructs herself according to her desires, conscious of her body as a commodity. One also notes a change from toxic to nourishing subject formation, contingent upon the dynamics of space. The final section, "Conclusions," reiterates the manner in which the nomadic journey of Alba resulted as a fleshing through of her experiences and working with this knowledge to actively form her subjectivity not in accord with prescription, but rather the recognition of her desires.

Chapter 6, "*Los placeres de Anastasia*: Sexing It Up!" delves into the biographical novel (2004) of Anna García. This particular chapter discusses the self-admitted sexual pleasures of the protagonist and her consumption of sex by way of her maneuverings, from ménage à trois to sex phone girl to famous porn star in Spain. While the construction of her subjectivity has the potential to be toxic, Anastasia experiences her sexuality as liberating. She is conscious of her body as a commodity for the voyeuristic pleasure of others, yet she accesses power and agency from this knowledge, and consequently within her chosen spaces, the protagonist forms a nourishing subjectivity that borders on liberatory.

The final chapter of this investigation is "Interconnections," which serves to draw parallels and underline contrasts among the novels under discussion. It aims to engage in a discussion regarding the multiplicity of female subjectivity through the convergence of the various cultures of consumption. This chapter draws together the diverging representations of woman as portrayed by Etxebarria, Bustelo, Grijalba, and Plané to underline the multifarious modes in which these women negotiate meaning by way of consuming goods that serve as articulation points of their identity. In sum, the results of the act of consumption are not clear-cut; they may be nourishing and function as a means for the active formation of self, or on the other hand, through consuming, the result remains a venomous and inert subjectivity. What does remain clear, however, is through spaces of contemplation, these women are agents that enact change, and for some, this may yield liberatory potential for female subjectivity stemming from autonomous self-creation. The chapter concludes by drawing connections between events of present-day Spanish reality and the novelistic production to suggest that the conjugation of these outlets potentially serve to destabilize and redefine the concept of Woman.

Notes

1. The novels of mainstream authors such as Rosa Montero and Almudena Grandes bear similarity to the novels under discussion as this corpus of female writers interrogate the representation of female subjectivity within Spain.

2. Ronald Inglehart, professor of political science at the University of Michigan, spearheaded a survey of eighty-one countries, interviewing 200,000 people between 1999–2001 with the purpose of measuring and comparing social values.

3. It is important to reiterate that the practice of identity formation vis-à-vis consumption choices is not exclusive to women. The contemporary Spanish writer Ray Loriga's novel *Héroes* (1993) evidences the relationship among cultures of consumption and masculine subjectivity. Moreover, there have been numerous studies that have treated male consumption and identity formation such as the article written by Gregson and Crewe, "Beyond the High Street and the Mall: Car Boot Fairs and the New Geographies of Consumption in the 1990s." Furthermore, as evidenced by Stella's article, "'Rebels without a cause': Male Youth in Italy around 1960," there has existed and continues to manifest an intimate relationship between consumption practices for both genders in the formation of becoming, or identity construction.

4. According to the theories of Held, McGrew, et al., globalization illustrates four stages of evolution. It involves an expansion of social, political and economic activities that traverse political and economic frontiers worldwide. Moreover, globalization

identifies with intensification evidenced through the interconnectedness and fluxes of trade, investment, migration, culture, etc. In addition, globalization may be intimately tied to the acceleration of worldwide interactions and processes, as the development of worldwide systems of transport and communication augments the velocity of the dissemination of ideas, goods, information, capital and people. And, furthermore, the growing intensity and rapidity of global interactions may hint at their significant influence and impact such that the effects of distant affairs may have profound meaning elsewhere, and likewise, specific local developments may yield global consequences. In this vein, the boundaries between local and global become fluid.

5. Hassan defines immanence as "the capacity of mind to generalize itself in the world, to act upon both self and world, and so to become more and more, immediately, its own environment" (qtd. Bertens 44).

6. Consumption played an integral role in the structure and dynamics of the Roman Catholic Church exemplified by the bacchanalian profusions of the carnivalistic rituals such as Mardi Gras and Lent. The cycle was initiated by the consumption of goods, a celebration of indulgence, and then stringent denial followed. Paradoxically, the community still consumed, if not of material goods then rhetoric and discourse.

7. Donna Haraway is considered to be one of the proponents of cyberfeminist theory, followed by theorists such as Anne Balsamo and Chela Sandoval.

CHAPTER TWO

Critical Framework

Overview

This chapter is dedicated to the exploration of key theories fundamental to the analysis of the literature under discussion as it relates to cultures of consumption and the female subject. The investigation contextualizes feminism and its struggles as well as its evolution within Spain in the twentieth century. Utilizing the discussion on feminist ideology as a foundation, this chapter proceeds to examine theories related to consumption in "Cultures of Consumption and the Female Subject." This section elaborates upon the divergent understandings of the term "consumption" and then works to locate consumption with the rise of mass consumer society since the 1950s through the optic of international conditions as well as those local to Spain. It critically analyzes the factors specific to Spanish society that aided the emergence of consumerism in Spain in the 1960s, and expands on the transformations in the relationship between female identity and consumption in Spain within the last fifty years. The last section of this chapter deals with "Cultures of Consumption: Imagined Communities and Neo-Tribes" which are collectivities—assembled and reassembled—by virtue of a desire to consume a like good. These "imagined communities" (Anderson) or neo-tribes (Maffesoli), which exist as fluid markers of identity, have emerged in the era of postmodernity through the globalization of cultures and economies and the progress of consumer capitalism. The patchworking and interweaving of the aforementioned theories establish a foundation for the analysis of the work of Lucía Etxebarria, Gabriela Bustelo, Silvia Grijalba, and Susana Plané.

Emergent Modes of Femininity

Feminism is the ideology of women's liberation that deems intrinsic in all its approaches the notion that women suffer injustice due to their sex. Under this broad umbrella, various feminisms offer differing analyses of the agents or causes of female oppression. Nevertheless, feminism is a sphere of beliefs, the nucleus of which is that women are oppressed and action must be taken to rectify their condition.

First wave feminism searched to include women in "humanity"; second wave feminism stressed the sexual difference of women, rejecting the notion of a general humanity. Third wave feminism looks at how the difference between men and women is constructed and also performed. Sexual difference can also be deconstructed. The supposed binary opposition between the masculine and the feminine relies upon a priori knowledge as well as an oppressive system of values. Third wave feminists, such as Donna Haraway and Rosi Braidotti, reject the binary model; they posit there are not two sexes but rather a series of sexual identifications and performances and there is no natural sex underlying our gender. Hence we only think we have a natural and precultural sexuality because of gender. Instead of the sex/gender distinction or the assertion of a common humanity, third wave feminism stresses polymorphous and groundless difference; that is, not a difference between men and women, but an unending and unstable difference that is common in postmodern writing.[1] Works of postmodernity, for example, refuse any notion of a natural humanity or a natural sexuality, opting for the argument that sex is textual; it is always in production and up for interpretation and questioning.

Third wave feminists rethink alterity as the fundamental goal of feminist theory and politics. The Italian philosopher Rosi Braidotti, among others, seeks through dissimilar ways, to radicalize and complicate the notion of difference, particularly sexual difference. In the 1970s, through the writings of Hélène Cixous, Luce Irigaray, and Julia Kristeva, sexual difference theory garnered attention. Collectively their works inspired radical change in feminist thought through their careful and insightful consideration of the workings and mechanics of language in their shaping and formation of our notions of masculine and feminine.

Third wave feminist Rosi Braidotti, in *Patterns of Dissonance*, grapples with the slippery history of the Enlightenment regime of "knowledge" and "truth" and the subsequent limits imposed upon human subjectivity from the reification of this paradigm.[2] The purpose of her analysis is to question the possibility of existence of the female subject within the masculine libidinal economic order as established in accord with the tenets of the Enlightenment. Braidotti initiates her analysis with the aforementioned period, an era in which man was associated with reason; she continues with Freud and Lacan's psychoanalytic theories and closes with a study of postmodernity. In fleshing out the various theories, she historicizes the specific relationship between the masculine, logic and rationality, revealing that Western society is both implicitly and explicitly overtly masculine. In the same vein, she demonstrates cogently that the feminine has unequivocally been associated with passive, irrational, and hysterical qualities (*Nomadic Subjects* 139). Braidotti affirms that women's historical heritage has been rooted in the practice of patriarchy; a practice that coincides with the production of a libidinal and material economy whereby the law is upheld by a phallic symbol that operates through the construction of supposed natural differences and the hierarchical organization of these differences. This results in the establishment of a binary opposition that Braidotti calls one/other (213). Through this dualistic, black-white ideology, patriarchal systems have equated woman with nature and the body, a force that must be tamed, bound, and secured. This dominant ideology furthermore produces a stigmatization of woman that renders her a foreigner, not one but always the other: "the borderline image, pointing to the outside of the cultural and symbolic order" (213). The masculine economy imagines woman as an absence or a lack. As such, the symbolic order is predicated on the sovereignty of the phallus and the absence of the feminine except as an object of male desire. This practice has operated and continues to operate through the construction of differences and the resulting hierarchy of these "asymmetries."

Braidotti's first objective is to enunciate the problematic questions that surround the structure of feminine subjectivity so as to challenge the dualism that traditional theories posit: the masculine as subject and the feminine as other (or other than).[3] This theorist challenges the political project of the Enlightenment—a project founded on equality and freedom for all—particularly objecting its essentialist, rationalist and humanist underpinnings.

The challenge that Braidotti presents is to rethink the idea of woman— only possible through the abandonment of the former regime—so as to (re)present Woman unbound and in flux. Within the masculine libidinal economy, the woman can only be other; she is the binary opposition of all that embodies man. In rethinking the subjectivity of woman, Braidotti, elaborating upon some of the major themes of Luce Irigaray's *This Sex Which is*

Not One, postulates the status of woman is transitory and fluid; it is identity in flux. In her essay "The Politics of Ontological Difference" (1989), Braidotti deals with the identity of woman, stressing that it is in a state of "becoming" instead of "being." She utilizes the word "becoming" so as to emphasize that identity and subjectivity must occur in a tense that is different from the both the past and the present manners of thinking.

> I would like us to adopt a special mode of thinking, trying to leave behind the centuries-old habit that consists of thinking in terms of identity and oppositions, thesis and antithesis. Let us think differently about this, in a mode that I would call, following Irigaray, the conditional present.
>
> If you look back to the early feminist theory of the 1960s and 1970s you could say that it is written in the simple future tense, expressing a deep sense of determination, of certainty about the course of history and the irresistible emancipation of women. The future is the mode of expressing an open-ended game of possibilities: half prophecy and half utopia and, above all, blueprint for action. The conditional mode, however, goes beyond the logic of ideology and of teleological progress. More akin to dreamtime, it is the tense of open potentiality and consequently of desire in the sense of a web of interconnected conditions of possibility. The conditional present posits the continuity of desire as the only unifying agent between self and other, subject and history. Desire determines the ontological plane on which the subject defines her-/him-self. Therefore the conditional is the mode of inscription of desire into the present, in the here and now of our speaking stance. (103)

Borrowing from Irigaray, Braidotti implements her concept of the conditional mode and utilizes it to challenge our concept of the present material reality. According to Braidotti, it is from the platform of this enunciative position that women negotiate the state of becoming. She asserts that subjectivity of woman is in opposition to the false universality edified in the Enlightenment. Furthermore, her approach to identity and becoming yields a positive affirmation of women's desire to assert and enact different forms of subjectivity. In this line, Chantal Mouffe, a French feminist, signals the polemical nature of the origins of 'Truth' since the Enlightenment, equating it to "the Enlightenment project of self-foundation" (Bertens 191). Mouffe argues that the traditional categories for subjectivity, based upon the Enlightenment project, cease to function as valid measures for female representation. She affirms:

> It is precisely the *ontological* status of the central categories of the discourses of modernity, and not their content, that is at stake; that the erosion of the sta-

tus is expressed through the 'postmodern' sensibility; and that this erosion, far from being a negative phenomenon, represents an enormous amplification of the *content* and operability of the values of modernity, making it possible to ground them in foundations much more solid than those of the Enlightenment project (and its various Positivists or Hegelian-Marxist reformulations). (190)

Thus, Mouffe seems to lend support to the enunciative position posited by Braidotti. This can be realized, she contends, through the dissolution of categories, in which the figure Woman is always other (other than the masculine), which will enact a further radicalization of the possibilities for the female subject. Her theory is an emancipatory politics of difference that rejects the universality of the Enlightenment of undifferentiated human nature (190).

Since the late 1980s through the present century, a new generation of theories grounded in sexual difference has emerged in scholarly writings from Europe, Australia, and the United States, including the well-known scholar Rosi Braidotti. These theorists aim to base, as their predecessors, sexual difference as the principal concept for the embodiment of the feminine subject.[4] At the same time, these theorists seek to empty the substantive and normative concept of terms such as "female" and "woman." Consequently, the feminist subject effectively escapes the dichotomous logic that Western culture has assigned to sexed identities. Braidotti's fundamental goal is to affirm feminine and women's difference without making any generalization regarding the nature of the female body or psyche. She asserts that the best exit from the dualistic logic is to *work through* (her emphasis) it. Braidotti elaborates:

> *Working through* the network of discursive definitions of 'woman' is useful not only in what it produces as a process of deconstruction of female subjectivity but also as a process, which allows for the constitution and the legitimation of a gendered female feminist community. (200)

As such, a key component of Braidotti's theory is countermemory. She posits that countermemory is a contingent to resist assimilation into dominant modes of representing the female subject as it endows the subject with the power to recall what has been learned and utilizes this cognizance for the future.

> Feminists—or other critical intellectuals as nomadic subjects—are those who have forgotten to forget injustice and symbolic poverty: their memory is activated against the stream; they enact a rebellion of subjugated knowledges. The nomadic tense is imperfect: it is active, continuous. (25)

According to Braidotti the feminist subject must begin by questioning existing definitions and representations of women so as to create new images of female subjectivity. She utilizes the term "figuration" to mean "politically informed images that portray the complex interaction of levels of subjectivity" (4). Hence, a series of experiences enact a *working through* or understanding that yields a consciousness on the part of the subject and allows for becoming-woman, the nomadic feminist subject.

The figuration refers to a mode of thought that evokes or expresses ways out of the phallogocentric vision of the subject.[5] The figuration that Braidotti employs to represent the female subject is the nomad. She employs this term because it reflects the situation of the postmodern subject, in which the nomad moves across experiences, blurring boundaries. She argues that the nomad is not determined through the literal act of transplantation, but through a subversion of set conventions or working within established conditions to the advantage of the feminist subject (Braidotti). Furthermore, the nomad does not represent homelessness or necessarily displacement; in becoming-woman, the nomadic feminine subject is located. Likewise, the nomad is a figuration for the subject who "relinquished all idea, desire, or nostalgia for fixity" (23). Accordingly, the subject expresses a desire for an identity composed of shifts, without essential unity.[6] From a nomadic perspective, the political realm is a form of intervention that acts on the discursive and material registers of the subject, thus bringing together many connections. The task of redefining female subjectivity requires the *working through* of the plethora of accumulated images, concepts, and representations of Woman—female identity—such as they have been codified by masculine economy in the Western culture.

In her work *Nomadic Subject: Embodiment and Sexual Difference*, Braidotti underscores an important question for sexual difference theorists: "Can we formulate otherness, difference, without devaluing it? Can we think of the other not as other-than, but as a positively other entity?" (123). She concurs with Irigaray that woman's real difference, her radical otherness, cannot be represented within existing cultural systems: "Woman as the Other (other-than) remains in excess of or outside the phallogocentric framework" (*Speculum* 143). The feminist philosopher Alice Jardine reinforces Braidotti's theory (*Nomadic Subject: Embodiment and Sexual Difference*) affirming:

> Is there a way to think outside the patriarchally determined Same/Other, Subject/Object dichotomies diagnosed as the fact of culture by Simone de Beauvoir thirty years ago, and, in the process, still include women as a presence? In

other words, do we want to continue re-organizing the relationship of difference to sameness through dialectics of valorization, or is there a way to break down the overdetermined metaphors which continue to organize our perceptions of reality? (214)

Braidotti effectively answers Jardine's plea through her theory of sexual difference. The goal, then, is not to deny difference or attempt to achieve gender equality. In doing so, feminist theory would endorse masculine sites of power and be forced to assimilate into the dominant libidinal economy. Rather, she posits, the goal is to recover the feminine within sexual difference.

The solution proposed by Braidotti can be described as a theory of sexual difference that affirms the importance and value of the feminine while refusing to endow it with substantive content. This refusal is consistent with theories on postmodernity as it can be read as an attempt to deviate from the establishment of "universal truth." Rather, the feminine subject resists definition, cannot be limited, and embodies multiplicity and otherness, in contraposition to the identification we know as Woman. She states,

> One speaks as a woman, although the subject "woman" is not a monolithic essence defined once and for all but rather the site of multiple, complex, and potentially contradictory sets of experiences, defined by overlapping variables such as class, race, age, sexual preference, etc. (4)

In this way the feminist subject is nomadic; it is intensive, multiple, embodied, and cultural. In her radical anti-conventional position, she posits that one speaks as a woman so as to be an example for other women, forming a collective empowerment, as agents for change. In light of these theories, the ideology of feminism is not about an essence of woman, but reclaiming and regenerating the notion of Woman. The dynamic multiplicity of Woman is patently obvious in our contemporary society; all we must do is look at groups such as the Riot Grrls, predominately teenage or early twenty-something-year-old women who subscribe to punk aesthetics, to other collectivities like the girlie girls who have responded to the second wave and their anti-feminine seriousness, and as such the girlie girls "have reclaimed girl culture, which is made up of such formerly disparaged girl things as knitting, the color pink, nail polish, and fun" (Baumgardner 80) and beyond. As seen through these examples, the concept Woman is not the naturalized binary opposition to man, rather through a recuperation of masculine spaces—music, pornography, and sexual pleasure, technology—women continue to defy patriarchy and add depth and breadth to the notion of the female subject.

Feminist theory is not just a movement of critical opposition to the false universality of the subject, but it is a positive declaration of women's desire to affirm and enact different forms of subjectivity. As such, Braidotti proposes the concept of the nomad—the itinerant—that does not conform to the naturalized model: "The nomad is a transgressive identity" (35). It involves a questioning of existing definitions and a creation of new images of female subjectivity. The process of becoming-woman entails nomadic thinking that involves expressing and naming different figurations for a de-centered subjectivity.[7] Within this framework, the subject connects, circulates, and moves on. That is to say that she does not form static identifications, but is transitory by nature. The ultimate concern is not to achieve sex-specific identity, but rather the dissolution of self into multiple subjects. Hence, as Braidotti posits, the rejection of universality of knowledge in conjunction with her theory of the nomadic subject results in a redefinition of the embodied nature of Woman that manifests in dynamic, transverse ways.

In the past century, Spain has undergone drastic changes, akin to countries in the Western world, the only difference is that Spain's pace was retarded due to nearly a four decade dictatorship. These radical changes have manifest in myriad territories: the political, the economic, technology, the social, and most importantly, the notion of Woman. With few exceptions, women within the Spanish culture have been consistent victims of marginalization and subordination in diverse arenas ranging from education to marriage laws and beyond.[8] A glance at their legislation further serves to reveal the absence that Woman represented. Article 57 of the Civil Code of 1889 stated: "El marido debe proteger a la mujer y ésta obedecer al marido" (33).[9]

The twentieth century in Spain was a period of extreme contrasts for the feminist movement. With the birth of the Second Republic in Spain in 1931, "both a symptom of and response to a national political crisis which mirrored the Europe-wide crisis of the 1930s" (Graham 99), processes of change were set in motion that modified personally and politically the family unit, and above all, women and their identity. This was a time period, not only in Spain but across the Western world, confronted with clashing perspectives on life: rural versus urban, religious versus secular, static hierarchies versus organized labor. These two distinct outlooks on life—tradition versus progress—produced crises proliferating in a plethora of realms: social, economic, political, and personal spheres.[10] The notion of Woman patently exemplifies the fissures between the dueling perspectives. While women were formally politically emancipated with the inception of the 1931 Constitution, the lived social reality was quite distinct.[11] The testimony of María Martínez Sierra at the "Ateneo de Madrid" in 1931 illuminates the political advances that women had achieved: "el gobierno provisional había hecho más por la mujer en quince días que cualquier otro gobierno desde el reinado de Alfonso X" (Scanlon 263). The inauguration of the Second Republic meant tremendous advances in equality and civil rights on behalf of the woman. Nonetheless, the social reality did not exactly mirror this testimony, as the advances in title did not translate in practice. According to Riera: "Pretender que en cinco años escasos se cambiaran los valores, ideas y tradiciones de siglos era esperar lo imposible" (35). It was, however, an enormous leap as it opened up new possibilities that previously were unattainable, starting the wheels rolling for the feminist movement.[12] The Second Republic fomented an atmosphere auspicious to the advancements of feminism in Spain. While some European countries were years ahead in their feminist movements, under the direction of the Republic Spain finally opened up possibilities for women that were not plausible a decade earlier. The Second Republic, though, was short-lived as it fell in 1936 with the end of the Civil War. Unfortunately, with the end of the war and the installation of the Franco regime, women as well as women's movements faced a dark, bleak future.

> Enseñaremos a las mujeres el cuidado del hogar, porque es una pena que mueran tantos niños que son siervos de Dios y futuros soldados de España. Les enseñaremos también el arreglo de la casa y a conocer las labores artesanas y la música. Les enseñaremos este modo de ser que quería José Antonio para todos los españoles, para que así ellas, cuanto tengan hijos, formen a los pequeños en el amor de Dios y en esta manera de ser de la Falange. (Pilar Primo de Rivera qtd in Riera 39)

Pilar Primo de Rivera, in May of 1939, uttered these words to ten thousand women of la Sección Femenina at a reunion to celebrate the victory of Franco. It is curious, though not surprising, the message disseminated by the female voice of the dictatorship: a woman's domain—her space—is the home. This suffocating atmosphere markedly contrasted with the vivacious ambience of the Republic in which women's social reality was brightening with each freedom won.

The inauguration of the dictatorship in 1939 produced swift changes that affected feminine identity. Almost immediately the regime retroacted the Civil Code of 1889, an exceedingly oppressive series of articles that were archaic when first established nearly fifty years earlier. Likewise, the regime targeted the liberal politics, abhorrent in their perspective, in zones occupied by Republicans. As a result of the horrific changes, it was as if overnight women were transported back five decades. No longer could a woman seek divorce, abortion was punishable by severe penalties, and moreover, birth control was deemed illegal. Essentially Woman, her body, and her identity were at the mercy of the dictatorship. The oppressive ideology of the regime enacted laws with the explicit intent to construct the female body according to the interests of the state and the church.[13] With such regimented control and legislation over the female body, from reproduction to education, woman fulfilled the role of the binary opposite of man—a lack.[14] In light of this, it is surprising that prostitution was not legally prohibited until 1956.[15]

As one could imagine, the social reality of life in Spain was tremendously oppressed by the Franco regime. Nevertheless, during the mid-1950s the economic realities facing the Spanish government echoed in very gradual transformations in feminine identity. The economic model utilized by Franco—autarchy—resulted in the impoverishment of the majority of Spanish citizens.[16] In 1960, the country was largely rural and agricultural, staggeringly behind in development and industry.[17] Due to the severe economic depression, Franco was forced to open, albeit it gradually, the doors to foreign investment and interests.[18] These capitalist ventures produced radical transformations in the Spanish society yet these alterations would still take longer to resonate among the female population.

If the Spanish economy found itself in dire straits at the end of the 1950s, within an eight year time span, the society had transformed at an accelerated pace.[19] In only eight years numerous evolutions occurred at diverse levels of society. If less than a decade earlier indifference and apathy plagued the Spanish society (in particular the students), Spain in the decade of the 1960s was about activism: "Vivir el 68 era luchar contra Franco" (Riera 60).[20] While the state was a primary target of the activists, the Catholic Church, being an extension of the regime, was the other. The Church, however, found itself in a precarious position, as there was pressure for it to separate from the Franco regime.[21]

While this was occurring in Europe, Spain in particular, experienced instabilities in population density. This occurred on two fronts in Spain: migration from rural pueblos to larger cities as well as population shifts from poorer regions to industrialized ones. The result of these population shifts removed Spain from its predominantly rural, agricultural status propelling economic growth through its incipient industry. It is significant that with these transitions (movements from rural sectors to city living and shifts from agricultural economy to industry) Spain not only witnessed better living conditions but also became a contender in the society of consumption. For the first time, Spanish citizens were owners of television sets, took vacations, edified large shopping centers, and were recipients of massive foreign tourism (Riquer i Permanyer). These changes brought new dimensions to the collective

Spaniard identity. While on a political level, the regime sought to differentiate itself through propagandistic measure such as the slogan "Spain is different," it became obvious that the official country (established through Franco's protocol) and the real Spain (as socially lived and experienced) were extraordinarily distinct.

During this time period, prolific advances were made directly affecting Spanish women. The economy in its upward spiral was forced by sheer necessity to open its doors to female employment. As a result, Fuero del Trabajo, the ideological instrument employed by Franco to keep women out of the work force and in the home, was unable to continue with this effort.[22] While the official discourse of the regime did not coincide with these new labor opportunities, the brutal reality required that the woman work (Larumbe). Even so, there was an ingrained hostility towards the possibility of a new social order that incorporated the female subject.[23]

> Conscientes las mujeres del Estado español de que ningún ser tiene derecho a realizarse a costa de otro, y de que la falta de libertades ha supuesto su marginación de la vida social en todos los niveles, afirman que para que la mujer pueda mayoritariamente adquirir una conciencia clara de sus problemas específicos, y como ser humano, debe participar activamente en la consecución de las libertades democráticas. (Resolución de las I Jornadas por la Liberación de la Mujer, Madrid 6–8 de diciembre, 1975 qtd. in Riera 68)

With the death of Francisco Franco on November 20, 1975, dreams of liberation became a legal reality for Spaniards—and in particular women. The following time period known as the "Transition" saw the installation of democracy resulting in widespread aspirations of freedom. In this new atmosphere, finally the word sex was not taboo; no longer did women have to secretly purchase birth control. Nevertheless, this victory came with some unforeseen negative changes.[24] Interestingly, though, the economic and political instability of the country contributed directly to the rebirth and development of the feminist movement with Spain.[25] Unlike other European countries, the fight for feminism in Spain did not have the mobilization from Spanish women predecessors.

From the perspective of Lidia Falcón, a significant figure to the upstart of the movement, the feminist movement began in Spain in the year 1975. In large part this emergence was attributed to other social movements concurrently transpiring within Spain such as: "el movimiento sindical, el movimiento vicinal, el inicio del movimiento de consumidores, los movimientos ecologista, pacifista, que alcanzan su auge al comenzar la década de los 80" (Falcón 15). The feminist movement emerged as a result of diverse leftist tendencies and subversive movements manifesting in the later years of the dictatorship; similarly, it organized itself as an alternative movement "enfrentado a partidos politicos, autónomo y revolucionario" (16). It is of great significance that the United Nations declared the year of 1975 as the International Year of the Woman. This initiative had an international character as it sparked numerous campaigns, conferences, and feminist groups. The women in Spain, while still subject to the dictatorship, took advantage of the opportunity to form various feminist groups, engage in debates and collaborate on work that would be presented at an international convocation.[26]

The period ranging from 1975 to 1981 was momentous in terms of recognition and advancement of the Spanish Feminist Movement. The evolutions that transpired effectuated on an organizational level as well as an ideological plane. To begin with, the Partido Feminista (which had its origen in los Colectivos Feministas and evolved to create the PF) was legalized in December of 1979. The creation of this political party is, perhaps, the most organized expression of feminism, a minority movement within this period. On other levels, per the Constitution of 1978, women were considered the equals of men, established in articles 14, 32, and 35.1. Likewise, women were gaining ground through the passing of three reformatory laws of the Penal Code. These laws eliminated the figure and treatment of the woman as a passive victim and evil influence. The principal reform was the Estatuto de los Trabajadores that expanded maternity leave to sixteen weeks and established measures to favor equality in the treatment of women in the workforce. The other two legislative reforms that benefited the woman were the equality of rights within matrimony and the ability to own and exercise control over familiar elements such as the administration and disposition of common goods. Despite these advances, the decade of the 1980s yielded disillusionment on the part of the woman, as she was legally an equal, yet in many cases, it remained only a paper truth.

The last years of the 1980s accelerated the bewilderment of the position of female subjectivity, but at the same time this epoch provided clarity for the need for an utter reformation of values. As official feminism appeared late in Spain, as compared with its earlier presence in countries such as the United States, Great Britain, and Australia, international models served as a guide for the development and strengthening of the movement with this country (Valiente Fernández). There continues to exist different feminisms within Spain as well as internationally. The diverse groups representing the various feminisms establish their own foci, yet at the nucleus associate for the liberty and autonomy of the woman. A contemporary polemic among Spanish feminists manifests in the current debate among feminism of equality (feminismo de la igualdad o feminismo socialista) and feminism of difference (feminismo de la diferencia o feminismo radical).[27] Both branches of feminism arduously work toward consciousness raising and the establishment of laws to better social conditions on behalf of the woman. Their primary difference rests upon how each collectivity envisions emancipation.

We may bridge the concept of feminismo de la diferencia in Spain with Western feminist theory, in particular that of sexual difference. Their politics involve a complete rejection of representation under the masculine libidinal order because of the explicit binary opposition: man/woman, subject/other. That dualist model will never yield equality because the woman cannot obtain subjectivity; she is always an absence. Despite numerous manifestations and the installation of new laws, woman cannot be emancipated within the very paradigm that rejects her as a subject, relegating her to a position of alterity. In sum, feminists of difference view the politics of feminists of equality as assimilation into the male symbolic order that ultimately is a form of colonization.

Feminists of difference such as Sendon de León, within Spain as well as internationally, have tried to unveil and subsequently extinguish this logic of thought composed of a system of relationships and codes. Through uncovering the exclusion inherent in this structure, this movement seeks an alternative epistemological ideology; one which is not binary, but in the words of Sendón de León, "analógica, es decir, que refleje la realidad y no una abstracción forzada de esa realidad" (40). Woman is not comprised of a singular essence nor nature; she is multiple and dynamic and for that reason a symbolic order must be created that introduces the variable of sexual difference into all facets of life. The variable to be introduced is not gender, which is a colonization of sex, but rather sexual difference. In sum, to achieve emancipation on behalf of women, difference must be the foundation for the establishment of new paradigm based upon the plurality of Woman; only through radical revolution can occur the necessary transformations for the realization of the female subject.

Cultures of Consumption and the Female Subject

With the advent of capitalism and the widespread technologization of global economies in the 1950s, all but the poorest groups (Bocock 21) saw the emergence of mass consumption within society. With the end of mass industrialization and urbanization, there arose an augment of employment in service and professional jobs and subsequently, a decrease in the manufacturing industry. The era of mass production or "Fordism" (termed by Gramsci in 1971 due to mass car production by Henry Ford) opened up possibilities for individual production. According to Spink, these changes were the catalysis for the growth in individualism. Moreover, he contends that political alterations since the 1970s have placed a heavier emphasis on private consumption. R. Bocock attributes the birth of consumer society to stabilization in socioeconomic factors within Western countries such as the United States, Great Britain, and France. The stronger economic arena stemmed from technological progress and globalization. In accord with Bocock, with disposable economic means, after providing for basic needs, consumers became aware of luxury objects such as televisions, stereos, cars, and vacations to which they now had access—needs that are not intrinsic but cultural. Bocock also notes that groups deemed poor (due to income or socioeconomic grouping) often did possess goods and take an active part in this novel era of consumption. In his analysis of mass consumption, Bocock parallels these changes occurring in society with alterations echoing at a worldwide level. Going further, Bauman, in his investigations on postmodernity and identity, affirms that identities in postmodern situations become more fluid, floating around in a state of flux. The decline in mass industrialization countered by the augment of employment opportunities in the service and professional sectors yielded new social realities both at the individual level and the societal. This rising pattern of consumption as opposed to occupation or class stood out as the decisive factor in establishing identity.

Stemming from sweeping transformations in technologies and globalization, consumerism has moved to the forefront not only in the lives of citizens but also has altered identity construction. According to Bocock: "Since the 1950s and more particularly during the 1970s and 1980s, new kinds of groups have emerged for whom consumption plays a central role in their way of life" (27).[28] Identity is negotiated by belonging to particular "imagined communities," arrived upon by the consumption and reappropriation of accoutrements. Bocock believes that in postmodern societies, identities are in a constant state of flux; as such, individuals maneuver freely from one cultural group to another, mixing and matching what formerly were distinct categories. He affirms:

> Under modernity, popular music, jazz, country and western, reggae and classical music had relatively distinct audiences, however, under post-modernity they have become mixed. Other forms of style consciousness in clothing, cars, interior décor, television viewing, types of food—which in modernity were clearly defined as distinct patterns for specific social status groups—have become more mixed up under post-modernity. (81)

Made patent through Bocock's affirmation, there has been a transformation in the negotiation and articulation of identity rooted in cultural shifts. Ceasing to be static and principally determined at birth, social and cultural evolutions—rooted in political and economic alterations—afforded the subject the opportunity to construct a selfhood that is in accord with desire, and moreover, constantly in flux. Furthermore, studies undertaken by market research firms during the 1980s resulted in a modification in the manner of looking at consumption and by extension consumers. Instead of linking consumption patterns to socio-economic levels, market researchers began to look at these paradigms through the optic of life stages. In "The Body in Consumer Culture" Mike Featherstone argues:

> The term life-style is currently in vogue. While the term has a more restricted sociological meaning in reference to the distinctive style of life of specific status groups, within contemporary consumer culture it connotes individuality, self expression, and a stylistic self-consciousness. One's body, clothes, speech, leisure pastimes, eating and drinking preferences, home, car, choice of holidays, etc. are to be regarded as indicators of the individuality of taste and sense of style of the owner/consumer. In contrast to the designation of the 1950s as an era of grey conformism, a time of mass consumption, changes in production techniques, market segmentation and consumer demand for a wider range of products, are often regarded as making possible greater choice (the management of which becomes an art form) not only for the youth of the post 1960s generation, but increasingly for the middle aged and the elderly . . . we are moving towards a society without fixed status groups in which the adoption of styles of life (manifest in choice of clothes, leisure activities, consumer goods, bodily disposition) which are fixed to specific groups have been surpassed. (83)

While many postmodern scholars have offered analyses claiming that society cannot be categorized as a consumer culture, other authors claim that in contemporary society people seek the realization of self and the formation of identity through lifestyles founded in consumption practices; the dynamic negotiation between consumption choices and respective lifestyles delineates with precision individual and collective identity. There is a culture of consumption, or more precisely, cultures of consumption that categorize social groups. As culture fragments into multiple sectors, there do exist diverse cultures of consumption through which people participate in society and infuse their lives with meaning.

Per Lury in *Consumer Culture*, "One of the most important ways in which people relate to each other socially is through the mediation of things" (1). This declaration is of fundamental importance to the exploration of identity vis-à-vis participation in economies of consumption. Made explicit, Lury highlights the intimate and complex meanings we forge through our interaction with the material realm. The author gives the term "material culture" to the study of animate-inanimate relationships as well as to the study of things-in-use. "Material culture" is a propitious term because it implies the existence of active relationships among the material and the cultural realms. It is, moreover, helpful to consider consumption in these terms due to the etymology of the word itself. The term "consumption" emerged in the Middle Ages and meant "devouring" or "eating up." Specifically, in that time period, the word referred to diseases such as syphilis and tuberculosis. In that understanding, the subject is passive, an object to be acted upon and ravaged. Likewise, consumption is related to the eating and metabolizing of food, a definition that also renders the subject passive. However, when considered in the realm of material culture, consumption becomes a form of communication to the self and to others, through which we as consumers navigate fluidly the landscape of our identity. Consumption as utilized in consumer culture, through the optic of the material, suggests a transformation, or "the manner in which people convert things to ends of their own" (Strathern 10). Adela Cortina in *Por una ética del consumo* affirms this concept:

> El consumo es mucho más que un momento en esa cadena de la actividad económica «producción», intercambio, distribución, «consumo»; es incluso mucho más que un medio de supervivencia. Es una forma de relacionarse los seres humanos, que intercambian regalos, van juntos al cine o a un concierto. Es una forma de comunicarme a mí misma y a los demás que he triunfado en la vida y por eso llevo un Mercedes o compro la ropa en Valentino, que no he fracasado como otros. Es una forma de demostrar a los presuntuosos vecinos, colegas, conocidos que soy por lo menos igual que ellos, porque yo también me voy del viaje al Caribe. Es una forma de sentirme yo misma en la ropa que he elegido, la casa, los muebles, haciendo caso a través de ellos al consejo de Píndaro «Llega a ser la que eres». (13)

As Cortina signals consumption must be considered beyond the scope of its relationship to the economy and production. She elaborates upon its intimate significance within the daily life of individual; through consumption, we negotiate and reconfigure codes rendering the body legible to the mass. Thus, consumption responds to various motivations and social beliefs such that the act of consuming can be considered an integral part of human existence. The process of identity formation is complex and involved, engendering a navigation, confection, and transmission of codes and images to the masses. These practices serve to metamorphose and signify the body (while rendering it legible to the masses) according to individual desire.

Having elaborated upon theories of consumption and the fundamental role of cultures of consumption in the formation of subjectivity, it is important to lend space to a cautionary discussion of the complexities of this concept as well as the divisive theories regarding consumption and emancipation. To begin with, consumption and subject formation are slippery notions. Through consuming an object, experience, memory, etc., the subject appropriates the good while assigning it meaning; this interaction produces meaning and identity. As such, it is an active process. Nevertheless, it is impossible to view consumption unilaterally as an empowering experience; as will be elaborated upon later, at times consumption practices may result in contradictory realities and consequently, in an unhealthy, inert subjectivity. This, however, is not solely the culpability of consumption, but rather how the individual appropriates the good. I argue that through consumption practices, the subject appropriates a good, produces and transmits meaning; as such, it is an active and dynamic identity construction (individual and collective) process that does also have liberatory potential, not rooted in class, but rather a molecular evolution of the female subject. This is arrived upon by way of a contemplation of experiences, fleshing through of encounters, and nomadic movements of the subject manifesting in the dynamic multiplicity of female subjectivity.

There has been much critique about the existence of the liberatory potential offered by consumption practices. The attack on consumption began with Marx and his severe critique of this system, which in his opinion represented a breach in the course of history and a movement towards a profane modern world steeped in values of production, distribution, and the consumption of commodities. As quoted in Best and Kellner, Marx affirms: "A commodity appears, at first sight, a very trivial thing, and easily understood. Its analysis shows that it is, in reality, a very queer thing, abounding in metaphysical subtleties and theological niceties" (Best and Kellner 50). In his line of argumentation, Marx asserts that the commodity existed prior to the inception of capitalism; however, its meaning and role in the lives of human beings and social values did not carry the same significance. He maintains that the system of capitalism places at the forefront the glory of the economy and subsumes while manipulating all aspects of social existence.[29]

In his understanding of capitalism, Marx arrives at the conclusion that every good (including person) has a price, and in his opinion, this commodification results in the loss of personal integrity, the absence of all that is human. To a certain extent, his statement anticipates the generation of consumer society and its importance to our everyday life. However, turning the focus away from the potential symbiotic and meaningful relationship among the subject and commodity, Marx asserts that the object arrives at the complete and utter domination of the subject. Instead of analyzing the potential for meaning making and creation, Marx posited that production—the birth of objects at the expense of human labor—only served to degrade the human:

> The more the worker produces, the less he has to consume; the more values he creates, the more valueless, the more unworthy he becomes; the better formed his product, the more deformed the worker; the more civilized his object, the more barbarous becomes the worker; the mightier labour becomes, the duller becomes the worker and the more he becomes nature's bondsman." (Tucker 73)

Marx outlines a vicious cycle rooted in the efforts of the worker. He asserts that the success that a worker achieves converts the subject into a fraud, living a distorted existence. In his perspective, the work and time invested in production by the human was akin to alienation or "loss of [human] reality," the ultimate consequence being the dehumanization of man: "Man . . . no longer feels himself to be freely active in any but his animal functions . . . and in his human functions he no longer feels himself to be anything but an animal" (74).[30] Marx contends that a system buttressed by capitalism quashes the potential for creativity, imagination, and revolution. As he insightfully understood, the material realm captivates humans as evidenced through the vigorous relationship among this world and the individual as well as collectivity.

> The bourgeoisie, by the rapid improvement of all instruments of production, by the immensely facilitated means of communication, draws all, even the most barbarian nations into civilization. The cheap prices of its commodities are the heavy artillery with which it batters down all Chinese walls. . . . It compels all nations, on pain of extinction, to adopt the bourgeois mode of production; it compels them to introduce what it calls civilization into their midst, i.e. to become bourgeois themselves. In one word, it creates a world after its own image. (Marx and Engels *Communist Manifesto* 9)

According to his theories, fundamental to capitalism are the assimilation of all cultures to the Western adaptation, the erasure of tradition, and the instilling of the desire to emulate the bourgeois class. While Marx, through his intrepid endeavor, utilized this trajectory to rouse the masses against capitalism and its dynamics, as witnessed through the past century, consumption has not only increased but has become "a central register of selfhood" (Twitchell 49). His theory on the relationship between capitalism and humans stultifies a coherent reading of subjectivity and the manner in which the subject actively engages with the material realm. Upon examination of his model, this cyclical theory assumes that the individual is not free to elect, but rather eternally subjugated to the whims of the capitalist economy, and as such are mere pawns of the system. If we embrace Marx's theory, we neglect to consider the potential for individual determination and the creation of a system of communication via consumption, one highly endowed with meaning.

> The compulsion to consume is not reducible to the power of manipulation, or emulation, or conspicuous display. Consumption is not just desire-purchase-disappointment-rekindled desire. When consumption leads to the generation of meaning, as it almost always does, it is an active and creative imaginative endeavor. (Twitchell 45)

What is important, then, is to examine the concept of consumption not through the optic of oppression, as it cripples a reading of unbound individual subjectivity. Rather this explore the role of consumption—an aspect central to everyday life—through the lens of its active dynamic construction of meaning and emancipatory potential, as consumers form a community (composed of various collectivities that subscribe to distinct cultures of consumption) that continually negotiates meaning, forming and transmitting messages by way of their consumption practices. Concurrently, this activity extends into their interpretation of significations projected from the mass. "Consumers are just another interpretative community. They are readers" (47). This is of fundamental significance to consumption; through the navigation of codes, the subject confects selfhood, and subsequently transmits the code via the bodily text made legible to the masses.

Fundamental to consumption practices is the adoption, re-appropriation, and subsequent transmission of the image. The symbols one elects and how they are exacted determines what is desired and how it is used. Gottdiener remarks that this social use "lay in the symbolic meanings that could be invested in the . . . commodities, its ability to signify the status, interests, affinities" (203). According to the French philosopher Jean Baudrillard, "In the postmodern world of culture, the image becomes central" (*Simulacra and Simulation* 18). Baudrillard asserts that image dominates as the fundamental vehicle of communication in present society. This philosopher critiqued the ideas of Marx concerning the system of production and consumption in capitalist society, as he maintained that Marx's perspective did not give sufficient importance to the aspect of consumption, focusing overwhelmingly on the elements of production and labor and their effects on subjectivity. Unlike Marx, who defined the stages of society according to their modes of production, Baudrillard envisions societal transformations according to the dominant modes of representation in society. He affirms:

> The passage from the form-commodity to the form-sign, from the abstraction of the exchange of material products under the law of general equivalence to the operationalization of all exchanges under the law of the code [i.e., the semiological structure that governs all meaning, reducing value to merely utilitarian form]. With this passage to *the political economy* of the sign, it is not a matter of simple "commercial prostitution" of all values [as Marx says]. . . . It is a matter of the passage of all values to exchange-sign value, under the hegemony of the code. That is, of a structure of control and of power much more subtle and more totalitarian than that of exploitation. *For the sign is much more than a connotation of the commodity*, than a semiological supplement to exchange value. (*The Mirror of Production* 121–22)

According to Baudrillard, the referential realm of the commodity and what that entails—needs, use value, and labor—has been displaced in postmodernity by the triumph, proliferation, and all-encompassing grip of the sign. Power ceases to be centered in the commodity itself, but rather is an abstraction dependent upon "autonomous development of the sign" (Best and Kellner 100).[31] He affirms that the reality that we consume is composed of signs or images. Going beyond Marx, who stridently finds fault with the system of capitalism based upon the terms of production, Baudrillard affirms that it is impossible to critique the capitalist system without seriously considering the value of the spectacle or "sign value," profoundly imbricated in society, which plays out in the commodification of culture.

While both theorists formulate conclusions that relegate the subject as isolated victim, Baudrillard's theory has a twist. He asserts that the market has the power to instill values and needs—in the name of profit—which extend past material goods, but rather shape our social dynamics. As Baudrillard contends, everything is spectacle and reality is being purely represented via the image due to its own commodification. In this vein, he asserts that the utter saturation of the spectacle in society will ultimately lead to the demise of Western culture due to its implosion.[32] He argues:

> The masses scandalously resist this imperative of rational communication. They are given meaning: they want spectacle. No effort has been able to convert them to the seriousness of the content, nor even to the seriousness of the code. Messages are given to them, they only want some sign, they idolize the

Critical Framework 43

> play of signs and stereotypes, they idolize any content so long as it resolves itself into a spectacular sequence. (*In the Shadow of the Silent Majorities* 13)

His critical reproach of the ability of the masses to rationalize suggests a partial approximation negating the autonomy and creativity of the consumer, the very aspect of production involved in the process of consumption. At the same time, his theory posits that the consumer's desire is to emulate high society, which is not always the case as evidenced by the blossoming of subcultures throughout the globe (and will be elaborated upon later). Furthermore, his theory fails to consider how sexual difference and gender operate within the system of signs, as well as the resulting embodiment of the subject, opting instead to relegate all consumers as passive receptors in a world bombarded by the spectacle. It is undeniable that not all consumers attain liberatory potential via consumption practices; nevertheless, subjects, as consumers, are actively selecting, re-appropriating, and encoding their bodies and lives vis-à-vis what they consume and the manner in which it is embodied and transmitted.

Although the image is of fundamental importance to the study of consumption, one must critically examine consumption as an aspect central to the life of both the individual and society and consider the type of relationships created via one's autonomous interaction with consumables (material or abstract). This paves the way for an exploration of the manner in which the subject negotiates meaning by way of her appropriation of the object and resulting embodiment. Concurrently, it examines the liberatory potential for subjectivity stemming from autonomous self-creation vis-à-vis consumption practices, while acknowledging the unhealthy subjectivities produced as well. As Twitchell contends, "The process of consumption, therefore, is creative and even emancipating. In an open market we consume the real and the imaginary meanings, fusing objects, symbols, and images together ... the object of self-realization via consumption is no longer preordained by class but results from a never-ending shifting of individual choice" (47). As Twitchell elaborates, through consumption practices the subject, according to desire, may confect identity that is not in accord with class, rather stems from dynamic individual decisions. His argument arrives at this conclusion through the following assertions: "Humans are consumers by nature. We are tool users because we like to use what tool using can produce. In other words, tools are not the ends but the means. . . . Consumers are rational. . . . They are often fully aware that they are more interested in consuming aura than objects" (22). As such, the subject does not consume simply for the act of consuming. Rather, it is an intricate process whereby consumable are tools;

they are signs that speak to the self and the mass, result in selfhood, and the formation of groups that share like affinities. These concepts lead him to probe the dynamics of the role of the consumer within commodity culture; he interrogates and debunks the notion of consumer as passive, while (drawing attention to and) reconsidering the connection that exists among consumption and production, "for they are more alike than separate, and occur not at different times and places but simultaneously" (22–23).

Today's society is one in which both production and consumption are important in the dynamics of culture of consumption. While consumption is a global phenomenon, it appears that the dominant culture of consumption roots itself in goods exported from the United States.[33] Nevertheless, there exist many sub-cultures of consumption that differentiate the globalized population. Postmodern consumption involves consumers who are producers in constructing selves, self-images, and meaningful experiences; Cortina argues, "En la sociedad a la que se ha dado en llamar «posmoderna», a falta de nombre más creativo, se difuminan las identidades fijas, establecidas por el nacimiento, la clase, la etnia o el sexo, y una de las formas de crearse la propia identidad es el lugar en el que se compra" (92). Cortina argues that in postmodernity, the identity of the subject is freed from diverse constraints that existed in the past such as social class, ethnicity, and birth. Due to the shifts in cultural systems, identities de-stabilized and became constructed via the outlet of consumption. This act, then, can be an exercise of individual liberty; by consuming, we construct and reconstruct, according to our pleasures, subjectivity. In our postmodern world of consumption, undeniably image is at the forefront. In this line, goods and services that lie at the heart of the material realm cease to be directly linked to use-value, but rather these objects-in-use convert to symbols or signs. People respond to these goods not purely based on their use-value, but rather their symbolic possibilities. "Beyond social positions, the consumption of goods as images constitutes a process of *representational positioning*" (Gottdiener 19). Gottdiener succinctly asserts that consumption practices yield representation or identity construction. We may signify ourselves through how we appear to be, who we emulate from mass culture (Ewen), and culture itself is now about image (Kellner). But not just image in and of itself; we meaningfully consume and produce our selves through our appropriation of goods. The process, indeed, is not the terminus. Similarly Gottdiener professes, "Consumption practices have increasingly become the domain within which people explore and define their own identities" (22). Spaces with which one associates become potential contingencies for the fabrication of selfhood. Moreover, he asserts that spaces of consumption are articulation points of individual psychology, social pressures, the media, fashion, and the realization of belonging. Hence the pursuit of distinctive lifestyles through consumption may represent a means of developing a sense of self and of actualizing identity politics. I view this as consistent with Rosi Braidotti's desire to create positive categories. Through autonomous self-creation and pursuit of distinct lifestyles, one could also seek a more positive, multi-faceted identity.

While these theories are building blocks for a solid foundation on consumption, they neglect to consider the affectual bodily text. In other words, while goods possess a sign value (Baudrillard), the consumption of these objects can be a mode of self-expression embodied on the textual subject that is contingent upon the nomadic becoming-woman. As mentioned previously, the act of consumption must not simply be understood as "devouring" or "metabolizing." Rather, I suggest a shift in the understanding of consumption that entails a re-examination of the active female role within the realm of consumption. As Rachel Bowlby argues, with globalization of cultures, mass media, advances in technology, and access to consumption: "Consumption . . . has offered women new areas of authority and expertise, new sources of income, a new sense of consumer right; and one of the consequences of these developments has been a heightened awareness of entitlement outside the sphere of consumption" (16). From this point of view, Bowlby understands the realm of consumption in two dimensions: as a space in which to negotiate and resist the passive absent feminine identity, as assigned through sex roles, and furthermore as the ongoing process of the creation of identity that embodies the nomadic subject. With respect to cultures of consumption, these aforementioned analyses provide a basis for becoming-woman or the feminist subject as these cultures afford women a libidinal return on their investment that is often experienced as liberating, and one which, I argue, can be seen as positive in feminist terms.

The study of consumption contextualized with feminism is of particular significance in contemporary Spanish society, as not even three decades have eclipsed since the fall of Francisco Franco's regime and the subsequent installation of democracy. During the dictatorship, there were varying degrees of control over all aspects of life that immobilized free expression of self. The last fifteen years of the regime, 1960 to 1975, stand in stark contrast to the previous twenty; in a decade and a half the country of Spain massively transformed from a predominantly agricultural economy to one that could be considered developed and capitalist. Borja de Riquer i Permanyer argues: "Spain went from being a backward agrarian country on the periphery of international capitalism, to one which could be considered fully industrialized, with a strong service sector, fully integrated into the global economic system"

(259). Within a short period, the economic and political dynamics of this country radically transformed. These adaptations, not always necessarily rooted in Franco's policies, emerged as a result of internal and external tensions. Internationally, the economy of the Western world was experiencing unparalleled growth while within the country, this only added to the growing tensions which stemmed from the collective desire to emerge from the autarkic isolation (Riquer i Permanyer).

Due to alterations in Spanish foreign trade policy, new products, and ideas, people entered the country, which inevitably had an impact. The Spanish economy experienced tremendous success along with capitalist growth. After decades of isolation Spain imported "machinery, technology, raw materials, and energy resources on a massive scale" (260). If this were not already astonishing, the country was also able to fund their foreign interests through currency obtained from tourism.

The result of these economic transformations is significant. Household income increased significantly as did production.[34] Another dimension of the overwhelming economic success manifests in the redistribution of the working population within Spain. As the country shifted gears from a primarily agrarian economy to industry, the number of people working on land dropped drastically. Along with this shift, Spain saw parallel deviations in the population centers. This transfer in physical position from the external, rural zones to urban locales is significant as it portended a new social reality. As a result of these transformations, metropolitan centers such as Madrid and Barcelona experienced rapid growth and expansion.[35]

The transformations experienced in Spain from 1960 to 1975 were of significance in terms of number and quality. As stated previously, within this decade and a half in Spain, the country experienced drastic economic changes that reverberated throughout other spheres of daily living. As employment in the agrarian sector dwindled and opportunities soared in the industrial sector, a new urban accommodated class emerged. The rise of this privileged class was intimately connected to the newly established interests in banking, tourism, construction, and foreign capital. "The greatest fortunes made in these years were amassed by figures such as Areces, with El Corte Inglés; Koplowitz, with Construcciones y Contratas; Banús, with Puerto Banús on the Costa del Sol; Barrié de la Maza, with Fenosa; Meliá, with hotels; Barreiros, with road haulage; or Ruiz Mateos, with banking and wine" (Riquer i Permanyer 264). With the development of the industrial sector, job opportunities arose across the board, ranging from those requiring a university degree, such as managers or administrators, to those requiring few professional qualifications. It is at this level we note the emergence of a new working class composed of young people of rural origin, who just a few years earlier would have been relegated to the impoverished conditions of agricultural life, but were now contenders in the financial sector.

These transformations occurring throughout Spain in the 1960s led to its introduction into a full-blown consumer society. As money flowed into the country from foreign investments, tourism, and the creation of a new economy, citizens also became consumers. Borja de Riquer i Permanyer elaborates:

> This speed of this process (consumer society) is exemplified by the impact of television. Spanish Television did not begin broadcasting regularly until 1959, but by 1974 70 per cent of homes had a TV. The same year saw 85 per cent of households in possession of a washing machine and a fridge. Car ownership rose even more rapidly. The SEAT factory in Barcelona, which turned out 30,000 saloon cars in 1960, produced over 360,000 by 1972. Spanish levels of car ownership rose from 500,000 (one car for every fifty-five inhabitants) in 1960, to over 3,300,000 (one for every nine) in 1974. (265)

Spain witnessed a new social reality with the introduction of mass consumerism. Not only did technology aid in the completion of mundane chores, but also the arrival of the television bears particular importance. It served as an asset that was an aperture to popular knowledge about the world and increased visibility of other socially lived realities.[36] While other European countries were absorbing into consumer society alongside Spain, the emergence of this culture was experienced in a distinct manner for the Spanish. To begin with, it occurred at a very accelerated pace, due largely to the television which provided instantaneous access to other cultures. "Spain passed rapidly from high levels of functional illiteracy to TV saturation without passing through intermediate stages of cultural development" (Riquer i Permanyer 265). The velocity of this process did not permit the Spaniards to pass through an intermediate stage, rather the society transformed from one extreme to another. To an extent, consumerism and the dictatorship were becoming compatible in the formerly autarkic country that just recently opened its doors to trade, yet the dictatorship still retained power. While Franco and the regime purported the country was in a period of *aperturismo* or liberalization, this was nothing more than a mask.[37] The "freedoms" (there was little freedom of speech and thought in the Spanish mass media) associated with consumer society, in particular the television, were greeted with further acts of repression manifesting through censorship, prosecutions, and propaganda, nevertheless, this mass culture had the ability to alter significantly the Spaniard's perception of daily social, economic, and political life. Through the television, citizens were bombarded with images of new products and status symbols of the Western world. This projection of worldwide images permitted them if not the "freedom to purchase," the freedom to consume and fantasize. It created an educational space—previously nonexistent in the regime—that opened up the dictatorship for critique, as the worlds and images they witnessed were not in accord with their social reality.[38]

> Television, despite the rigid political control to which it was subjected, turned itself into a genuine window onto the world, indirectly helping to break the stranglehold of the cultural and informational 'autarky' enforced by the regime. Similarly, the youth culture of the 1960s had a startling impact on the rigid social world of Franco's Spain, where enthusiasm for the Beatles or Bob Dylan, or emerging Spanish protest singers, represented a more overt political statement than in democratic societies. (Riquer i Permanyer 265)

Indeed the introduction of the television into Spain produced drastic transformations in the society concurrently with the boom in the economy. The existence of the modern television within households gave way to globalizing influences and postmodern cultural fragmentations. The arrival of mass culture as experienced through the television (although heavily censored), converted the citizens into consumers of images. The soar in the economy allowed them to exercise their liberty and own one these images.[39]

Reflecting on consumption, we only need remember the brilliant movie made by Luis G. Berlanga, ¡Bienvenido, Míster Marshall! (1952): a film that portrayed the American dream and filled the heads of Spaniards with the promise of future economic prosperity and consequent autonomy. Adela Cortina implies that the act of consumption may serve liberatory roles. She states, "Y si el acto mismo de consumo pertenece al reino de la libertad, tanto más serán miembros de ese reino las formas de consumo, y entre ellas, las formas de consumir productos del mercado" (29). Overall, the introduction of mass culture into Spain had profound effects on experienced social reality that translated into the questioning of self-identity. In his article Borja de Riquer i Permanyer describes the ambience of this period as one of growing skepticism especially among the "younger generation that had not lived through the civil war. This increasingly critical attitude was based on two fundamental principles: better information about world affairs and the decline of traditional religious values" (266). The television exposed the culture, especially the youths, to exhilarating experimentation, from the rock and roll of the Beatles to the emergence of the pop style. This window revealing aspects across the globe is a form of technology that permitted the spectator to travel and experience cultural identities and different worlds without leaving the confines of the home.

The gradual erosion of the influence of the Catholic Church and the politics of Franco combined with new economic opportunities created a space for the contemplation and critique of the traditional power structure. The death of Franco in 1975 and the subsequent inauguration of the new Constitution in 1978 resulted in spectacular growth in areas ranging from mass culture to individual autonomy. A natural result of the political developments within Spain was greater freedom, as they were now citizens of democracy, but concurrently Spaniards, in particular the youth generation, were able to exercise further liberty in the realm of consumerism.[40] Navarro claims: "El consumo se ha convertido así en uno de los primeros comportamientos autónomos que comienzan a ejercerse desde la infancia, y para muchos casi la única conexión con el mundo de los adultos, fuera del sistema escolar y la familia" (qtd. in Amando de Miguel 168). While Navarro's argument underlines the totality and centrality of consumption in an individual's life, his argument may also imply that consumption is an inherent human activity.

Much like the television, magazines became another venue by which one, particularly women, could absorb into mass culture. In particular, fashion magazines such as *Ama*, *Telva*, and *¡Hola!* converted their predominantly female readership into consumers of images, products, and new ways of life. The introduction of these magazines into society in the 1960s offered a new ideal for women, one in which she is represented as autonomous. Nonetheless, from their inception into Spanish culture until the year 1976, these women's magazines followed the dictates of Franco first and their commercial agenda next. For instance, the magazine *Ama*, which had a diffusion of 180,000 in 1970 was linked to the Opus Dei, the ultra-conservative technocratic body governing with Franco. As a result the principal themes treated were "niños, pedagogía, reportajes, actualidad, artículos, decoración, trabajos manuales, modas, hogar, belleza, libros, discos, cocina, consultorio sentimental, de belleza y religioso" (Rivière 140). *Telva*, founded in 1963 and also linked to Opus Dei, intended to import external elements and adapt them to the Spanish society. In its presentation, it appeared much like the French magazines *Elle* and *Marie Claire*. Similar to *Ama*, *Telva* focused on fashion, interior design, gastronomy, and social concerns. These magazines, while they did promote gender differences, also were a medium to present images of women for the consumption of women, rather than men. This arena, akin to the television, provided a space for consumer empowerment as the magazines, through their articles and advertisements, extended an invitation to its readership to own the feminine body as one's self.

In consideration of the relation among consumption and the female subject, scholars such Angela McRobbie rethink the role of the concept

Woman. She postulates that consumer culture, in general, and fashion in particular, offer women the means of satisfying desires and pursuing pleasure. Her theory, however, does not focus merely on bourgeois status, but rather on youth subcultures that exist, stemming from the pursuit of various cultures of consumption. McRobbie additionally researches the role of female magazines—targeted primarily at youth culture—and their active interplay in the stimulation of the female imagination. Likewise, their consumption in this realm may be considered an exercise in and affirmation of autonomy. She agrees that the female youth culture:

> Do not want to be represented in a humiliating way. They are not dependent on boys for their own sense of identity and well being. Magazines (like *Jackie*) which continue to offer this passive stereotype of femininity will simply lose their readers. As young consumers girls are therefore able to exert some power in the marketplace. They will buy a magazine as long as it presents an image of themselves which is compatible with those selves that exist outside the text. . . . There is also a re-definition of the feminine self. It can be endlessly constructed, reconstructed and customized. ("Shut up and Dance: Changing Modes of Youth Femininity" 8)

McRobbie recognizes the capacity and desire on the part of young women to be portrayed as active agents that participate in identity formation through the adoption of codes that are compatible with their ideologies and affinities. As McRobbie argues, the process of purchasing and marketing commodities does not transpire in a void; rather the process entails the formation of a connection of "much longer chains of meaning and value systems" (14). Through an exploration of these affiliations, one can garner an understanding of the intricate and sophisticated pleasures associated with consumption practices. Not only does this investigation yield important awareness of the creative operations that it entails, but also unveils the rich multiplicity of subjectivities at play, each texturized by the autonomous elections of the consumer.

It must be noted that other scholars, such as Susan Bordo, maintain that consumer culture oppresses women, while masking as a discourse that animates subjects to "imagine the possibilities and close our eyes to limits and consequences" (39). Bordo's line of argument addresses political, social, economic, and ideological situations that demean, oppress, and limit the value of woman. Likewise, she focuses on the homogenization and consequential normalization of images and signs disseminated in mass cultural representations. Bordo affirms:

> First, the representations *homogenize*. In our culture, this means that they will smooth out all racial, ethnic, and sexual "differences" that disturb Anglo-Saxon, heterosexual expectations and identifications.... Consumer capitalism depends on the continual production of novelty, of fresh images to stimulate desire.... Second, these homogenized images *normalize*—that is, they function as models against which the self continually measures, judges, "disciplines," and "corrects" itself. (24–25)

Bordo calls for a change in focus away from the body as a semiotic signifier; nevertheless, this fails to acknowledge the complex dialectic occurring between the subject and object. As a result, her theories neglect to consider the manner in which women appropriate and own these images. Bordo centers on the institutional context of consumption and their participation in the creation of the illusion of power, while never endowing the subject with agency. She argues against the liberating role of consumption stating: "The fact is we are not empowered in this way by our culture; indeed, we are continually being taught to see the body that reflects back to us in exactly the opposite way—as wrong, defective, 'a caricature, a swollen shadow, a stupid clown'" (299–300). In placing the focus on the institutional, the focus on the individual is smoothed over, and consequently, functions as little more than a token, made to desire, aspire to, and consume the whims of higher authority reflected in the institutional practices of commercial culture.

The aforementioned feminists illustrate two poles, a radical optimism versus a totalizing critique; nevertheless, the truth remains in the gray expanse between the opposed essentialisms. In consideration of the potential agency endowed to the female subject by way of her participation in cultures of consumption, particular ambiguities must be signaled. To begin with, the patriarchy has constructed the female subject as a sex object with a specific use-value; she is other (Bordo). Some feminists believe that woman is unable to escape the binary opposition of mother/prostitute, and therefore the reproduction of this representation (woman as commodity) cannot support the feminist aim of emancipation. Nonetheless, upon exploration of the manner in which the subjects experience their female sexuality or their subject as a commodity, the totalizing critique becomes clouded. Furthermore, it begs for further examination of the realm of consumption and re-appropriation of these goods. In so doing, this may open the possibility for the female subject to draw attention to the identity she articulates. Power can be derived from her ability to manipulate images and confuse gender/moral codes. Although her desired representation may be perceived as seductive or insubordinate to hegemonic norms, one must also consider the power and pleasure she gleans from her sexuality, which disrupts essentialist explanations. Consumer culture may afford women distinct opportunities for the approximation of self-creation. Vis-à-vis knowledge and interaction with the material realm, each woman as nomad, makes meaningful negotiations, communicating to the self and the collectivity. This dynamic interaction is also ongoing; the female subject traverses territory, negotiates meaning, and assembles and reassembles identity.

Cultures of Consumption: Imagined Communities and Neo-Tribes

In the epoch of postmodernity, an era infused with globalization of cultures and homogenization of customs, identity ceases to be defined according to traditional categories. Rather, there is a growing emphasis in society on lifestyles and individual interests as a designation of who one is and as a manner to connect and unite with others. Gottdiener argues, "Now people increasing relate to each other through commonly held consumption practices such as their preferences in sports, vacations, music, films, restaurants, and not the least, modes of shopping itself" (21). These activities and exercises do not merely represent marginal elements of consumer culture, but actually, in their aggregate, they eclipse other aspects of society. A vested interest in particular lifestyles divides society into agglomerate groups; these groupings express a desire for the consumption of a like good. In considering the emergence of this conglomeration of assemblages, which I argue can be viewed as what Benedict Anderson denominates "imagined communities," it is fundamental to outline his theory to be followed by an explication of its synthesis to the present investigation.

In his investigation of the concept nation and nationalism, Anderson utilizes the term "imagined communities" to signify "the nation: it is an imagined political community—and imagined as both inherently limited and sovereign" (6). As evidenced through his definition, his notion of nation departs from the mere geographical, political, and economic dynamics traditionally conceived of alongside this term.[41] The dynamics of Anderson's theory of "imagined communities" may expand to the concept of cultures of consumption. Cultures that arise and edify themselves due to consumption practices may be considered "imagined communities." His concept of "imagined communities" does not stem from political alliances or diplomatic assumptions; rather he asserts that at the heart of the community exists interplay between cultural dynamics that presuppose political structures. He proposes that: "nationalism has to be understood by aligning it, not with self-consciously held political ideologies, but with the large cultural systems that preceded it, out of which—as well as against which—it came into being" (12).[42] Hence, it is the sign that unites groups across the expanses and their ability to read and identify with that sign renders them part of the same community.[43] Through consumption, we produce and transmit meaning via the sign, legible to those who partake in the same communion of goods. The diverse social groups that encompass the globe, regardless of their locality, ethnicity, or historical heritage, unite by way of common interests (facilitated by advanced technologies). At the core of the bond is the consumption of an object that converts to sign and not only is made legible but also communicates to the masses. Cultures of consumption become articulation points of identity, and these various cultures manifest in diverse "imagined communities" increasing the possibility for the creation of autonomous self-construction.

Anderson's concept of "imagined communities" can be patch worked with the notion of neo-tribes posited by Maffesoli.[44] The conjoining of these theories provides a deeper understanding of the manifestation "imagined communities" of cultures of consumption and also lends further support to the argument that via consumption practices, one has the potential to shape subjectivity and identify with a global community. While the two theorists employ distinct terminology and have different approaches, they both investigate contemporary identity—utilizing historical antecedents—and its relationship to the cultural and social realm. While Anderson explores the creation of "imagined communities" through the global spread of print capitalism, Maffesoli investigates the existence of contemporary cultural communities that he denominates neo-tribes. He applies this term to categorize groups that reflect various cultures of consumption such as sports, hobbies, and fashion, to name a few. These tribes, akin to "imagined communities," are constructed and dependent solely on the desire for the metabolic consumption of the aforementioned good(s) or idea. Through these spaces, one produces an identity, namely through techniques of the body, as the body is an instrument or tool to be fashioned and created; Foucault argues, technologies "permit individuals to effect by their own means or with the help of others a certain number of operations on their own bodies and souls, thoughts, conduct, and way of being, so as to transform themselves in order to attain a certain state of happiness, purity, wisdom, perfection, or immortality" ("Technologies of the Self" 18).[45] Hence, through consumption practices, individuals have the capacity to actively confect their identity through the assemblage and reassemblage of accoutrements that serve as contingencies in the articulation of selfhood.

Cultures of consumption are lifestyles associated with a more or less stable community that feeds off of shared rituals and norms, and are inflected with social order, and also share a language. Consequently, these ways of life lend a social identity to individuals within the context of established life forms. Cortina argues:

> Los consumidores no forman una clase, ni tampoco diversas clases. Se organizan en diversos estilos de vida, en los que se integran gentes de forma poco cohesionada y con intereses diversos desde el punto de vista profesional, intelectual, espiritual. (137)

By way of consuming one forms lifestyles. The goal of self-realization by way of consumption is no longer dictated by caste nor bloodline, but stems from the continuous shifts in consumer choices and options. One ceases to be simply defined by work, religion, or ethnicity; consumption, in a lucid manner, defines individual and social identity and potentiates the formation of new "imagined communities." To this end, the theorist Maffesoli contends that aspects such as class, race, and age are no longer viable to describe these groups, some being short-lived, and others traversing across existing categories. As such, the individual is not static, but a fluid subject which moves freely across neo-tribes, modifying her interests and behaviors as she maneuvers. Furthermore, Maffesoli points to "the importance of the immaterial in the very heart of the material" (11). In the process of joining tribes, the individual self-fashions (idea of the body as a text that can be read) so as to create an identity within the tribe.[46] He states:

> Whether trendy exercises in sensory isolation, or various forms of bodybuilding, or jogging, or Eastern techniques of one sort or another, the body is being constructed as a value, even to the extent of its epiphany. . . . Note, however, that even in its most private aspects, the body is being constructed only in order to be seen; it is theatralized to the highest degree. Within advertising, fashion, dance, the body is adorned only to be made into a spectacle. (18–19)[47]

The body converts to a commodity to be read by the masses through the adoption of one form of lifestyle or another. This is further reinforced in Cortina's argument:

> A partir de los años cincuenta del siglo XX surge un conjunto de grupos que se visten, calzan, escuchan música, viajan o se divierten de una forma determinada. Y precisamente a través de su peculiar forma de consumir es como «expresan» su identidad y, sobre todo, como se «forjan» su identidad:

los patrones de consumo constituyen el mecanismo de inclusión y de exclusión del grupo. (98)

The scholar essentially reiterates Maffesoli's claim regarding the commodification of the body engendered by consumption practices, which suppose intimate ties with a particular community, albeit temporal.[48]

Gazing at the various members of society, it becomes apparent that there are myriad groups erected purely by their like to consume a similar good or idea. Undoubtedly, certain milieu desire to imitate those who occupy positions of power; it may be said that these people intend to "keep up with the Joneses." Notwithstanding, there exist reference groups, tribes, or "imagined communities" that may also be denominated counterculture. Groups that embody counterculture practices seek to resist identification with society's prescribed norms. Perhaps they achieve this through body dressing that is anti-establishment such as jeans, ripped T-shirts, and army boots. Other groups may speak out against war, capitalism, and other vices of our technological society. As Twitchell contends: "Expressions of material discontent, far from being an indication of decline [of consumer society], are the way a consumer society balances conflicting demands and indulges different behaviors" (3). Through their boycott of prescriptions of mass consumption society or their choice to be anti-materialist, they still remain consumers. Thus, "imagined communities" or reference groups are diverse and multiply constantly. As such, each group maintains a distinct way of life that necessitates different forms of consumption.

In sum, the theories postulated by Anderson and Maffesoli provide strong evidence for the idea that each subject belongs in a loose sense to "imagined communities" or multiple neo-tribes, by which she partakes in collective experiences that serve as a locus for the articulation of identity. Each feminine subject functions as part of a whole; however, she still operates as an individual self, an active "figuration" composed of a multiplicity of selves, the not-one. In that vein, she is the owner of her experiences, stories, and her body. Wielding the power, she is not only disqualified from a mass identification but also paves the way towards an embodiment of the nomadic subject. Having said this, it is important to note that this investigation is not postulating Woman as a monolithic and homogeneous group, thereby essentializing the feminine. Rather, each subject acting as consumer traverses through spaces, albeit collective, yet comes to embody the multiplicity of the feminist subject through the working through of experiences coupled with the awakening of her consciousness.

Notes

1. The term postmodern is contentious as it has been described and re-described from multiple and varying standpoints. This investigation adheres to the notion that the postmodern encapsulates heterogeneity, discontinuity, and destabilization, as Ihab Hassan points out (later to be conceded by Jencks and Lyotard). Characteristic of postmodernity is the absence of determinancy:

> Compounded of subtendencies that the following words evoke: heterodoxy, pluralism, eclecticism, randomness, revolt, deformation. The later alone subsumes a dozen current terms of unmaking: decreation, disintegration, deconstruction, decenterment, displacement, difference, discontinuity, disjunction, disappearance, decomposition, de-definition, demystification, detotalization, delegitimation (Hassan 9)

The postmodern is connected with the breakdown of belief in universals, encompassing scientific truth and objectivity. Many scholars link this epistemological fragmentation to the fall of the hegemony of Western culture, while others see the age of information as fundamental to this shift.

2. Braidotti further develops these theories in her later works *Nomadic Subjects: Embodiment and Sexual Difference* (1994) and *Metamorphoses* (2002).

3. Braidotti offers a plethora of examples demonstrating the dualistic relation among man and woman. For instance, man = rationality, agency, logic, whereas the feminine = passive, invisible, irrational.

4. The word "predecessors" refers to the first generation of sexual difference theorists such as Cixous and Irigaray.

5. This mode of thought entails a move beyond dualistic conceptual constraints.

6. Braidotti comments on the persistence of the nomadic trait in contemporary political movements, from "hippies" to the "new age gypsies," the peace camps, the music festivals, and feminist happenings (26).

7. Braidotti views the concept of becoming-woman as a positive category. It is within this space that woman has agency, and as such can fluidly negotiate the systems of power.

8. In 1900-01 "51.111 alumnos cursaban estudios medios y 17.186 superiores por 5.557 y 1 alumnas, respectivamente" (Riera 33). Riera's evidence highlights the weak participation of women in the academic environment.

9. Historically in Spain the law has imposed upon the woman a position of inferiority and passivity; as such women—due to an utter absence of options—consumed the dictates of the masculine libidinal order. Woman in Spain was to be a subservient commodity caring for the home and the needs of her husband.

10. To begin with, there was an obvious attraction to tradition due to the familiarity and comfort it bred and the stability it invoked. Helen Graham suggests that this conservative attraction was based on anxiety and tension produced by new conceptions of living. It is interesting to note that "the central impulse of this social-cultural conservatism was often directed at re-imposing or reinforcing traditional gender

roles on women—the social and in particular reproductive) policies of Italian and German fascism being just the most widely known examples" (100). This model was also developing in Spain as well, but was temporarily displaced in the late 1920's by the collapse of the Primo de Rivera military dictatorship (1922-1930), and the proclamations of the Second Republic.

11. These reformations were enacted institutionally from the top down, instead of from the bottom up or by means of grass root movements. The way in which these were enacted had an effect on the recognition of women's legal equality for many reasons. To begin with, Spain was a largely rural country with few urban centers, which underscores the clash among traditional and progressive modes of living. These rural units, coined "la España profunda," were disconnected from the urban centers and progressive modes of thinking and being, and following their traditional customs that provided them with a sense of stability and familiarity. Furthermore, women encountered other familiar obstacles; those that desired to enter the work force were also faced with the double burden of caring for the family as well as employment outside of the home. Added to this, many women were forced to exclude themselves from the economic sector due to a lack of education:

> Es lógico, pues, que a primeros de este siglo el 71,5 por 100 de las mujeres fueran analfabetas (frente al 56,6 por 100 de los varones) y que en 1930 este porcentaje no bajara del 58. La instrucción pública, ya de por sí raquítica en cuanto a recursos, no podía despilfarrarse en una formación totalmente inútil. Como máximo había que enseñarles las tareas «propias» de su sexo. (Riera 32)

And those women fortunate to have an education—albeit limited—to enter the work force were faced with other obstacles such as the hostility of masculine dominated economic order. In sum, tradition, customs, and morality marked as other the woman and justified her inferiority based upon her sex.

12. This movement in Spain was protagonized by Clara Campoamor, one of the two female high-ranking officials in government. She championed the arduous task of amending the Constitución of 1931, implementing modifications in favor of the condition of the woman. Instead of reading "No podrán ser fundamento de privilegio jurídico: la naturaleza, la filiación, el sexo, la clase social, la riqueza, las ideas políticas ni las creencias religiosas," it was modified to "reconocer en principio la igualdad de derechos de los dos sexos" (Riera 36). She also stridently defended women's suffrage, making remarkable advances despite the opposition from not only her own political party but also the only other woman in parliament, Victoria Kent. Nevertheless, the Spanish society in general, and women in particular, were not fully prepared or comfortable with this responsibility.

> Los pocos años de la II República significaron un avance espectacular en la igualdad de los derechos de la mujer y en su consideración como persona. Se dice que los cambios se produjeron desde «arriba», que la sociedad española y, más concretamente, las mujeres no estaban preparadas para estas reformas; que el voto sólo sirvió para que ganara el derecha en 1933; que se concedió el divorcio pero que casi nadie lo utilizó. (35)

13. In 1937 the Catholic bishops collectively signed a letter stating their support of Franco and his military coup against the Republic. The most enthusiastic supporters were Cardinal Gomá and Cardinal Pla Daniel. Pío XII additionally acknowledged the Catholic Church's support of Franco. The support of the ecclesiastical hierarchy elated Franco. Buttressed by the Church, Franco reinforced his ideology in multiple spheres of social life.

14. In April of 1942, the Minister of Education declared women unfit for higher education. He stated:

> Mi opinión es que debe alejarse a la mujer de la Universidad, quiero decir que el sitio de la mujer, en mi opinión, es el hogar. Y que por consiguiente, una orientación cristiana y auténticamente española de la Enseñanza Superior ha de basarse en el supuesto de que solo excepcionalmente debe la mujer orientarse hacia estudios universitarios. (Signo 1942)

The regime solemnly preached that women did not need an education if their purpose was to remain in the home, married and pregnant. Nevertheless, the economic reality that faced women could not support the lifestyle demanded by the regime. This forced women, who had little or no education, to work in stores, as maids cleaning homes, and other poorly paid odd jobs.

15. This suggests and further supports the claim that under the Franco regime women and their bodies were a means to an end, fulfilling the masculine order's desire while at the same time, highly regulated and under surveillance.

16. This model based upon closed borders, complete isolation, and self-sufficiency was deteriorating the social, political, and most importantly economic well being of the country.

17. "Todavía el 43 por 100 vive en poblaciones de menos de 10.000 habitantes y un 41 por 100 de la población activa se concentra en el sector primario. Las condiciones de vida en los hogares rurales son muy duras: solo un 37 por 100 tienen agua corriente y un 20 por 100 baño o ducha" (FOESSA 211).

18. Due to the enormous deficit and impoverished state of Spain, Franco instituted a *Plan de Estabilización*, a set of economic reforms intended to open up the economy to capitalist interests. Nevertheless, opening the country to foreigners could potentially make the regime and its politics vulnerable. Hence, Franco found a group—el Opus Dei—that would help him to achieve both goals: maintain the image of Catholic Spain while promoting capitalistic interests. The ideology of Opus was exceedingly conservative and connected with the Catholic Church. At the same time, the group promoted economic qualities such as development, consumption, and efficiency.

19. At this time, events occurring worldwide opened possibilities for progress and new patterns of thinking. These social phenomena included major expansion of universities, the Vietnam War met with fierce opposition among United States students, and intense political upheaval in France.

20. This activism is attributed to many causes principally, though, the critical eye of the press. Newspapers, while subjected to the scrutiny and censorship of the Ley Fraga, were the principal disseminators of knowledge and fighters for freedom. For instance,

> Los medios de comunicación (no TVE, claro está) hablan de huelgas (aunque todavía se utilicen los eufemismos de paros y de productores en lugar de obreros), de los juicios del Tribunal de Orden Público, de las multas a la prensa, de los continuos incidentes estudiantiles que son controlados por el regimen con detenciones, expulsiones, cierres y en enero del año siguiente, con el Estado de Excepción. (Riera 60)

21. As such the church was divided: there were bishops that continued praising the efficiency and effectiveness of the dictatorship and yet dissension was growing among the priests seen through their support of those persecuted by Franco "los curas se manifestaban y las parroquias cobijaban asambleas y reuniones de todos los grupos ilegales y perseguidos por la dictadura" (60).

22. The most notable sector affected by female employment was "servicios, con un crecimiento muy notable de empleadas de oficinas y vendedoras" (62). Likewise, there was a marked augment in the number of young females (aged 20 to 24) entering the workforce. In 1960, 28 percent of women in this age group maintained employment outside of the home. By 1968 this number had grown astonishingly, yet there does remain discord among the actual number. In either case, one notes the definite infiltration of the workforce by women; according to the census in 1970 the number was 39 percent, however, the EPA projects a higher number, tallying 47 percent of this age group with new economic resources (Riera).

23. Not only did the State work through legal means to limit woman's labor rights, the press and media portrayed women in a manner unsuitable for the workforce. The media disseminated popular images of women; two in particular are: "la «Tía Leo», que anunciaba el caldo concentrado, y una despampanante rubia que, montada en un caballo blanco, incitaba a los hombres a beber coñac, una de cuyas marcas consideraba que ese licor era sólo *cosa de hombres*" (Larumbe 148). The disseminated image of the woman as a sexual object or an animal not only functioned to nullify female subjectivity, but also further isolated her from the workforce due to the explicit devaluation of woman.

24. From 1975 to 1981, the country experienced stagnations in the economy leading some to believe that they were no better off under the democracy than they were under the dictatorship. For example, the unemployment rate among the Spanish population was 6.2 percent (7.1 percent among women); in total 832,400 citizens found themselves in this situation, 274,200 of them women (Riera 78–79).

25. The unstable political environment gave way to a substantial level of tolerance and permissiveness.

26. Perhaps not surprising, the Sección Femenina strongly desired to charge itself with the direction of the project; nevertheless, progressive women challenged their

request as they did not want the situation of the women in Spain to be represented by one of Franco's instruments. Hence, other feminists groups such as the MDM (Movimiento Democrático de Mujeres) spearheaded the efforts to portray Spanish woman's reality from a very distinct optic.

27. Since the Enlightenment, the theme of equality has garnered abundant attention. Feminists of equality utilize as their conceptual framework the tenets of equality as established by masculine philosophers in the Enlightenment. This branch contends that equality will be achieved once we comprehend the notion of the "universal subject." Their belief is that in an androcentric society, wiping away sexual difference, women can incorporate into the patriarchal model and be an equal.

28. In his study of the dynamics of these new consumer groups, Bocock underlines the importance of the internal dynamics, stating that it is these factors that have played a role in the social construction of a sense of identity. While the external features of these groups were also new, for instance age, socio-economic, gender, he points to identity as a process which "may make use of consumable items such as shoes, designer trainers, clothing, music, sports activities, and belonging to clubs or soccer clubs" (29).

29. In his analysis of capitalism, he traces three fundamental yet differing stages: Middle Ages, early capitalist period, and a highly developed era of commodification. In the first stage, he asserts that only when there was surplus in production—that which would be nonessential to sustain simple needs—was bartered; in the second phase, the sphere of industrial goods entered the realm of exchange. The last era—that of commodification—represented a time:

> When everything that men had considered as inalienable became an object of exchange, of traffic and could be alienated. This is the time when . . . virtue, love, conviction, knowledge, conscience, etc.—when everything finally passed into commerce. It is the time of general corruption, of universal venality, or to speak in terms of political economy, the time when everything, moral or physical, having become a marketable value, is brought to the market to be assessed at its truest value. (Marx and Engels *Collected Works: Vol VI* 113–14)

30. Within the cycle of capitalism, he posits that man is animal and can be nothing but this figuration due to the beastly nature inherent in the system and man's need to constantly perform for meager pay.

31. He differentiates himself from Marx in numerous ways; Marx argued that the "mass" was dominated by artificial and false ideologies, while Baudrillard, on the other hand, articulates that the "mass" already recognizes that the prevailing ideologies are false, and rather is dominated and controlled by the spectacle: "the spectacle is the affirmation of appearance and the affirmation of all human, i.e. social, life as mere appearance" (*The Mirror of Production* 10). This theorist does not focus his attention so much on the political economy and its relationship to consumption, rather he places emphasis on what he calls "sign value."

32. The concept of implosion was first articulated and discussed in the modern era by Nietzche; however, it was presented as 'nihilism.'

33. There does exist a plethora of cultures of consumption. However, we may condsider the U.S. consumer culture as a dominant force behind the globalization of cultures of consumption. In large part, these cultures of consumption stem from lifestyle orientations.

34. Borja de Riquer i Permanyer illustrates the noteworthy alterations through four compelling statistics.

> Between 1960 and 1974 the average income per capita tripled, rising from $400 to $1,350 per annum. The GDP grew during the 1960s at an average of 7.5 per cent per annum, a rate surpassed only by Japan. Growth in industrial output in 1960-7 was the fastest in the world at 10.5 per cent per annum. And real industrial wages increased by 40 per cent in this period. (262)

35. From 1960 to 1975 the number of urban centers with populations over 100,000 doubled from twenty in 1960 to over forty in 1975.

36. Further evidence of the inauguration of consumer society in 1960, made patent in the *Real Academia de la Lengua*, was the incorporation of new words in the dictionary such as: televisor, lavadora, financiación, and aparcamiento.

37. An example of this is the acceptance of Buñuel's movie, *Viridiana*, to the Cannes Film Festival, in which it won an esteemed international award but was subsequently banned in Spain due to its controversial content.

38. In large part these reactions and movements were protagonized by the youths of this period. What perhaps began as a rebellion against the parental authority converted into revolution against all figures of authority, as witnessed through the slogan of the student movement of 1968, "haz el amor y no la guerra."

39. In his survey undertaken in 1960, Amando de Miguel interviewed his participants about the goods they consume. His results reflect their attitudes and desire to appropriate goods for their own comfort and pleasure. Certain objects saturated Spanish households; eight out of every ten owned a radio and had running water. Nevertheless, the objects of consumption represented the existent socio-economic inequalities persistent among the population. While certain commodities were prolific: "hay otros que no llegan al 10% de los hogares de varones: frigorífico eléctrico, coche o televisor. El consumo realmente masivo de esos tres artículos iba a ser el «sueño» de la década de los años sesenta" (35). These luxury items, a television, refrigerator, and car, echoed the American dream as seen through North American movies, and remained symbols for the Spaniard.

40. According to Amando de Miguel, the youth generation of the 1950s had little if any access to money due to the severe economic hardships experienced throughout the country. The decade of the 1940s was denoted "década de hambre" by the Spanish because of the tremendous poverty. However, this sociologist found

that youth generations following 1960 had some pocket change that allowed them to experience autonomy as consumers.

41. His study begins with a definition of key terms for the comprehension of what constitutes 'imagined' community; these terms include: *imagined, limited, sovereign,* and *community*. Anderson postulates that a community is *imagined* because one is incapable of knowing all of the people that are members; nevertheless they joined as "in the minds of each lives the image of their communion" (6). As such, a nation is not defined simply as political entity, but developed and molded by culture. Communities are also *limited*; this is attributed the fact that there are diverse interests and pursuits among the various global populations. A feature of these communities is that they are *sovereign*, a notion that arose with the Enlightenment, an era that challenged the validity of the ancient regime of deific authority; consequentially this clash led to the debilitation of "the divinely-ordained, hierarchical dynastic realm" (7), as well as the aperture for the possibility of freedom. The last term fundamental to Anderson's concept is *community*. Anderson asserts that the community is composed of a nation "conceived as a deep, horizontal comradeship" (7). He, furthermore, justifies this notion, regardless of the disparity that may exist among the members offering as example people prepared to give their lives for their vision.

42. To comprehend the concept of his theory of nationalism, he begins the exploration with the examination of cultural evolutions that have shaped and informed it. He analyzes the two aggregates integral to the cultural realm until the epoch of the Enlightenment—the *religious community* and the *dynastic realm*. In his discussion, he highlights the strengths of these two systems and commented on their instabilities that ultimately led to their downfall. To begin with, the religious community—while composed of many different territories and an array of religions—was able to assemble as an imagined group and interact with their comrades via the reciprocal ability to comprehend the sign. Anderson affirms:

> Christendom, the Islamic Ummah, and even the Middle Kingdom—which, though we think of it today as Chinese, imagined itself not as Chinese, but as central—were imaginable largely through the medium of a sacred language and written script. Take only the example of Islam: if Maguindanao met Berbers in Mecca, knowing nothing of each other's languages, incapable of communicating orally, they nonetheless understood each other's ideographs, because the sacred texts they shared existed only in classical Arabic. In this sense, written Arabic functioned like Chinese characters to create a community out of signs, not sounds. (13)

Anderson's modern day notion of 'imagined communities' also stems from an investigation of the dynamics of the dynastic realm, focusing particularly on the model of society in which, at the center, lies monarchy. He comments: "Kingship organizes everything around a high center. Its legitimacy derives from divinity, not from populations, who after all, are subjects, not citizens" (19). In a system ruled by a hereditary sovereign with more or less unlimited powers, a monarch maintains a dominant position indoctrinated with supreme power and sovereignty. This model of cultural system functioned for centuries, increasing territory and power through rivalries and marriages among kingdoms. Nevertheless, while distinct from the religious cultural system and its relationship to nation, leadership stemming from divine right was challenged during the Enlightenment, yet continues to exist in various countries to this day. Interestingly, both types of communities communicated through the word, the sign.

43. The conception of modern 'imagined communities' is due to a series of factors and did not come about as a substitute for cultural systems of antiquity. Rather there were widespread changes occurring in the eighteenth century that affected the framework of the conception of community and nation: "Beneath the decline of sacred communities, languages and lineages, a fundamental change was taking place in modes of apprehending the world, which more than anything else, made it possible to 'think' the nation" (22). This transformation was occurring by way of the emergence of print media: "the novel and the newspaper. For these forms provided the technical means for 're-presenting' the kind of imagined community that is the nation" (25). Through these two media, one could participate in the community through experience acquired by reading. That is, while the member may not have previous awareness of what is being described in the newspaper or personal knowledge of the theme elaborated upon in the novel, she could imagine and create and share in the experience, as well as connect, via the word.

Of course, the process of the formation of modern 'imagined communities' intensified with the appearance of print capitalism as well as transformations in technology. As a result of these developments, the possibility for the new creation of communities is endless, especially taking into consideration the globalization of cultures. "What, in a positive sense, made the new communities imaginable was a half-fortuitous, but explosive, interaction between a system of production and productive relations (capitalism), and a technology of communications (print)" (Anderson 42-43). The confluence of capitalism and print technology facilitated communication between the masses; concurrently, this promoted an exchange of ideas and also a sense of individual and collective identity. As Anderson contends: "These fellow-readers, to whom they were connected through print, formed, in their secular, particular, visible invisibility, the embryo of the nationally imagined community" (44). By way of the ability to have access and read print media, one could form a kinship with another, without respect of race, age, or profession. Rather, the word bridged a connection among diverse groups of people and the result is the manifestation of the budding of communities whose commonality was the printed word. Accessibility to information has become widespread and the possibility to connect globally and form a horizontal kinship with another has been made possible by these technologies; a series of advances that have exploded the possibilities for "a new form of imagined community" (46) fashioned by contingencies unique to each group.

44. The theorist Maffesoli in his work *The Time of the Tribes* presents an analysis of heterogeneous fragments of contemporary society with respect to consumption; groups that distinguish themselves by their shared lifestyles and tastes through cultures of consumption. The term, *tribes*, is not intended to signify 'tribes' in the traditional

anthropological sense. Rather according to Maffesoli's usage of the term, these neo-tribes do not exemplify the longevity or the fixity of traditional tribes. The community, or tribe, that Maffesoli proposes is characterized less by a future project, than by a communal sense of belonging. As Maffesoli asserts:

> Overall, within massification, processes of condensation are constantly occurring through which more or less ephemeral tribal grouping are organized which cohere on the basis of their own minor values, and which attract and collide with each other in an endless dance, forming themselves into a constellation whose vague boundaries are perfectly fluid. (12)

Neo-tribes are marked by their fluidity: they are locally concentrated, dispersed and periodically assembled. Neo-tribes are momentary condensations in the flux of everyday consumer life. While they are fragile, ephemeral and unstable, they elicit intense affective and emotive involvement from their members. Nevertheless, the inner organization, aims and aspirations of neo-tribes are not important. Common desire is the only purpose they require; in other words, there is no admission procedure. Neo-tribes exist by virtue of individual decisions to "sport the insignia of tribal allegiance" (21). The premise of Maffesoli's argument recalls Anderson's four basic tenets for the definition of "imagined community": *imagined, limited, sovereign,* and *community.*

45. Techniques of the body refer to corporeal modifications such as fashion, comportment, gait, and any other body adornment, as a result of conformism or anti-conformism.

46. It is the argument of this study that cultures of consumption and various neo-tribes that emerge demonstrate practices of self-fashioning, individuation, and privatization of the body. Maffesoli, however, postulates the opposite. While the theorist Maffesoli provides a comprehensive study of the concept of the neo-tribe, beginning with its historicity through the present day, he arrives at political conclusions that do not recognize the experience of the individual feminine subject on various levels, opting instead to discuss the proliferation of neo-tribes within the purely social realm. With the rise of neo-tribes, Maffesoli suggests that there has been a decline of individualism in mass society. "As for the metaphor of the tribe, it allows us to account for the process of dis-individuation, the saturation of the inherent *function* of the individual and the emphasis on the *role* that each person is called upon to play within the tribe" (6). Nevertheless, his theory neglects to acknowledge issues such as sexual difference, self-affectivity, self-consciousness, embodiment, and the mode in which these corresponding dynamics unravel within neo-tribes.

47. The notion of self-fashion has been treated by many scholars, including theorists who view the phenomenon from a position of sexual difference such as Entwistle and McRobbie.

48. Amando de Miguel, in his second survey of the Spanish youth undertaken in 1998, noted the prolific existence of neo-tribes in the Spanish culture, constructed and perpetuated by the consumption of particular material goods.

Hoy día, cada grupo etáneo tiene sus modas y un tipo de atuendos determinados. Los jóvenes en concreto, sufren los efectos del «marquismo» y el «fetichismo». Esto es, gustan de consumir más que ropa, marcas determinadas. La marca es símbolo de exclusividad, de prestigio y por tanto de clase. (174)

Through sporting name brands or consuming a range of goods, youths are expressing themselves via a series of operations and practices that not only serve as articulation points for individual identity, but also determine social associations and groups. Thus the consumer looks for a references group—imagined community—one for which she has a particular affinity. However, one cannot speak in unilateral terms; there exist many groups, one carrying no more prestige than another.

CHAPTER THREE

~

Amor, curiosidad, prozac y dudas: The Raver, the Cyborg, and the Housewife

Cultural Context

Of Basque origin, the author Lucía Etxebarria was born in Valencia, Spain, in 1966. At a later date, she relocated to Madrid where she currently resides in the old working-class Lavapies neighborhood. Due to these shifts in territorial location within Spain, Etxebarria has gleaned a unique perspective, one of distance, on what it means to be a woman living in contemporary Spain. She affirms: "Este no ser de aquí y no ser de allá me ha negado la conciencia de una identidad nacional y me ha proporcionado, en contrapartida, una amplitud de miradas a la hora de examinar nacionalismos, sexismos, extremismos, chauvinismos y otros ismos, derivada de la distancia impuesta" (http://www.ctv.es/USERS/patxiirurn/cero/biolucia.html). Etxebarria's scholastic career took place at the Universidad Complutense de Madrid where she earned a degree in journalism and English philology, while her professional background encompasses a mosaic of jobs ranging from a waitress to translator and an interpreter to a gopher in a musical production company. The literary course of this author began with *Aguanta esto*, a book that treats the origins of the grunge movement through the optic of the problematic relationship of Kurt Cobain and Courtney Love.[1] Etxebarria began to receive recognition for her writing with the publication of her first novel, *Amor, curiosidad, prozac y dudas* (1997) that was initially titled *Exceso de testosterona*, later changed due to the opposition on part of the publishing house. She has been awarded many esteemed literary prizes such as the *Premio Nadal* in 1998 for her third book *Beatriz y los cuerpos celestes* and the *Premio Primavera* in 2001 for *De todo lo visible y lo invisible*. Other works of Etxebarria include *Nosotras, que no somos como las demás* (1999), *La Eva futura* (2000), *La letra futura* (2000), *En brazos de la mujer fétiche* co-written with Sonia Núñez Puente (2002), and *Una historia de amor como cualquiera* (2003). She has also published a collection of poetry entitled *Estación de infierno* in 2001 as well as cowritten several movie scripts such as *Sobreviviré* (1999), *Amor, curiosidad, prozac y dudas* (2001), *I love you baby* (2001), and *La mujer de mi vida* (2001).[2]

The literary production of this author provides a fecund landscape to investigate the output of contemporary women writers in Spain. Her position is not exceptional as she was a child of the Franco regime and spent her formative years, that is to say her youth, in transition between two contrary worlds: dictatorship and democracy. Hence, it is interesting to analyze how Etxebarria, and other women born at this time, envision the identity and role of woman in contemporary Spanish society. The intense shifts experienced by Lucía Etxebarria, not only territorial relocation but also serious transformations in the political paradigm which resonated from top to bottom, accords the reader with a credible measure of change. As a youth, the writer was witness to the evolving roles and identity of woman. From the Transition and beyond, she further attested to the numerous struggles facing women, as woman was deemed a legal equal of man under the 1978 Constitution. Yet in practice woman does not achieve full emancipation due to a hodge-podge of factors such as oppressive societal norms stemming from a society steeped in machismo. As a result of her socially lived experience, consistent among the work of Lucía Etxebarria is the perpetual questioning of the traditional hierarchy of knowledge in conjunction with the turning upside down and inside out of conventional categories. In doing so this author highlights the fluidity of identity in our postmodern era as well as proposes alternative spaces for the female subject. In the study of this writer's production, the portrayal of female subjectivity is analyzed through the optic of consumption, focusing on various cultures such as drugs, music, fashion, sex, and technology. Concomitantly, the investigation will explore the resulting embodiment that emerges vis-à-vis the personal election of the consumer.

If we keep in mind Braidotti's framework of the nomadic subject, we note the multiplicity of feminine postures that Etxebarria creates in her literary production; each a territory in which women occupy, negotiate, and shift the notion of the self. In Lucía Etxebarria's writing, we see the nomadic subject wandering and fashioning her identity in accord with her particular social reality. Some of the protagonists, such as Cristina Gaena in the novel *Amor, curiosidad, prozac y dudas*, are active agents conscious of the power system in which they maneuver and as such exploit these spaces to their benefit. While others, such her sister Ana, a married housewife with one child, glorifies her pursuit of happiness through the absorption of the ideology disseminated by the Franco regime and its female sector the Sección Femenina of "Angel del hogar," yet on the other hand feels trapped by this traditional prescribed feminine role. Nevertheless, all of the characters, through contemplation and *working through* (Braidotti's emphasis) experiences, reach a consciousness of self, resulting in various figurations, and arrive at the embodiment of nomadic feminist subjects.

This chapter explores the dynamics of the Gaena sisters—Cristina, Rosa, and Ana—to flesh out the multiplicity of the female subject. When the novel was published in the late 1990s, Spain had already hosted key international events that not only brought them important worldwide recognition but also led to the influx within Spain of a globalization of cultures. According to Francisca López:

> Para muchos españoles, 1992 marcaba simbólicamente la culminación de un proceso de renovación, dada la convergencia en tal año de una serie de acontecimientos de diversos grados de relevancia a nivel internacional: las celebraciones del quinto centenario, Madrid como capitalidad europea de la cultura y Barcelona y Sevilla como sedes de los Juegos Olímpicos y de la Exposición Mundial, respectivamente. Tales acontecimientos ayudan a lograr el reconocimiento de esta España moderna fuera de nuestras fronteras y este reconocimiento refuerza, a su vez, la propia identificación con los procesos de la modernidad a nivel local. (1)

The combination of the aforementioned events—economic development, new political paradigms, and fluid contacts with the exterior—propelled the acceleration of socio-cultural transformations, which began in the late years of the Franco regime and resulted in a new order which supposed new challenges for subject formation. By way of this analysis, various cultures of consumption will be called into question, each a fundamental component through which the respective protagonists establish a notion of home. This exploration brings to the forefront the paradigm of the politics of location and the various neo-tribes or "imagined communities" to which these women subscribe, that consequently influence the embodiment of each female subject. In the process of becoming-woman as postulated by Rosi Braidotti, the starting point for this conversion is the politics of location, which implies a critique of dominant ideologies and identities in which the concept and determinacy of Woman is codified. The central argument is that each woman traverses through varied spaces or territories that run parallel to the selected cultures of consumption and thus unfold into personal lived experiences and stories. As a result of the interconnection of experiences and knowledge gained along the journey, each arises to a consciousness of self and comes to embody the nomadic feminist subject.

From the inception of its publication in 1997, the novel *Amor, curiosidad, prozac y dudas* achieved great success and launched its author, Lucía Etxebarria, into the orbit of immediate fame, which was echoed into its movie adaptation in 2001.[3] A platform for revolutionary ideas in a conservative world, through the novel Etxebarria reveals her controversial and transgressive personality. The work, dedicated to women at the end of the twentieth century, hooks the reader from the beginning to the end, bearing a plot that diverges into three stories: one for each of the Gaena sisters. Written in colloquial style, the novel employs explicit language and vulgar terms evidenced from the opening of the first chapter in which Cristina describes one of her disappointing sexual experiences with a guy who "lo tenía minúsculo" (13).[4] The three sisters narrate fragments of their life; these fractions are divided into chapters whose titles are especially seductive: in alphabetical order, each chapter begins with a letter and a word bearing that particular letter. For instance, the first chapter carries the title "A de atípica," the second is entitled "B de bajón," and this continues through the entire alphabet until the final chapter "Z de zenit." The reader of the novel is addressed as a woman who shares the protagonists' divergent lifestyles of shopping, capitalism, and the underground bar scene. Often written in the first person, their tone is one of shared confidences. The reader is assumed to be an adept consumer, to have a familiarity with designer labels, and is expected to have the knowledge to recognize the sophisticated brand names that fill the pages of this novel. As such, the novel is written for women who are skilled and experienced in contemporary discourses of consumption. As Rachel Bowlby has outlined, consumption has been associated with women since the development of the large department stores in Europe in the late nineteenth century. Sean Nixon, in "Have You Got the Look? Masculinities and Shopping Spectacle," extends this argument stating:

> The very spectacle of consumption—the windows filled with goods, the lighting, the displays, the other shoppers, the places to meet—has historically been signaled as a feminine domain, and associated with femininity. From the department stores at the turn of the century with their clientele of middle-class ladies, to the 'consuming housewife' of 1950s advertising, the dominant imag-

ined addressee of the languages of consumerism has been unmistakably feminine. Consumption, associated with the body, beautification and adornment in particular, has historically spoken to a feminine consumer, producing her as an 'active consumer' but also as a 'spectacle' herself. (151)

The protagonists of this novel are certainly active consumers, but not only in the interest of creating themselves as "spectacle." Their pleasure in consumption is not limited to fashion and cosmetics for their own adornment, but extends to the consumption of ideas, men, technology, and aesthetics; these aforementioned items become contingencies for the formation of female subjectivity through the subject's active process of negotiation and reappropriation of meaning.

Cristina Gaena: From the Multinational to Planeta X—the Consumption and Embodiment of Counterculture

Cristina Gaena, the youngest of the sisters, is a single, twenty-four-year-old English philology student and waitress at Planeta X. As the youngest of the siblings, Cristina experienced a unique formation—in comparison with her sisters—in that she was not as susceptible, nor easily swayed by discourses of Truth. Unlike her older sisters Rosa (thirty years old) and Ana (thirty-two), Cristina's generation was not raised beneath the pressures and extreme influences of the Franco regime, hence, the notion of tradition—from the macroscopic to the microscopic level—stood in stark contrast to her lived reality (belief system). From infancy, her generation has witnessed the confluence of the global and the local; as López contends: "la inmensa mayoría de sus [Cristina] referencias culturales, de películas a grupos musicales, actores y actrices, son extranjeras; su lenguaje está plagado de palabras en inglés (broker, overachiever, patchwork, grunge, etc) y de expresiones de este idioma directamente traducidas al español" (13). The influx and saturation of foreign culture in Spain has virtually created a dynamic space within which to question and negotiate the role and sustainable importance of convention in Spanish society. Throughout her story, Cristina, non-conformist and rebellious to explicit authority, develops as a contentious individual in defiant opposition to grand narratives. She quickly criticizes the code of morality that the "monjas" imposed in school and without hesitation will target psychology and its dogma: "los psicoanalistas creen que tus problemas pueden arreglarse si logras aislar el Gran Porqué, si logras encontrar el hecho particular que te convirtió en lo que eres" (278), a field in which she claims to be well-versed, as her mother sent her to a range of psicoanalysts and psiquiatrists due to her "problemas mentales" (176) with regularity throughout her childhood. The twenty-four-year-old astutely attributes her problems to the same factors that may have catalyzed her older sisters' issues: the abandonment of the Gaena father at an early age and, particular to Cristina, the purported sexual abuse she suffered from her cousin Gonzalo, thirteen years her senior. Nevertheless, it is interesting to note that unlike her sisters who both regularly consume an arsenal of prescribed chemical enhancements, she refuses to accept the potential validity of claims offered by the psychiatric institution, perhaps viewing their discourse through an optic of oppression, that is their possible colonization and subsequent erasure of her self, much like the totalitarian control of the Franco regime.

The two issues—the rejection from her father and "violation" by her cousin—shaped profoundly Cristina's conception and enactment of her sexuality. As the novel opens, Cristina makes a dual confession: (1) that it has been one month since she broke up with her boyfriend Iain, with whom she had an intense sexual relationship and (2) she just had her first sexual experience since Iain, which resulted botched for multiple reasons.

> En primer lugar, lo tenía minísculo. . . . Total, que lo hicimos de la forma tradicional, enroscados y babosos como anguilas. Nuestras pelvis entrechocaban una y otra vez . . . pero aquel micromiembro se restregaba patéticamente en mi entrepierna, resbalando una y otra vez entre mis labios, y cada nuevo empujón no era sino otro intento vano por introducirse en una sima cuya hondura—de dimensión y de apetito—le superaba. (14)

This vivid description reveals her consciousness and perhaps assertion in the appropriation of her sexuality. The choice of words used to describe both the male and female genitalia categorize them through oppositions; yet, the binary dialect employed transgresses—in some ways—the traditional conception of male/female sexuality. He is "minúsculo," lacking creativity, and pathetic; she, however, surpasses him not only in size but also in her voracious appetite. Throughout her personal narrative, Cristina makes reference to her desire and almost addictive need for sex: "necesito una polla entre las piernas" (39). Etxebarria employs the myth of the femme fatale, the woman who devours men, manifest in Cristina. Yet, she does not simply consider the woman in black-and-white categories, rather Cristina embodies a twist of this myth; she has a super-charged sexual appetite, not normally associated with women, but is not diabolical nor scandalous in her efforts; she is a woman feeling a sense of emptiness in the accelerated culture surrounding her. Thus, aware of how the economy of desire functions as well as her power,

Cristina works from the margins to achieve the desired effect. This ranges from sexual games with lovers to attempted suicides.[5] Self-destruction represents a form of manipulation used to control those who surrounded her. This patchwork of revelations exemplifies the narrative of Cristina's life and also lends evidence to her dynamic nature of working through experiences via the continual interrogation of universal truths.

Prior to obtaining the waitress job at Planeta X, Cristina worked for a multinational corporation translating documents into English and then sending them to various technological magazines. In that capacity, Cristina, unlike her older sister Rosa, experienced an absence, a loss of her self replaced by the advances in technology. In the chapter "C de curro," she offers her understanding of the capitalist setting, citing that progress "ha superado al Dios original en todo, incluso en crueldad" (33). López argues that Cristina quickly learns the two rhetorical strategies fundamental to the success of the capitalist rationale: "1) el esfuerzo será reconocido y se traducirá en la mejora de estatus y sueldo y 2) por cada empleado hay cuatro parados dispuestos a hacer lo que sea necesario para conseguir un puesto" (14). The ideology espoused by this paradigm runs in complete opposition to Cristina's dissident nature and her utter aversion to the growing affinity among technology and humans, which emerged internationally as a result of the globalization of cultures and instant ability for communication. She states:

> Controlaba perfectamente términos como interface, tarjeta VGA, puerto paralelo, driver, puerto de serie b, slot de 16 bits, filtros digitales para audio, transferencia térmica de cera o microprocesador. Me pasaba allí la vida, sentada en mi cubículo, mi punto de engorde, un espacio de apenas dos metros cuadrados acotado por dos mesas de formica dispuestas en forma de ele. (30)

The politics of location is entangled by many factors: physical dimensions, feelings of being enclosed, and the emotional element. As Cristina illustrates, the multinational dehumanized her existence, technologically colonizing her self. This is evidenced through her emphasis on the de-naturalized human space "los cubículos" and "punto de engorde" (33) of the capitalist empire, again pointing to the politics of location. Moreover, she criticizes this male-centered site signaling lack of space, poor lighting, and a meager salary.[6] Nevertheless, her male boss who "cobraba un millón de pesetas al mes" (31) earned eleven times her salary to chit-chat with his "girl of the month" which changed as frequently as one switches perfume. Cristina argues: "se pasaba el día llamando por teléfono a su amante de turno, porque las iba cambiando como cambiaba de colonia: Davidoff, Fahrenheit, Calvin

Klein, Ana, Lucía, Loreto . . . ¡hay que estar siempre a la última!" (31). From her discourse, she further suggests the role consumer culture has infiltrated and commodified all arenas of life: from products such as perfume to humans; we are not just purchasing a material good, rather a series of packaged images and people circulate as commodities. Furthermore, this boss who possesses a master's degree could not speak English nor be bothered with his accent marks in Spanish; this remained Cristina's responsibility. Yet, by virtue of being born male, he is the "ganador de la lotería demográfica" (31). From Cristina's perspective, the environment of the capitalist regime embodies artificial, de-humanized, machine-like qualities, consequently codified in the subject.[7] She states,

> Se me jodió la vista a cuenta de pasarme los días forzándola, cegada por la luz fantasmal del ordenador, y la claridad excesiva de las lámparas halógenas y la constante inclinación forzada sobre el teclado me provocaron unos dolores de espalda espantosos. Dos dioptrías y escoliosis, así de golpe. (30)

The job at the multinational enterprise not only affected but also structured her life, as she started at 8:00 A.M. and did not return until 8:30 P.M., completely exhausted. As such, per Cristina, her life was devoid of quality. While Cristina had many legitimate reasons for leaving her position, the motivating factor was the despotic practices of the "compañía machista." Cristina affirms:

> ¿qué coño hago you aquí? ¿QUE COÑO? Fue la llegada de aquella subnormal profunda, que acababa todas sus frases con un ¿sabes? Y para la que todo era como muy ideal o como muy algo, lo que me convenció de que me habían estafado, de que estaban engañándome como a un burro con el viejo truco de la zanahoria y el palo, y una mañana que bajé a la farmacia a comprar buscapinas porque ya no podía con aquel dolor de espalda, el sol me dio en la cara para avisarme de que estaba malgastando mi vida, la única vida de que dispongo, porque soy una mujer y no un gato, y caí en la cuenta de que llevaba dos años sin sentir la caricia dorada del sol en la nariz, de que se me estaba yendo la juventud encerrada en un despacho de ventanales blindado. (33)

After profound realizations, she purposefully entered work one day, hit "«Delete All» " (34) and walked out on her job certain, liberated, and utterly ecstatic. This defining poignant moment in shift in location points to a shift in the self, a resistance—one that is particularly active—and demonstrates her ability and desire to *work through* her experiences to her benefit, to arrive at a feminist embodiment of self. No longer willing to be codified according to the tenets—logic, rationalism, technology, and absence of affect—of an affected, accelerated culture, Cristina seeks to explore and define her own identity in a distinct territory. As Gottdiener qualifies, spaces of consumption are articulation points of individual psychology, social pressures, the media, fashion, and the realization of belonging. Hence, the pursuit of a distinctive lifestyle through an alternate via of consumption may represent a means of developing a sense of self and of actualizing identity politics; it can be seen as an emancipatory process, each choice indicating resistance, subversion, and empowerment.

This history of Cristina leads to an exploration of the proxemics of the rave culture as seen in her current place of employment, Planeta X. As her personal narrative indicates, first and foremost, it must be noted that Cristina leaves a patriarchal institution for another: the location of the multinational corporation for the underground bar; however, immersed in this space she feels empowered and liberated.[8] All the while, she is an active agent, embodying nomadic subjectivity, because of her understanding of the dynamics of the power system coupled with her ability to appropriate this territorial shift to her advantage. She confesses: "Parezco la Kate Moss, pero con tetas. Muy grunge, muy trendy. Por algo soy camarera, porque a los tíos les gusto. Muy machista, lo sé, pero de algo hay que comer, o, en mi caso, no comer. Lo siento mucho, la vida es así, no la he inventado yo" (37). Interestingly, she cites verses from a popular song of the eighties, "El jardín prohibido," written by Sandro Giacobbe; the melody, entrenched with masculine tones, is dedicated to his girlfriend whom he just betrayed by sleeping with her best friend. His response to her is: "Lo siento mucho, la vida es así. No la he inventado yo." With glaring irony, Cristina quotes this popular saying to explain her position and movements within the power paradigm. She acutely recognizes the dynamics of the hegemonic economy, yet her quote implicity hints at her exploitation of the system through her own means.

As Braidotti posits in *Patterns of Dissonance*, men have maintained and authorized control over the feminine through the power of the patriarchy, or the power of the father (Braidotti). This paradigm of power subjugates women to masculine domination through the symbolic such as traditions, language, myths and the socio-political, which effectively has silenced the female and converted her into an object without a concrete exchange value. Irigaray affirms these ideas as she contends:

> In our social order, women are 'products' used and exchanged by men. Their status is that of merchandise. . . . Women's social inferiority is reinforced and complicated by the fact that woman does not have access to language, except through recourse to 'masculine' systems of representation. (223)

To escape this symbolic violence of the masculine paradigm in which man is not the enemy but rather the phallocracy, Braidotti calls for the opening of new paths for contemplation; one which, in her words, does "not conceptualize the feminist position as that of the 'guerrillera' fighting a holy war" (279). But rather, she envisions as fundamental the necessity for the rethinking and redefinition of the subject. "As in postmodernism, the conceptual challenge consists in upholding the idea of the subject as a dazzling collection of integrated fragments, while also defending the specificity of the female subject as a theoretical, libidinal, ethical and political agent" (282). Working with this conceptual framework, Braidotti conceives of the notion of sexual difference as delineating the absence of symmetry among the sexes which subsequently raises the question of women in terms of the modifications and merits they carry to a culture embedded in crisis. Elaborated in these terms, she offers a radical alternative to the centrality of the masculine economy, purporting that female subjectivity, or the process of becoming-woman in postmodern times, entails a type of fluid nomadism that seeks to question from the position of sexual difference, dominant identities as well as conventional power structures. She affirms:

> This possibly enables them to make a breach in the code of symbolic representation. In the name of the repressed, which is where they have been positioned, women are capable of producing a 'boomerang effect,' opening the way to the return of the repressed, that is, to new forms of representation. (279)

In consideration of Braidotti's theories, we may conclude that Cristina's rejection of the culture of the multinational and subsequent immersion in the culture of the rave, redefines the embodied nature of Woman or Cristina. She possesses no notion of changing the power system, but rather works within this structure to her benefit, as evidenced through her representation. She is dynamic and in transit.

It must be noted that in raves, cultures of consumption, musical production, event distribution, and hence profit-making are predominantly qualified as male sites of experience. Nevertheless I agree it represents a liberating experience, and is one that can be seen as positive in feminist terms. To begin with, Cristina earns more as a waitress in this environment than she did while working in the multinational. Likewise, this profession imposes fewer constraints on her time; she now assumes ownership of her life.

> En el bar gano más de lo que ganaba en aquella oficina, y mis mañanas son para mí, para mí sola, y el tiempo libre vale para mí más que los mejores sueldos del

mundo. No me arrepiento en absoluto de la decisión que tomé, y nunca, nunca jamás volvería a trabajar en una multinacional. Antes me meto a puta. (34)

Her words exemplify a profound understanding of power dynamics as well as her ability and intense desire to work through her experiences to her benefit. While some may read "Antes me meto a puta" as a mere phrase, upon consideration, the declaration reveals: she is conscious that she maneuvers within a patriarchal economy, and as such, she participates within the economy, yet on her terms. The vocalization of the fact that she would rather earn money for sex than prostitute herself to the capitalist masculine dominated society clearly demonstrates her utter despisal of being a mere pawn of capitalism. Futhermore, it may represent a critique of the exploitation of women's labor within the capitalist system. Earning a living as a prostitute, then, is better than being a "multinational" prostitute. What stands out here is the emphasis on the issue of agency, even if this could represent a submission to the symbolic. While both options remain within the realm of the patriarchy and could be read by some feminist scholars as submission to the symbolic order, I view Cristina's consideration of her job as a waitress as well as her joke regarding becoming a "puta" as both professions (she still remains within the dominant economy) that permit her to exploit the masculine economy to her advantage, as well as access active female agency. That is to say, she is not a prisoner of a cubicle that has the same dimension as a veal pen; likewise, she has an abundance of free time which she appropriates as she feels necessary.

> Que me mola ser una camarera y no veo nada de malo en ello por mucho que mis hermanas se empeñen en decir que debería dedicarme a algo más serio. Por lo general les respondo que si pudiera ya lo haría, que no soy tonta. Y tengo que dejar claro que, al contrario de lo que la mayoría de la gente cree, lo de ser camarera en un bar de moda no quiere decir que sea idiota, no señor, que así tengo más tiempo para leer o para acabar mi tésis que si me dedicara a otra cosa, y de momento estoy muy a gusto con mi trabajo, aunque no tenga seguridad social ni contrato fijo ni estabilidad de ningún tipo, ni esos detalles que tanto valoran mis hermanas. Pero, qué coño, es un trabajo, y me da para vivir, que es lo importante. (20)

It is interesting to note how Cristina embodies her job on an affectual level. Whereas in the multinational, she exuded the principles of the information saturated culture such as rationalism and logic, her body and self metamorphose in a distinct manner in conjunction with the location of the bar. She describes herself within this space stating: "Y aquí estoy ahora, en mi bar del alma, en este bar que para mis hermanas supone la mayor vergüenza social, limpiando botellas con la energía de un huracán" (42). What is significant, then, is that through her expressions of capitalist malcontent, she is not indicating a rejection of consumption; rather, she is balancing paradoxical demands and indulging in behaviors particular to the community with which she finds affinity.

The physical space of the rave culture which emerges from the chic bar scene of Planeta X gives rise to an alternative female subjectivity, one that partakes in the maximization of auto-erotic pleasure stemming from more intimate levels of involvement. Cristina reveals:

> En los escasos momentos en que la barra queda vacía cierro
> los ojos e intento concentrarme en los sonidos sintetizados,
> visualizando la música como una cebolla iridiscente a la que yo,
> lenta y concienzuda, voy arrancando capas, una tras otra, hasta dar
> con una diseñada especialmente para mí: el regalo de la rave. (35)

In consuming the rave culture, her experience signals how her body becomes a home. It is a location—a site of liberation—in which the sounds and the music are a meditation that flow through the body providing a mental bliss. The penetration of these accoutrements provokes the disintegration of the bound female, suggesting the unraveling of the barriers of the body that subsequently permits Cristina to delve into the profundity of her self.

While material goods possess a sign value, their consumption is a mode of self-expression embodied on the textual subject, which must not simply be understood as "ravaging." Rather, Bowlby suggests a shift in the understanding of consumption that entails a re-examination of the active female role. As an illustration, the rave culture in which Cristina participates demonstrates how the feminine subject is an agent who can enact change and evolution. That is, we must look at the shifts as experiences that go far beyond symbols or mere images of delectation. Rachel Bowlby argues for a rethinking in the relationship among consumption and the female underlining that: "Consumption . . . has offered women new areas of authority and expertise, new sources of income, a new sense of consumer right; and one of the consequences of these developments has been a heightened awareness of entitlement outside the sphere of consumption" (16). From this point of view, Bowlby understands the realm of consumption two-fold: as a territory in which one can ponder and rebuff the passive feminine identity and also as the ongoing process of identity creation that embodies the nomadic subject (Bowlby). With respect to cultures of consumption, this analysis provides a foundation for becoming-woman or the feminist subject. In particular, it is springboard to illustrate how the rave scene affords women like Cristina a libidinal return on their investment that is often experienced as positive and liberating. While she is not earning the astronomical salary of her sister Rosa, nor does she have the luxurious privileges of Ana, her oldest sister, through consumption of experiences and goods, Crisitina illustrates patently Bowlby's affirmation of women's heightened consciousness of legitimacy outside of consuming conventional doctrine.

This leads us to an analysis of the rave assemblage in the culture of Planeta X: "ese espacio tecnificado y cyberchic que constituye el escenario de mis noches" (121). The first component is time; the events at the bar occur at night. Followed by time, we must consider the space or layout of the venue, and finally the body and how it is used; for instance, the dancing, emotion, and use of drugs which occur in the venue. Cristina clearly describes the aforementioned material and discursive elements as they work upon and produce her self. She states:

> Y cuando la [la rave] encuentro, la hago ascender a través de mis venas, mis capilares y mis arterias, recorrer mi cabeza mezclada con mi linfa mi sangre, ascender hacia mi cabeza, inundarme por completo. Me diluyo en música, me borro, me extiendo, me transformo, me vuelvo líquida y polimorfa. De pronto llega un roll on, un cambio radical de ritmo seguido de una secuencia prolongada que comienza muy, muy lentamente y luego se acelera de forma paulatina hasta retomar el ritmo del techno, machacón. Insistente, acompasado a los latidos del corazón. La oscuridad me invita a dejarme llevar y arrastra hacia el altavoz que vomita una música monótona, geométrica, energética y lineal, suavizada en mi cabeza por el éxtasis. (35)

This dance-drug scene re-appropriates socially lived reality; it reinvents what anarchist Hakim Bey describes as a "temporary autonomous zone." Such zones, Bey suggests, are "successful raids on consensus reality, breakthroughs into more intense and more abundant life" (115). The primary artistic expression of the rave culture, the music, offers a consistently transforming sonic narrative, enacting feelings that surpass linguistic abilities. It is depicted as a culture with choices instead of rules. As Braidotti posits, the process of becoming-woman in postmodern times entails a type of fluid nomadism that seeks to question from the position of sexual difference, dominant identities as well as conventional power structures. Cristina's total immersion into the rave culture redefines her embodied nature as Woman. Within this context, she experiences a sense of autonomy unknown to her within the capitalist confines of the multinational, evidenced through the fluidity of her body as it transforms in accordance with the free form of the music.

The rave culture—embedded in energetic music that utilizes samplers to create audio collages, fragmenting visual stimuli and the drug ecstasy—is composed of a collectivity that shares in the maximization of libidinal pleasure stemming from intimate levels of involvement rooted in empathy and friendship (Collin). This reveals another intrigue with respect to the production of the self: the neo-tribe or imagined community. The theorist Maffesoli presents a deconstruction of conglomerate atomizations of contemporary society that differentiate themselves via a similar lifestyle and the desire for the metabolic consumption of similar goods. According to Maffesoli's usage of the term neo-tribe, these groupings do not have longevity or the fixity of conventional tribes, rather they share a communal belonging based upon the here and now:

> Can we extrapolate and make a link with the puissance of the masses? I believe it is legitimate to do so, especially since the essential characteristic of religion, in its different manifestations, remains nevertheless intangible: its transcendence. Whether it can be situated in a great beyond or whether it is an 'immanent transcendence' (the group, the community transcending individuals) does not alter the truth of the matter. My hypothesis, as distinct from those who lament the end of great collective values and the withdrawal into the self—which they falsely parallel with the growing importance of everyday life—is that a new (and evolving) trend can be found in the growth of small groups and existential networks. This represents a sort of tribalism which is based at the same time on the spirit of religion (re-ligare) and on localism (proxemics, nature). (40)

Imagined communities or neo-tribes are marked by their fluidity: they are locally concentrated, dispersed, and periodically assembled. Maffesoli points to the importance of aesthetics or the "immaterial in the heart of the material." In the process of joining tribes, the individual self-fashions.

> Whether trendy exercises in sensory isolation, or various forms of bodybuilding . . . the body is being constructed as a value, even to the extent of its epiphany. . . . Note, however, that even in its most private aspects, the body is being constructed only in order to be seen; it is theatralized to the highest degree. Within advertising, fashion, dance, the body is adorned only to be made into a spectacle. (18–19)

Cristina's engagement within the rave culture reveals how this space represents a liberating positive experience. I consider the narrative of Cristina's experience as a member of this culture gratifying and freeing, as illustrated via the material aspects such as the lights, music, drugs, as well as aspects of location, the body, and affective manifestations. Through examining these elements, I contend that Cristina's experience within the rave is embodied in a dynamic nomadic subject. The following quotation is a testimony to the discursive and material angles of the rave culture.

> El DJ es el nuevo mesías; la música, la palabra de Dios; el vino de los cristianos ha sido sustituido por el éxtasis y la iconografía de las vidrieras por los monitores de televisión. Es el regreso del tribalismo ancestral, heredado genéticamente, dicen, en el inconsciente colectivo. (36)

This tribe, a reminder of the subconscious need to belong, establishes its own religion in which fixed borders among the participants are diluted. The music and ecstasy percolate through the dancers' brains—trying to play their body chemistry—creating a homology between sonic texture and the chemically elevated cortex (Collin). They partake collectively in the ecstatic fluid celebration yet can be read individually as each participant brings her own personal history and experience and therefore embodies her own figuration, in Braidotti's terms, of the nomadic subject. "Yo también participo en este rito común, y una vez bendecida por el DJ al que va dirigida nuestra alabanza, le imploro de corazón que me funda con el resto" (36). Cristina, a figuration partaking in the neo-tribal rave scene, admits that while it is a collective act signaling us to Maffesoli's theory—a location of a communion of believers—she still retains her individuality and moreover, the elements both discursive and material are embodied on her self:

> Siento que las luces de la pista son tangibles, y que la música se traduce a imágenes. Vuelve a ascender la música en capas envolventes intentando anularnos con su voluntad ensordecedora. Desde la barra vislumbro un tejido irisado de brazos y piernas y camisetas brillantes, una masa humana y multicolor de cabelleras, ondeando al ritmo de mil tambores atávicos. Ramalazos de luces surgen de la nada, flash, y desaparecen al segundo de cegarnos, negro, y otra luz cegadora vuelve a surgir coincidiendo con un nuevo latido de nuestro corazón. Cuando tengo que cruzar la sala para ir dejando limpias las mesas erizadas de vasos y botellas me siento un nadador contra corriente. Alrededor de mí los cuerpos, comprimidos y multiperforados, se empujan los unos a los otros, las personas ya no son personas porque la identidad de cada uno se funde en el crisol de la masa, y lo que siento alrededor es un magma en ebullición, con pequeñas burbujitas que de vez en cuando emergen a la superficie. (39)

The space of the dance floor is a decisive element of the grammar of Cristina's identity. This territory is distinctive because it contrasts the individual experience with that of the masses, or identity opposing the abysm of anonymity. It is within this location that Cristina articulates her notion of self, focusing not so much on the content or the rationality of the experience but rather the feeling imbued: she is in constant movement. This new consciousness surpasses linguistics; she felt it with every cell of her body, without the distortions of language intervening. The prevailing mentality of sensation and sound is interwoven and defined by the set and setting of the participants, which itself is interwoven with the prevailing social mood of the 1990s in Madrid, Spain. That is, identity formation ceases to be rooted solely in the local; rather due to technological advances and globalization, it becomes enmeshed in other practices:

> Es fácil localizar temporalmente el fenómeno. En la transición entre el siglo XX y el XXI los grandes estados, las grandes ciudades y, en general, las sociedades complejas se desarrollan sobre espacios muy amplios, casi mundiales, en los que resulta muy difícil marcar fronteras y límites. Estas mismas entidades no logran ya—recuérdese que estamos en la sociedad de la información y del libre comercio—frenar lo que viene de fuera, lo que obviamente, les lleva a confundir lo propio con lo extraño. . . . Entonces resulta ya mucho más difícil distinguir a los enemigos, a los oponentes, a los auténticamente extraños, a los que pertenecen al espacio propio y a los que provienen del espacio ajeno. (Costa 29)

In a society entrenched with globalized information and progressive consolidation of free commerce, no longer functions the traditional constitution of identity: space delineating social status. The weakening of conventional identity founded on the one's own space gives way to self-formation in alignment with the conditions called for in our twenty-first century: consumption, fashion, technology, and the spectacle. Pere-Oriol Costa in *Tribus urbanas* affirms a transformation in identity politics stating: "El panorama urbano español de este turbulento final de siglo y de milenio no difiere, en el fondo, de los demás centros metropolitanos de nuestro planeta" (36). This is realized through the bombardment of public announcements in their constant attempts to awaken us to achieve our full potential. "La publicidad no cesa de dirigirse personalizadamente a ese individuo—un individuo que desea—mediante la modalidad del imperativo seductor: "«compra», «usa», «haz», etc." (Costa 40). These public announcements conjugated with the consumer negotiate the subject-formation, such that each subject feels she is both owner and planner of her existence. Costa contends:

Pasear por las calles de una gran ciudad, con la mirada errante, si es posible sin prisas, es una experiencia en la que se obtiene la impresión de que miles de neones, carteles, pancartas y vallas publicitarias tutean al sujeto y captan su atención en una celebración constante de ese triunfo del individuo. (40)

Hence mass media, through the creation of superficially intimate ties (use of the informal tú address) with the consumer, reveals to the subject multifarious options for the fashioning of selfhood. So, while there are those who seek to edify their identity through the exaltation of designer labels, such as Cristina's older sister Ana, others, Cristina being the obvious example, choose to adopt a distinct aspect, codified with anti-capitalist, anti-consumer language. Costa associates this behavior with the term *anomia* stemming from a-nomós in Latin, meaning "ausencia de reglas, normas, y consecuentemente, inobservancia de las leyes" (38).[9] He further contends that this phenomena tends to surface in a society in transformation whereby traditional values conflict with emerging ones, generating an endemic frustration. He states:

Caducidad de los viejos valores e inexistencia (o fragilidad) de los nuevos. En su acepción más evidente, todo esto significa que en un contexto urbano como el actual, en el que se manifiesta una oferta plural de bienes materiales y culturales, se genera fácilmente irritación y frustración entre quienes no tienen los medios— no sólo económicos sino también (y, tal vez, sobre todo) simbólicos—para alcanzar dichos bienes. La reacción puede ser entonces de tipo anómico. (38)

Thus, dissidents—those manifesting anomic qualities—toy with the margins and produce a social discourse distinct of the dominant rationale, reflected in the individual narratives. Cristina, walking out on the capitalist multinational, broke with the establishment, going off into the bar; nonetheless, it must be noted that she is not outside of the masculine economy. She not only made the physical but the emotional break with the reality that she knew. Her experiences within the underground scene of Planeta X have reinforced the break; no longer relying on tested narratives, vis-à-vis the rave culture, the neo-tribe and, by extension, Cristina explore creative channels that new technology affords. This particular location, Planeta X, constitutes a special time when normal rules are suspended; it unfolds as an idealized, peak experience that allows space for utopian dreaming and acts as a catalyst for events to come (Collin). Through adoption of a new lifestyle (Planeta X), Cristina altered her vision of stable security; wealth and traditional status represented linear authoritative control. Yet within the scene, the plethora of accoutrements acts as rhythms that induce a different relationship between the self and body: one that is more sensorial and sensual.

Visibility is a key component of identity construction in contemporary society. The image or particular style of "mask" is a fundamental feature of identity that affords each individual visibility. Costa argues its instrumental functionality stating:

> Insistimos en la importancia de la dimensión del aspecto y de la apariencia, bajo un punto de vista complementario: trans-parentarse, es decir ver lo que aparece a través de una superficie. La sociedad contemporánea, más que todas las que la han precedido, parece obsesionada por la idea de verlo y/o mostrarlo todo, de transformar el mundo en algo literalmente transparente. (50)

The image, constructed through the articulation of body dressing, represents a synergy among feelings, clothes, signs, and senses. Fashion, furthermore, is the syntax of body language that charges the body with meaning; its value remains not in the use of the clothing but rather its communication. Patrizia Calefato contends in *El sentido del vestir*, "en el propio vestir según la serialidad de la imagen de moda, subsiste siempre un gesto arquetípico carnavalesco que consiste en travestir, en disfrazar, en 'escribir' el cuerpo y sobre el cuerpo para que éste se introduzca en la circulación 'de las calles y del placer,' para que el cuerpo sea 'para los otros'—y para sí mismo—como si uno fuera otro" (10). Dress, then, is a body "disguise," codified with social meaning, lending weight to pictorial representation of identity, albeit fluid. From this symbolic language, what then emerges is a sense of who one is and who one is not. Fashion, a world affording a visual, nonverbal vocabulary for the construction of truths, provides for a constant negotiation of identity and its borders due to its intrinsic nature; every season and year is greeted with a new, if not recycled, trend. Cristina's fashion consumption further indicates the minding and construction of her subjectivity. Her body dressing of choice oscillates between two outfits, yet both embody a style "desenfadado." As the body is a symbol of cultural location, the dressed body is always situated within a particular context. In the bar, she "prescindido de los pantalones de campana y las camisetas por encima del ombligo" (74), and on the street she sported a "camiseta blanca, vaqueros nuevos, sin remiendos ni nada, botas de cuero" (74). Both options effectively inflect the body with meaning, underlining her sexuality, yet at the same time, her informal nature; in the same way she expressed dissention against capitalist systems, the protagonist also achieves this through her clothing. Furthermore, by way of sporting jeans or cargo pants, Cristina embodies a laid-back yet slightly rebellious subjectivity that stands in contraposition to her body as text within the multinational. The fashion that Cristina elects serves the function to attract the male gaze, for instance, within the bar she wears a tank-top that reveals her stomach. Yet it must be emphasized that while her body converts into a commodity, it is not a passive object. Rather, Cristina actively produces it through routine and practice.

As a means of clothing, adorning or decorating the body, fashion operates at an affectual as well as symbolic level. It aids in the construction and reconstruction of individual subjectivities while forging an affectual or experimental relationship between various actors. Cristina's choice of clothing does not simply symbolize rebellion, but it has a serious impact on how she savors and relishes her lived-body and her body-in-use. Whether dressed in jeans or her bar outfit, she has a commanding presence. "Soy una chica como cualquier otra, que no destacaría en un concurso de belleza. Y, sin embargo, por la calle todos los hombres me dedican adjetivos más o menos amables, más o menos procaces. Quizá sea más guapa de lo que creo yo" (73–74). This can also be noted within the context of the bar; Cristina, as the bartender, works from behind the bar and is the focal point of this venue. That is to say, as the chief distributor of libations, her body converts to a commodity, but she still maintains power. While selling drinks, Cristina places herself on the market, not explicitly for amorous purposes, but to bolster her income. Her body-in-use, then, is located in this affective structure—a convergence of music, lights, drugs, bodies and fashion—within the economy of give and exchange, and articulates, reinforces, and reflects the social lived reality of this scene. One of the most powerful examples of the use of her body as a material within this construct is the scene in which her sister Rosa pays a visit to Planeta X. As the two siblings are embroiled in the continual spat regarding Cristina's job selection, a customer enters described as "un tipo bajito y repeinado, que no debe de tener más de treinta años. Lleva un polo rosa, pantalones de pinzas y zapatos italianos. Apenas supera el metro setenta. Un pijillo" (49). As Cristina approaches him, he lets her know that he would like a whiskey, but not just any; he questions: "¿Cómo se llama el de aquella botella marrón que está en lo alto del estante?"(49). After Cristina explains to him the specific liquor he requested was not a whiskey but actually a gin— a very expensive one—and, moreover, that it would be difficult for her to access the bottle as it was not within reaching distance, he forcefully tells her that he is the customer, and as a worker, she is obligated to fulfill his request. Only, within this economy, he was not simply asking for the drink, rather a peek "el muy cabrón está aprovechando la ocasión para mirarme el culo" (50) as her body was a component of the bar assemblage. Interestingly, his request, which was being fulfilled by Cristina, represented a point of contestation for her older sister Rosa, who promptly informed the customer: "¿Te importaría dejar de mirar el culo de mi novia con semejante descaro?" (50). Rosa enters the situation, albeit subversively, with a handful of motives: to remove Cristina from the realm of pure spectacle and to make her aware that she does indeed work in a patriarchal institution.[10]

In the dimension of the bar, a zone of pleasure, commodities circulate and meanings are appropriated, re-imaged, and retooled for consumer consumption. It is in this location that Cristina articulates her identity through the symphony of music, lights, drugs and fashion, which works to produce her body, a body that communicates and may be understood through the grammar of signs. This language connotes a specific ideology or set of cultural meanings that speak of one's identity; in Cristina's case, an individual who works from the margins in a collectivity, distinct of that of capitalism, to access and feel the emancipation otherwise denied to her in the space of the multinational. So, it is interesting to note how she appropriates this discourse outside of Planeta X; that is, her autonomy is not exclusive to the rave scene, although this particular ambience offers new possibilities for the invention of the self. Likewise, the commanding and exercising of her identity outside of this realm gives evidence to, in Braidotti's term, the working through of experiences to one's benefit.

Cristina's closest friends, Line and Gema, embody a similar ideology regarding contemporary life in Spain. Her best friend Line, who suffers from an eating disorder, proclaims as her holy trinity: "Los éxtasis . . . , el chocolate. . . . el sexo anal" (160). This collectivity of women, through cultures of consumption, embodies dissidence; they rebel against socially prescribed norms for the female subject and thereby create alternative subjectivities. One particular occasion that exemplifies their questioning of tradition is in the chapter "I de intolerancia." This specific chapter treats the construction of alternative female identity and the manner in which it is received by patriarchy. Cristina, in much detail, describes a morning bus ride shared by herself and Line in which they were returning home after a night of much partying and no sleep. She provides a vivid illustration of their attire:

> A Line y a mí, monísimas, tal que salidas de un catálogo de Don Algodón. Todo en nuestro aspecto (el modelito compuestísimo, el maquillaje corrido, las carreras de mis medias . . .) delata que venimos de una fiesta y que todavía no hemos dormido. (91)

From the outset, these women symbolically represent the erosion of traditional values as their highly sexual yet disordered appearance suggests. Cristina is wearing "un traje negro ceñido que revela con el mayor descaro las curvas vertiginosas de mis cincuenta y ocho kilos" (91), an outfit that offers her the means of gratifying desires and pursuing pleasure; nonetheless, her body resembles that of an adolescent: "Me estoy quedando en los huesos. Parezco recién salida de Dachau" (37). Thus, her look alludes to the complex balance between social control and self-gratification. Her body as an object constructed thorough consumerism is an important element in feminine culture that is a commodity—transformed and sold. The paradox between her "on the move" look and size takes on new dimension with the way she embodies this combination on the bus. For example, the way she sits: "me siento con la planta de un toro de la ganadería de Pablo Romero: poderío y bravura cincelados en negro" (91–92) reflects the power she receives (perceived or real) from her body dressing. Her friend, Line, contrasts sharply with Cristina due to her angelical, childlike look: "cuarenta y tres kilos, camiseta rosa talla doce años con estampado de la Bola del Dragón, flequillo, dos coletitas sujetándole los cabellos rubios y unos enormes ojos azul cielo que la confieren un aire de perpetuo asombro" (92). Upon pure consideration of image, Line's look could be cast as passive; nevertheless, her body refuses effacement, asserting its independence from the clothes that cover it. On the bus, these two friends begin a critical conversation about men, focusing on their sexual relationships. As the remaining passengers were men, including the bus driver, they eavesdropped on the women's conversation about their sexual escapades. Cristina begins the conversation inquiring about Line's night, to which she responds: "No mucho. HE ESTADO FOLLANDO" (93), each word resounding louder. As if this were not enough to cause discomfort for this conventional crowd, she retells with minute detail her experience: "No gran cosa, hija. ¡Menudo coñaazo de tío . . . ! Y encima nos lo hemos hecho en la cama de sus padres, con el crucifijo en la pared y la foto de su mamá en la mesilla. Bueno, bueno . . . ¡me daba un maaal rollo! Todo el rato con la impresión de que la foca esa me miraba con cara de mosqueo" (95). Not only do these two women discuss their evening, but they also admit that they were quite disappointed in the performance of their partners. The conversation elaborates further on past sexual experiences and also sexually transmitted diseases, which Line says were pure torture. In her own words: "soy una adicta al sexo. No pasa una semana sin que lo intente otra vez" (98). Their discourse collides with the prevailing tradition that prescribes and enforces gendered identities. Yet, these two continue to question conventional roles as manifest in sexual experiences; Line elaborates: "Ellos, los muy cabrones, sí que lo tienen fácil, porque al final no importa que la cosa les salga mejor o peor, el caso es que siempre se corren, mientras que nosotras . . . es como jugar a la lotería" (98). The discourse demonstrates their major preoccupation with the formulation of the fulfillment of their needs and desires defined in their own terms, which sharply contrasts with society's constrained conception of female pleasure. This is poignantly displayed through the men's reactions toward their personal conversation. To begin with, the bus driver nearly avoided two accidents due to his intense focus on their conversation, to which he could only offer: "Mira, guapa. La culpa es tuya por no bajar el volumen. ¿O te has creído que los demás estamos aquí para escuchar vuestras vulgaridades? (99). Or other trite responses from workers: "A éstas me las llevaba yo a la obra y se les iban a quitar las ganas de cachondeo. . . . Mira, rubita [Line]. Tengo una hija que debe de tener tu edad, y te aseguro que si alguna vez la oigo hablar como tú, le doy cuatro hostias y le lavo la boca con jabón" (100). Thus, in the attempt to have a personal conversation in which they relate their sexual experiences and frustrations in contemporary society, these women are met with resistance and the threat of punishment. These responses underline the prevalence in contemporary society of containment of women in the binary opposition of Eve, the temptress, or Mary, the holy mother of God. The women, though, utilize this situation to their advantage; instead of allowing their comments to produce negative effects such as feeling ashamed or embarrassed or silencing themselves, they speak out against the unjust stereotypes hurled at women. Line responds to the men firmly and succinctly all the while maintaining intense eye contact: "No hagas caso a estos RE-PRI-MI-DOS. Mejor nos bajamos. Prefiero seguir andando que quedarme en este autobús lleno de MA-CHIS-TAS" (100). Line and Cristina repossess bodily space through their denunciation of men's attitudes and exiting the bus. As Braidotti contends:

> The body as a site of interaction of material and symbolic forces is the threshold of subjectivity; it is not a biological notion, but marks, rather the non-coincidence of the subject with his/her consciousness and the non-coincidence of anatomy with sexuality. (282)

In this view, essentialism no longer clothes the body as it is now positioned between the sign and biology. The women, through the appropriation of the body, explore multiple and non-binary experiences through lived practice. Armed against the notion that Woman is one, Cristina and Line create a new set of possibilities for the embodiment of the female subject. In fact, their heterogeneous representation is evidence of the multiplicity of female subjectivities, as T. de Lauretis affirms:

> What is emerging in feminist writings is . . . the concept of a multiple, shifting, and often self-contradictory identity, a subject that is not divided in, but

rather at odds with language; an identity made up of heterogeneous and heteronomous representation of gender, race and class, and often indeed across languages and cultures; an identity that one decides to reclaim from a history of multiple assimilations, and that one insists on as a strategy. (9)

Through resistance and rejection of the hegemonic model, Etxebarria's writing redefines the concept of the knowing subject, which suggests support for the notion that a new image of both knowledge and subjectivity is not necessary, rather essential to the regeneration of the concept of woman.

Rosa Gaena: Techno-colonization, the Cyborg, and Emotive Harmony

Rosa, the middle child of the Gaena sisters, is a highly successful single thirty-year-old director of finance for a large multinational company. As third wave feminists seek to resist the essentialism of woman, opting to define women through a multiplicity of figurations, the characters of Cristina and Rosa shed light on their statement vis-à-vis their distinct ideologies on what it means to be a woman in Spain in the last decade of the twentieth century. The character of Rosa—mediated by various discourses—serves to highlight the shortcomings of the second wave of feminism; the modus operandi of that particular generation of feminists was to achieve equality among the sexes through the assimilation of women into the patriarchal structure. Unfortunately, as evidenced by the confessions of Rosa as well as the discourse of Cristina, women while legal equals under the Spanish Constitution of 1978, were subjected to different standards and continued to suffer ill treatment in the workplace. Rosa recites, as if by memory, the unwritten code of comportment for women in the arena of the office.

> Si desea tener éxito como mujer de negocios póngase de pie con tanta frecuencia como sus colegas masculinos y en las mismas situaciones que éstos. No permanezca sentada cuando alguien entre en su despacho o se reúna con usted ante su mesa. No importa lo que digan los manuales de urbanidad: si quiere usted igualdad de oportunidades e igualdad de trato, debe ponerse en pie como un hombre, literal y figurativamente hablando. (215)

Peppered with the rhetoric of equality, Rosa's discourse promotes masculine politics whereby the woman must adhere to norms of the male economy and sacrifice her internal liberty. Equality in this paradigm supposes a definitive triumph of the patriarchal structure. Sendón de León argues the ineffective nature of these strategies citing the work of Simone de Beauvoir.

> Siendo consecuentes con lo que plantea Beauvoir, la propuesta de la igualdad y emancipación desde semejantes presupuestos solo puede lograrse negando la diferencia sexual femenina en beneficio de un «sujeto universal y neutro» que, lógicamente, sería masculino, por más que incluyera tanto a hombres como a mujeres en la etapa gloriosa de la igualdad. (21)

This theorist of sexual difference underlines the absurdity of locating emancipation of the female subject within the dominant model; equality realized under this paradigm—one of colonization—only annihiliates the possibility of autonomy and serves to perpetuate fundamental inequality. This is further evidenced in Rosa's interior monologue: "Compórtese como un hombre. Controle sus sentimientos. No llore en público. Que sus gestos siempre sean adecuados y aceptables con arreglo a la situación concreta. Sincronice las palabras con las acciones" (216). The list of commands she flips through like a rolodex file seems much more appropriate for a military person as opposed to a woman in business, yet she justifies her rhetoric stating: "Recuerde que, por lo general, cuando las mujeres se encuentran al frente de la dirección siempre son blanco de críticas que nada tienen que ver con su capacidad profesional" (216). As she discovers, biology is the determining factor for women in the workplace, as opposed to their efforts. While the feminine is explicity located at the heart of the commodity culture, a traditionally masculine script of ambition and achievement is reconstructed through the figure of Rosa. A quandary for Rosa is her intense desire to succeed in a masculine economy at the expense of utter negation of her emotions and nature. Following this line of thought, Rosa declares that to be successful in this: "mundo en que solo tienen cabida los triunfadores" (219) is to join them and "sacrificar casi todo lo demás" (219).

As opposed to her younger sister Cristina, who walked solemnly out of the capitalist economy after having intentionally crashed the hard drive, Rosa consumes and is consumed by the world of capitalism and technology.[11] In the late twentieth century, advances in scientific culture and technology have made possible the dissolution of the neatly bound human. Shedding light on this is Rosa as she represents a hybrid identity, part machine and part human; in the words of Donna Haraway she is a "cyborg" or a mix of "machine and organism" (2), a figuration which illustrates the contemporary social reality of our Western world. The term cyborg was initially coined by Manfred Clynes and Nathan Kline at the beginning of the sixties to describe man-machine systems. However, since then, the concept of the cyborg has been theorized in a manner to consider the relationship among human beings and technology, as cyborg technologies ambiguously reconfigure human subjectivity. Of specific concern to the cyborg is its constituency; unlike the patriarchal hegemony, the cyborg is a crafted fabrication. It represents the melding of the machine and the mind, expansion of consciousness and intelligence. The cyborg fuses the organic and the hi-tech, and as such is a boundary breaker.

However, this theory engenders conflicts. According to Haraway, the cyborg does not submit to the symbolic law, as the role of the father is inessential: "The cyborg does not dream of community on the model of the organic family, this time without the oedipal project. The cyborg would not recognize the Garden of Eden; it is not made of mud and cannot dream of returning to dust" (3). In her line of inquiry the cyborg, a potentially subversive figuration, possesses no historical memory nor is grounded in the dominant economy. Negating social and historical background results problematic; in "erasing" history, one denies differences and experiences among marginal groups. Furthermore, the theory supposes that body and mind convert to a tabula rasa to be developed through the melding of flesh and circuits, again denying voice to individual experience as well as brushing over historical accountability.

Encoded on Rosa's body—rationality, order, and logic—manifest and concurrently demonstrate the conflation and resulting hybridization of organism and machine. Rosa defines herself: "idéntica a mi ordenador, que dispone de una batería de emergencia que se conecta automáticamente en caso de un fallo en la corriente eléctrica. Diseñada para durar. Programada para seguir adelante" (220). As a cross between machine and organism, Rosa is coded in such a way to produce confusion among boundaries of female identity. What is missing in this new identity—to a certain degree—are the insipid forms of oppression that historically have been naturalized by the libidinal male economy (Haraway).

> Palabras que me definen. Equilibrio tecnológico. Correo electrónico. Memoria Ram. Balances. Presupuestos. Informes por triplicado. Curvas de campana. Capital riesgo. Mínimo amortizable. Comité de dirección. Plan de crecimiento. Inyección de capital. Versión alfa. Fase beta. Proyectos. Equipos. Multimedia. Liderazgo. (163)

The terms she employs to describe herself coincide with the notion of the melding of machine and flesh: e-mail, RAM, capital risk, expansion plans, and leader. This thirty-year-old woman has essentially come of age in an increasingly technological and materialistic bureaucratic society, where discourses collide and communities are fragmented. Consequently, her subject is the product of her upbringing and experiences. Amidst sensations of alienation and fragmentation, the cerebral Rosa organizes her life both personally and professionally according to high technology principles that are encoded in her subjectivity. Her memory mimics technological information systems as she emphasizes the transition from the old hierarchical economy to the new network of information systems. "Ha llegado un punto en que mi memoria está duplicada, y la memoria exteriorizada en archivos y bases de datos supera a la almacenada en mi cerebro biológico" (125). Her discourse problematizes and subverts the integrity of binary oppositions steeped in the masculine ideology.

> Una gran cantidad de información está guardada en mi computadora. Para acceder a ella hace falta teclear una clave de acceso que solo yo conozco. Otra parte, menos confidencial, se archiva en disquettes, guardados bajo llave. Los disquettes y la memoria RAM contienen cifras y datos precisos, archivados por orden alfabético en carpetas y subarchivos fácilmente localizables. Esta información procesada en dígitos binarios conforma mi identidad laboral, la que me identifica frente al mundo. (125)

Analyzing the connections between Rosa's subjectivity and technology points towards an exploration of her identity, one that extends itself beyond mere hardware. With the influx of technologies in the information age, significant alterations in patterns of human activity are occurring; the subject addressed by these technologies is not the familiar modern subject, centered, coherent, stable, on whose actions, initiated in individual consciousness, society is based; instead, it is unstable, multiple, and fragmented. The body is principally reconfigured through communications technology and biotechnologies, consequently: "these tools combine and enforce new social relations for women world-wide" (Haraway 14). The articulation of this world is not bound by the symbolic language of the patriarchal hegemony as it creates its own common parlance: code. This notion is of particular interest to the theorist Donna Haraway because as this sector is not tightly bound by the masculine libidinal economy, it represents a common point of potential resistance for women against the heterosexual dynamic: "the translation of the world into a problem of coding, a search for a common language in which all resistance to instrumental control disappears and all heterogeneity can be submitted to disassembly, reassembly, investment, and exchange" (14). Communication technologies have fundamentally obscured the boundary between the machine and organism. This occurs by way of the unity of the mind and body with the tool. Consequently, social relations are reconfigured.

As Rosa declares: "la vida se me va entre números y cuentas, documentos internos y disquettes de ordenador, y resulta difícil recordar que mi cerebro no está hecho de chips, que soy humana. Aunque cada día se me note menos" (132). The technological era has indoctrinated society with a new measure and source of power, one that has been feminized.[12] This power source may have the potential to rearrange the politics of gender, as fixed identities are destabilized and women are offered an escape from their naturalized essence, an escape from the masculine. Within the cyborg economy, the power of production and reproduction take on an entirely different form. Whereas the heterosexual economy naturalizes production and reproduction within the context of binary oppositions, with respect to the cyborg these are forged through the coalescence of flesh and machine. Within communications technology, though, the subject wielding the power is ambiguous: "It is not clear who makes and who is made in the relation between human and machine. It is not clear what is mind and what body in machines that resolve into coding practices" (Haraway 26). Due to the ambiguity of the cyborg hybrid, there does not exist the notion of one/other.

On an affectual level, Rosa embodies particular characteristics intrinsic of the intensified machine-body relations, which emerge through her experiences of her body-in-use. For instance, Cristina described Rosa's gait as she leaves Planeta X drawing attention to the control and near militaristic discipline exerted by her legs as they cross the dance floor in a few strides: "Cruza la pista en tres zancadas, marcial, solemne y estilosa" (51). Her body language mirrors the ideology of the culture of consumption to which she belongs. From the microscopic level—her footstep—to the macroscopic—her journey out of the bar, one notes the reproduction of the tenets of communications technology. Rosa's exit reflected purposefulness, as if it were a mission. Cristina comments: "la veo cruzar la pista con la velocidad constante de una flecha disparada a un objetivo claro" (51).

These principles of logic, rationalism, militaristic discipline, and minimalism manifest on multiple levels in the life of Rosa Gaena. As Rosa relates her personal narrative, we learn that she has achieved great success in her career, which has enabled her to enter into the realm of material consumption, taking special interest in luxury goods. Unlike Cristina who prefers apparel "desenfadado," Rosa consumes top of the line Spanish and foreign designer labels such as Philip Stark, Loewe, Armani, and Angel Schelesser. Her selection in name brands likewise parallels her ideology, as the production of these designers reflects a modern elegance through prudence and functionality. Schelesser's collection, in particular, illustrates the triumph of minimalism as seen in his "ropa bien cortada, sobria y descomplicada" (Figueras 140);

the other Spanish label, Loewe, is also of high distinction. This label, founded in Madrid in the nineteenth century, caters to the select few—those with resources to consume this line—who appreciate sober, clean lines with ever so slight strokes of trendy innovation. Josefina Figuera, author of *Moda española: una historia de sueños y realidades*, categorizes the work of this label as: "una moda de altura en la que domina siempre la piel pero que da también cabida a toda clase de tejidos y líneas que alternan su clasicismo habitual con toques de vanguardia" (25). Rosa's choice of consumption in fashion mirrors the dynamics that manifest within her professional environment: sober, lineal, and functional. The following description in which Rosa elaborates upon her work attire illustrates her clean, square thinking which is inscribed on her body.

> Me gustan los trajes sastre, también, porque resultan prácticos. Me basta con cambiar a diario de camisa y accesorios y puedo usar el mismo traje tres días seguidos. Eso sí, mis trajes son de la mejor calidad: Loewe, Armani y Angel Schelesser. Tengo tres: gris, azul marino y negro. Colores sobrios para una imagen sobria. (55)

Three pantsuits, somber in color and of very high quality, take turns dressing and infusing Rosa's body with their characteristics. According to Paul Sweetman in his article "Shop Window Dummies? Fashion, the Body, and Emergent Socialities," "Bodies and selves are made and remade in part through the ways in which they are adorned, and this is a process that involves 'carnal knowing' as well as 'cognitive apprehension'" (67). In light of Rosa's fashion consumption, the arena(s) in which she participates and their norms must be taken into consideration. Rosa is located in the space of the multinational, where she occupies a position of distinction. Despite the supposed equality of the sexes, she knows and understands the unwritten politics as they manifest in nearly every life decision. She cites John T. Molloy's *Dress for Success* which treats the appearance a woman should project in the business world: "«Las mujeres que llevan ropa discreta tienen un 150% más de probabilidades de sentirse tratadas como ejecutivas, y un 30% menos de probabilidades de que los hombres cuestionen su autoridad»" (55). Whereas a man's authority is implied, it is emphasized that a woman must earn hers not through her intellectual capacity but through the type of clothing she chooses. Effectively, the technological discourse of the capitalist economy has colonized Rosa's bodily text not only symbolically, but it also affects how she experiences the use of her body.

Rosa occupies, and maneuvers among, a predominantly masculine space, and as such the many facets of this territory form the architecture of Rosa's self. Through a very detailed description of her closet, we witness the amount of control, logic and linearity invested in her personal space. As a member of this collectivity—the community of the multinational—she reflects its extreme adherence to order and rigidity, hanging each object in its place. Indeed, there manifests a relationship between Rosa's closet and the masculine order. Similar to the ideology of the hegemonic paradigm, Rosa superimposes linearity and tyranny in the arrangement of her vestuary. Furthermore, this action reflects the binary hierarchical dualisms: rational/irrational, logical/illogical, linearity/nonlinearity. This afformentioned instance exemplifies how she assumes and inscribes onto her body and her intimate space—where one is free to be whoever—the tenets of capitalism and technology.

> El armario en el que almaceno mi ropa de trabajo exhibe un orden meticuloso. Los zapatos, alineados por parejas. Los trajes, cada uno en su percha correspondiente, en el lazo izquierdo. Las camisas, bien planchadas, en el derecho. De plancharlos se ocupa la asistenta, por supuesto, porque yo no puedo desperdiciar mi tiempo planchando. (55)

This location evidences a particular cleanness through its absence of qualities, the absence of stains; the closet is suffused with what Daniel Harris terms "machine envy" (150), or "the desire become our appliances" evidenced through the incorporation of technological principles onto Rosa's body and her space. Interestingly, in a separate closet, Rosa houses the rest of her wardrobe; shuffled away in a hodge-podge order are the clothing articles that do not correspond with her metabolic consumption of technology, order, and logic. In this other space, we witness disorder and clothing that are representative of a different culture of consumption, and thus neo-tribe. She mentions jeans, an article of clothing that would be utterly unsuitable for her high-ranking position, and other playful articles of clothing or jewelry that no longer correlate with her daily existence.[13]

> En el armario contiguo, el destinado al resto de mi ropa, reina el caos. De las perchas cuelgan pantalones vaqueros, camisas estampadas, trajes de noche y vestidos de verano mezclados en un batiburrillo de formas y colores. En uno de los cajones se acumulan un remolino de jerseys de lana. En el siguiente, la ropa interior negra, las bragas, los bodies, los ligueros y las medias. Y en el último, una masa informe de diferentes prendas. Gorros impermeables y sombreros de fiesta, camisas hippies y camisetas psicodélicas, cinturones dorados y bufandas. (56)

In examining the ideas, objects, and memories that Rosa consumes, it is interesting to mention what she excludes: frivolity, undefined boundaries, excess emotion, and sexual encounters. Through hiding every trace of femininity, Rosa projects a hyper-masculine look—an identity with neatly marked borders—perhaps because it allows her to feel that choices are more clearly defined. In negating her femininity, Rosa traverses a path that does not permit deviations; her choice is work, of course made easier through renouncing her feminine nature and absorbing masculine tenets.

The techno-colonization of Rosa occurs at the level of her body language, the organization of her personal space, as well as how it is reflected through consciousness of her sexuality. Unlike Cristina, who consumes and is consumed by sex, Rosa rejects this part of her female self, shedding more light on the unmitigatedly macho aesthetic of the techno-colonized multinacional. Through her participation in the communication arena, Rosa must learn to embody the dominant language and values of that zone: self-control, determination, cool, emotional discipline, and mastery. Her body speaks symbolically of this necessity through her pursuit of these virtues with single-minded, unswerving dedication. During a visit to Planeta X, Cristina and Rosa become embroiled in a conversation about the many negative qualities of Cristina's ex-boyfriend Iain, one of which was his over-exuberant flattery towards Line, praising her skeletal appearance and weight loss efforts. Cristina quickly defends Iain and Line claiming that while her friend may be quite thin, she does not fit the typical case study of an anorexic: "el caso es que tampoco, por lo visto, muestra el cuadro mental típico de una anoréxica, porque según el psiquiatra las anoréxicas suelen ser personas muy perfeccionistas e introvertidas, que renuncian al sexo" (45), as Line professes that aside from chocolate, sex gives her the most pleasure. Cristina buffers and redirects Rosa's attacks—basing her argument on the lack of universal truth-calling her older sister an anorexic. The medical terminology of anorexia refers to a person who refuses to eat and uses this as a control mechanism. In this vein, Cristina calls Rosa an anorexic for her lack of sexual appetite as well as the neglect she demonstrates towards her femininity:

> En primer lugar, que sepas que desde que ha aparecido la histeria de las top models y el culto al cuerpo parece que ya hay anoréxicas de todo tipo. En segundo lugar, si estás intentando meterte con mi amiga, te recuerdo que si solo hubiera que medir las cosas por ese rasero, entonces la anoréxica serías tú, que eres la que ha renunciado al sexo. (45)

Offended by her sister's re-appropriation of the word anorexic, Rosa justifies her lack of sexual activity through her independence, the same independence that forces her to deny herself an intrinsic part of her female identity, her sexuality. Yet, she feels she must keep under tight control the sexual economy because within the techno-colonized space of the multinational, bodies are erased. "Yo misma debería ser vicepresidente. Estoy mejor preparada, con mucho, pero con mucho, que el inútil que tiene el puesto. Pero soy mujer, así que no me ascienden" (46). Her discourse reveals the shortcomings of the second wave of feminism; in attempting to assimilate to the masculine model, women submit to a series of violations that make her intelligible in a normative regime that does not represent her (Butler 84).

Yet Rosa's bodily text is layered in contradictions and ambiguities. A product or child of the information circuit, Rosa illustrates the displacement of the hierarchical dualisms of naturalized identities. Like her sisters, she was colonized by the patriarchy; however, her experiences both inside and outside of the multinational present her with the possibility of reimagining herself. Returning home after intensely long work days, Rosa only desires to relax yet is disturbed on numerous occasions by mysterious phone calls in which the caller plays Henry Purcell's *La hora fatal*.[14] This baroque composition infused with affectations of real life relocates Rosa emotionally and spiritually to her childhood. Recalling the piece, which deals with the painful separation of loved ones, is an integral process in countermemory; it permits Rosa emotional vulnerability to flesh through her past experiences that have informed her selfhood. Decades ago Rosa was capable of singing this composition without missing a single note, as she was considered a musical prodigy. However, since her father abandoned the three sisters and their mother nearly twenty years ago, she has since blocked these lyrics from her memory. "No puedo explicar exactamente qué relación conectó las dos decisiones; la de mi padre de dejarnos a nosotras y la mía de dejar el canto, pero sé que tuvieron que ver entre sí. Si él no se hubiera ido, yo habría seguido cantando" (58). Singing, like writing, gives Rosa the power to signify, something that she had no desire to do after losing her father. Yet through her narrative Rosa arrives at a deeper understanding of her passion—singing—and the power it represents. Instead of searching to reclaim her lost innocence, intimately connected with her father's abandonment, Rosa begins to envision an interconnection among singing and the power to survive. The fleshing through of the memory permits Rosa to elevate her awareness of her selfhood and ultimately these shifts, resulting in a feminist nomadic subject, allow her to situate herself in a liberated state of passion. She relates:

> Y es que me hizo [la canción] recordar que hubo un momento en que yo era capaz de sentir pasión por las cosas, en que fui capaz de aprenderme nota a nota

una canción que ninguna alumna de mi edad se habría atrevido a solfear y mucho menos a cantar. Que hubo un tiempo en que luchaba por lo que de verdad quería. Que hubo un tiempo en que lloraba escuchando a Purcell. (265)

The mysterious phone calls work at the re-textualization of Rosa's cyborg body vis-à-vis the infusion of emotion, something she has denied herself for years. The combination of Purcell's emotive musicality and her techno-colonization situates Rosa on the border between human and machine. Donna Haraway argues: "Cyborg politics is the struggle for language and the struggle against perfect communication, against the one code that translates all meaning perfectly, the central dogma of phallogocentrism" (25). Hence, Rosa has released herself from the constraint of an "original dream of a common language or original symbiosis" (25), which frees her to further liberate herself from the notion of a unilateral identity. And, this situates Rosa within the realm of potential whereby she may acknowledge and understand herself beyond binary oppositions, as an intense multiplicity. Woman is not essence. Pondering and fleshing through experiences, woman has the potential to construct an active female subjectivity, which runs counter to the hegemonic economy. "Stripped of identity, the bastard race teaches about the power of the margins and the importance of a mother like Malinche. Women of colour have transformed her from evil mother of masculinist fear into the originally literate mother who teaches survival" (26). Situated on the boundaries, Rosa is machine and she is human; this hybrid identity collides with the neat categories popularized and naturalized throughout Western history of female subjectivity, as Haraway professes: "female embodiment seemed to be given, organic, necessary; and female embodiment seemed to mean skill in mothering and its metaphoric extensions" (29). Liberated from a unitary, conventional subjectivity, Rosa as cyborg exhibits a fluid identity of neither one, nor the other. The multiplicity she embodies challenges and subverts the patriarchal ideology and furthermore, suggests an alternative to the totalizing paradigm of heterosexuality.

An element that has mediated and worked Rosa's bodily text is her gratuitous use of Prozac. In Cristina's words, her sister lives "colgada" to this chemical. Rosa herself begins to question the type of stability her dependence on this drug offers her.

> ¿Es esa pastillita blanca y verde que me tomo cada mañana la que me ayuda a no llorar? ¿Esa pastillita que el médico me recetó, ese concentrado milagroso de fluoxicetina, es la que hace que las preocupaciones me resbalen como el agua sobre una sartén engrasada? ¿Es la paz o el prozack? No lo sé. (216)

Prozac, the trendy anti-depressent, actively works on the body—the brain—to stimulate and increase the levels of neurotransmitters called seratonin. The consumption of Prozac results in the increase of mental activity, the reduction of anxiety and fatigue, as well as the augment of the attention span. This particular chemical enhancement is closely associated with the capitalist world, as its effects supposedly increase the overall productivity level of the individual. While its primary effects are quite attractive, its secondary effects have not been as widely commented, such as the reduction of libido and appetite and the creation of, at the least, a psychological addiction. Prozac mediated, and to a certain point created, subjectivity for Rosa compliant with the dominant economy's dictates. A statistic from Lucía Etxebarria's personal website confirms: "Las mujeres son el sexo drogado. El 75% de las consumidoras de drogas psicotrópicas legales (sedantes, tranquilizantes, antidepresivos y reductores del apetito) son mujeres" (http://teleline.terra.es/personal/luciaetx/drogas.htm). This statistic suggests the over-medicalization of women, yet for what purpose? In the age of information, a world suffused with technology, the hierarchies of universal truth are under scrutiny and their validity is being questioned. Prozac has been utilized to try to relocate the patient emotionally and psychologically, so that she may fit neatly within society's defined limits. However, Rosa renounces Prozac; hooked to the chemical balancer, she meandered through life and its experiences anesthetized. After contemplation, which arose in part from the mysterious phone calls playing Purcell's *La hora fatal*, Rosa decides to quit cold-turkey the anti-depressant, despite medical warnings against this sudden method, yet she suffers no ill effects. One night, after discontinuing the medicalization, Rosa notices the changes that her body, mind, and self-experience.

> Busqué entre mis discos viejos aquella canción de Purcell, cantada por James Bowan, descolgué el teléfono, me senté tranquilamente en el sillón y me puse a escuchar la misma canción, una y otra vez, recordando en cada nueva escucha las notas una por una, las palabras, los acordes, los arpeggios…Cada nota golpeaba como un puño en mi interior y esos golpes transmitían tal calor a mi corazón que éste explotaba y se disgregaba en fragmentos dispersos. La música bullía dentro de mí, galopaba por mis venas, contenía el mundo, y dentro del mundo a mí misma, a mi verdadero yo que había permanecido dormido allí dentro de tantos años y acababa de despertar furioso, emborrachado de entusiasmo. (265–66)

Flushing the flouxicetin out of her system regenerates an integral part of herself that she had denied for much time: the ability to feel, whether it be pain, sorrow, or joy. A song that she had forgotten for so long textualizes her body with striking traits of exuberance, ecstasy, and irregularity. Her decision to live life to the fullest—her quest for survival as opposed to one of salvation—can be read as a rejection of dominant ideology and an exploration into the profundity of her inner self which leads to the trusting in her own intuitions. Her decision to free herself is a step on her journey toward the feminist subjectivity posited by the scholars Haraway and Braidotti.

Ana Gaena: Consumption and Embodiment of the Angel del hogar

Ana, the oldest of the Gaena sisters, is a thirty-two-year-old mother and housewife who maintains an identity completely distinct of her other two siblings. As the Gaena sisters were abandoned by their father at an early age, and relegated to the care of their ineffective, bitter mother, the oldest sister, Ana, from a young age, was charged with the care of her two sisters as well as the domestic duties in the household. As her sister Rosa comments: "esa obsesión que Ana tenía con el orden y la limpieza nos ahorraba a las demás tener que preocuparnos de limpiar el polvo, hacer las camas o planchar la ropa. Teníamos criada gratis" (67). The narrative of Ana takes great pleasure in conspicuous consumption, as she is in a financial position—married to a wealthy successful man—to afford it. The assessment of clothing, interior design and commodity consumption in her monologue frequently borrows from the language of lifestyle women's magazines. That is, there is a direct crossover between her narrative and fiction journalism.

Ana's discourse in *Amor, curiosidad, prozac y dudas* revolves around themes impregnated with consumption such as design, style, and fashion. As she derives this information from pop culture media, she consistently assesses situations in terms of prescribed norms taken from magazine blurbs and shopping habits:

> Para arreglar una abolladura sobre la madera hay que aplicar un trapo blanco húmedo, procurando que empape la madera. Acto seguido hay que colocar otro trapo grueso, también humedecido, y aplicar la plancha de vapor caliente, porque la acción del calor dilatará las fibras y las nivelará. (84)

Her life is molded by her consumption of suitable goods, and her love for her husband and child are expressed through the care with which she chooses furnishings for their home. Ana articulates her anxieties about her marriage and child and expresses her disdain for her life, entirely in terms of commodities and a stratification of brand names:

> Las cortinas de Gastón y Daniela están hechas una pena, sobre todo por los bordes. Eso es porque el niño se dedica a colgarse de ellas con las manos grasientas. Tengo que decirle a la asistenta que se encargue de lavarlas. Gracias a Dios, como son de hilo se pueden lavar en lavadora y después no hace falta plancharlas. Se centrifugan y se cuelgan. El propio peso hace que queden impecables. (85)

Pierre Bourdieu affirms that material goods are by no means simply a matter of style, rather they assert class difference and superiority. Ana herself acknowledges that her own lifestyle is distinct from the women who wear "una especie de imitación de Chanel de baratillo con botones dorados con el que esta mujer debe de creer que va muy elegante y que se parece a la Consuelo Berlanga" (113). Her profound knowledge of brand names distinguishes her own taste from that of the ordinary consumer, sporting a couch from "Roche Bobois" (76), crystal fabricated by "Vilches" (76), place settings designed by "Agata Ruiz de la Prada" (77) and a purse brand-named "Farrutx" (117). Every object mentioned not only has a use value, but more importantly, a sign value. By way of the name brand, Ana carefully constructs herself as a woman that is adept in not only consumerism, but also is exceedingly familiar with luxury goods (as she possesses them) and name brand. By way of consuming these particular goods, Ana negotiates and re-appropriates them via her bodily text. In doing so, she defines herself, which is also a process of differentiation or exclusion. Bourdieu elaborates: "The competition for luxury good, 'emblems of class,' is one dimension of the struggle to impose the dominant principle of domination" (232).

Through her first person narration, Ana is eager to express her knowledge of contemporary style throughout her story; she presents herself as someone in a position to recognize "emblems of class." Ana, a thirty-two-year-old married housewife, is the daughter of a mother who was "niña de familia bien de San Sebastián" (82) and a father who "malvivía en un cuartucho desfondado de una pensión de la calle Huertas, en la que el frío era tan intenso que pegaba dentelladas y por la noche lo obligaba a dormir con dos jerséis puestos y un gorro de lana" (84). Yet, this protagonist declares herself product of her mother's family: "La familia de mamá es mi familia. Los abuelos que me han criado y con los que he pasado todos los veranos en el caserón de San Sebastián" (85) as she professes that with respect to her father's family "no sé mucho" (86). From a very tender age, Ana identified herself with her mother's family and, being the oldest sister, was intensely influenced and conditioned by traditional discourses on decency and proper comportment for women, which she succinctly illustrates in the following analogy.

> Alguien me podó a mí, creo, y por eso soy como soy, ordenada y de buen aspecto. Ninguna rama ha crecido por donde no debía. Soy un arbusto podado que ha crecido merced a las indicaciones de los otros. Una tijera se llevó por delante las yemas rebeldes, los futuros capullos, las rosas cubiertas de espinas (90).

Using the comparison of pruning bushes, she indicates that her body and self, much like the roses, were plucked and shaped by her upbringing so as to be the perfect woman and all that it constituted, so that nothing unfit would nor could emerge. Her mother is described as a woman of means and taste, connoted by the luxury brand names that she was able to consume as well as her stunning physical aspect: "mamá tenía dinero de sobra para pagarse un traje de Scherrer si quería. . . . Mamá es guapa. Muy guapa. Los chicos de su clase la apodan la Sueca por lo de la melena lacia y rubia y los ojos grises" (83). Ana's mother bequests to her the blond mane of hair. More importantly, though, her legacy to Ana is cultural capital. Ana's mother provides for her daughter, as well as the reader, an image of secure bourgeois and propertied marriage. This image clearly represents what Ana's mother anticipates for her daughter and Ana for herself.

Although Ana is self-described as an attractive, married young woman her narration begins from the assumption that there must be more to life than how hers has unraveled. The first chapter that gives Ana voice is "H de hastío" in which she tediously describes the monotony and profound sadness of her life, also hinting at her unhealthy formation of subjectivity.

> Cristina se ha marchado y ha dejado en el aire su perfume, un aroma dulzón que no sé identificar. No es una marca conocida. Será pachuli o algo así que habrá comprado en un mercadillo de esos modernos. Habría podido decirle muchas cosas, y sin embargo he pasado la mayor parte del tiempo sin abrir la boca, revolviendo inútilmente la cabeza en busca de un tema de conversación. Creo que al final se ha marchado porque no me aguantaba más. La aburro, o la de primo, o ambas cosas a la vez. Y la verdad es que no la culpo. Me ha dejado sola en este salón. Sola, como paso casi todas las mañanas. Borja está en el trabajo y el niño en la guardería. No tengo de quién cuidar, excepto de mí misma. Y ni siquiera eso sé hacerlo bien. (81)

Ana represents a case of the contradictory realities of consumption. The location that defines Ana is her home, and this space holds the promise of a distinctive lifestyle. Yet as the reader comes to understand, Ana's implicit needs cannot be fulfilled by the bourgeois comforts. Likewise, no man, lifestyle nor house can provide her the active subject-formation she desires.

While Ana did study and prepare herself for a profession, "decidí estudiar secretariado porque algo había que hacer" (180), her true aspiration was to be cared for financially so that she could remain a housewife: "no podía pasarme el día metida en casa fregando y planchando y ordenando, por mucho que eso fuera lo único que me apeteciera hacer" (180). Furthermore, Ana maintains a very traditional fantasy of femininity; the white wedding remains her dream, despite her mother's bitter admonishments.[15] In spite of this and the fact that she was not a virgin, she is consumed by having a white dress ceremony in San Fermín de los Navarros, a very old church in Madrid, with maids of honor and a reception at the Mayte Commodore, an upscale, fine dining establishment with a tradition of more than forty years.[16] It is ironic that as she confesses her desire for tradition, Ana switches it up with the contemporary glamour of the designer name. Her pursuit of the traditional white wedding, though, is not that innocent; she wanted the world to know, especially Antonio, her former heartthrob, that she indeed was worthy of consuming the fantasy:

> El hecho de que Borja fuera amigo de toda la vida de Antonio, el saber que Antonio acabaría por enterarse que había quien valoraba lo que él había despreciado, que me valoraba hasta el punto de querer hacerme la madre de sus hijos, de querer reconocer ante Dios y ante los hombres que yo valía la pena. (181)

Ironic, also, is that she reunited with her husband—at that time he was a friend from her childhood summers spent in Donosti—at the major chain of department stores in Spain, El Corte Inglés.

In Ana's perspective, marriage, like the wedding, is frequently imagined in terms of commodities. Despite profound changes in the identities and roles of Spanish women in the last thirty years, Ana confesses the conventional nature of her aspirations; her desire is for a male provider:

> Estuvimos saliendo durante cinco años, y prácticamente desde el principio se dio por hecho que nos casaríamos en cuanto Borja acabara la carrera, y yo, que sabía muy bien que nunca haría otra cosa que dedicarme a mi casa y a mis niños de la misma manera que llevaba dedicándome a la casa y a mis hermanas desde que se había marchado mi padre. (180)

As made patent through her revelations, the expectation of a traditional marriage remains ultimately unchallenged.

Amor, curiosidad, prozac y dudas evokes a sense of dissatisfaction in women's lives, a dissatisfaction that is manifest in Ana's dull, monotonous routine mixed with prescription chemical enhancers, which are assumed to be answered by a man. Ana sorrowfully articulates the impossible combination of desires. The prevalence with which these anxieties are articulated in contemporary popular women's writing suggests that these irreconcilable demands are material contradictions in the expectations of femininity in the late twentieth century. As manifest in this novel, it seems that contemporary femininity is expected to be, and women are demanding of themselves that they be, concurrently glamorous and maternal, cosmopolitan and homemakers, modern women and stay-at-home wives. The manner in which this is internalized in Ana, results in the production of an unhealthy subjectivity.

In Ana's situation, consumption is offered as a means of reconciling these conflicting demands and of achieving a resolution; the protagonist is presented as a contemporary woman with an apparent infinite variety of lifestyle choices—as exemplified through the other Gaena sisters –and the choices are presented as consumer choices. Lauren Langman contends that the pleasures of consumption are in the possibilities of a multiplicitiy of modes of being. She affirms that shopping can provide:

> Commercially produced fantasy world of commodified goods, images and leisure activities that gradually have transformed desire and provide packaged self-images to a distinctive form of subjectivity. A decentered selfhood has become a plurality of intermittent, disconnected, recognition-seeking spectacles of self-presentation. (40)

Ana's narrative, similar to that of Cristina's, is about packaged self-images that celebrate the commodification of desire; yet, while they are 'disconnected,' they can be read to promote a specific presentation, as there are definite recommended modes of self in Ana's narrative—from images portrayed in *Elle* (193) to packaged concepts in *Mía* (157). Elaborating upon and extending the theories of de Certeau, Rob Shields has contended that consumption is via for the active production of self. He asserts: "There is a need to treat consumption as an active, committed production of self and of society, which rather than assimilating individuals to styles, appropriates codes and fashions, which are made into one's own" (2). Indeed Ana is an active and compromised consumer inextricably preoccupied with the construction and production of self. The repetition of her consumption acts in conjunction with the dominance of brand names points to the construction of self within an exclusive grammar of consumer goods. An object-in-use or material good is never simply anonymous; rather it is a "Farrutx" or "Gastón y Daniela" (76), and if not carrying the brand name, then its origin is that which endows the good with an air of distinction, such as the the bronze faucets she imported from Trentino, Italy. The name brand even carries over to the realm of the grocery store which further suggests the strict hierarchy of labels in her narrative: "Scotch Brite Fibra Verde con esponja (3x2 precio especial), fregasuelos Brillax, latas (melocotón familiar en almíbar Bamboleo, champiñones El Cidacos, espárragos de Navarra al natural Iñaqui, guisantes Gigante Verde, huevas de lumpo Captain Sea, atún claro Calvo pack de tres latas)" (115). She does not only purchase these goods for pleasure or simple sustenance; the goods should be recognized as signifiers of class and style.

This housewife character must work through a problematization of the home, which propels Ana to examine her subjectivity as it is intimately linked to the domestic. Ana questions whether the home offers a space for the realization of the female identity. Topical representations of her home can be read as equating the domain with requiescence. Like decorating magazines, Ana presents a vision of home immaculate, so clean it denies the existence of a family that inhabits it. There is little evidence of human occupation except for the odd mention of a material good falling victim to her child. Her pride and joy that was birthed—not her son but a room forged in her image—through consumption articulates a mismatch of perspectives: there is movement articulated through the vaults and niches paired with a traditional aire due to the antiques. Cristina describes the room in erotic detail:

> El sofá Roche Bobois. Las cortinas del salón, de Gastón y Daniela. . . . Arcos, hornacinas y diferentes alturas de suelo y techo dan movimiento a un interior dominado por el blanco. Toda la carpintería y metálica la ha realizado Vilches. . . . Un costurero de pino viejo comprado en una almoneda y restaurado . . . hace las veces de mesilla. Sobre él, un teléfono antiguo, adquirido también en una almoneda y elegido para no desentonar con el resto de la decoración, un armatoste negro y brillante que parece un escarabajo megaatómico. (76)

The description of the room, forged according to her intimate desires, outlines the paradox of homemaking and housekeeping argued by Janice Radway (1984) as "ideological seams" where theory and reality conjoin in a mishmashed manner provoking the emergence of contradictory desires in women: establishing a home for familiar comfort versus making a home in a sexy vision so as to erase all traces of the inhabitants. Due to the fact that ideology, in concept, is not rippleless and smooth running, Radway utilizes the term "patchwork quilt" to define ideology as it is composed of "institutionalized but variable power relations, practices and activities" (109). This theory is significant as it highlights the areas that in practice do not mesh fluidly with the presuppositions of discourse, yet are mixed together and thought to be organic. Nevertheless, the sections that are unevenly bound together signal turbulence among varying desires, all of which are mediated by a patriarchal ideology that does not esteem nor permit a woman to be whoever she is. This situation is further aggrandized via the bombarding of packaged images by mass culture, which liberates and constrains the female subject. In sum, this theory advances a series of fundamental concepts: the junctions illustrate a mismatch of ideals that compose our desires, which is also the locus for contemplation of problematization in the ideological understanding that conforms our desires; nevertheless, as the symbolic is "driven by conflicts, slippages and imperfect joinings" (109–10) a perfect fit among desires and junctions cannot be reconciled.

Ana herself feels the effects produced by the uneven conjoining of the contradictory ideologies: "me siento como la pieza de un rompecabezas que apareció por equivocación en la caja que no correspondía. No encajo" (113). She is plagued by the constant demands and realities of her household life, exemplifying the contradictory reality of consumption. On the one hand, she confesses that her dream has always been to be a wife and a mother, caring for the home. Yet, on the other, she finds herself severely depressed, "no puedo pasarme la vida encerrada en casa, sola, llorando como una Magdalena" (113), almost to the point that it paralyzes her life. Ana confesses:

> Tedio y tiempo empiezan por la misma letra, y las horas y los días pasan sin hacer nada, como una sucesión inacabable de hojas en el calendario. Es muy aburrido vivir cuando no tienes nada que hacer y nadie en quien apoyarte. Mi marido y mi hijo, ya lo sé, pero ya no me basta. Aquí encerrada en casa todo el día. (149)

For a time Ana, through her consumption of fashion and design/decoration magazines, could barricade herself from feelings of inadequacy and extreme isolation.[17] Reading this genre of magazine served as an escape hatch for Ana from the continuous demands of daily life. Within the space of her home she could fashion and consume imaginaries—which fit in well with her daily routine—through partaking in the world of material goods, while securing for herself a personal space of albeit temporary relief. Through her consumption of luxurious, fine items, Ana was able to escape tensions surrounding her marriage and associated with her identity as a mother; hence, she is liberated from constraints imposed due to gender while simultaneously permitting her to fit perfectly within them. This defense mechanism is evident in her monologue as she consistently flips between two discourses: one in which she relates conflictive troubling memories and another where she elaborates upon cleaning methods or her collection of fine home goods. This measure—detailing the beauty of a room or the procedure of cleaning a particular item—can be read as a mode to congeal time, if only temporarily, so as to feel control within one's life (Golombisky). Moreover, through her tedious efforts of decoration and housekeeping, Ana may arrange and perfect each room, albeit unoccupied, so it is reproduction of her self—clean, in order, under control, and of high quality.

> Yo siempre he estado orgullosa de este salón. Lo he mantenido pulcrísimo, y tampoco es que sea tan fácil. Hay que pasar la aspiradora una vez al mes, como mínimo, por sillas, sofas y cortinas. Hay que lavar los visillos también una vez al mes con agua y jabón, sin frotarlos ni retorcerlos. Para darles consistencia una vez limpios hay que sumergirlos en agua con azúcar y colgarlos todavía húmedos a fin de eliminar cualquier arruga. (82)

The space of the home—the area that defines Ana—is maintained perfectly to the senses: there is not even a speck of dust nor a slight wrinkle to tarnish the appearance. She received the utmost satisfaction from cleaning up a stain. Through her consumption of these high-end products, all of which are white, Ana's body can be read as a text of purity that is maintained by her continual upkeep of these goods and practices.

Nevertheless, while participating in the community of the yuppies, those who have achieved immense financial success and display that through their many material belongings and aire of elitism, Ana is immensely distraught. Through contemplation of memories and her personal history this Gaena sister questions her existence: "Si la vida se pudiera limpiar igual que unos visillos, si pudiéramos hacer desaparecer nuestras manchas en una lavadora, todo sería más fácil" (82). While consuming the role of housekeeping and homemaking, Ana buys into the patriarchal belief that the house constructs her home; it is her territory of influence. According to Kim Golombisky, the act of homemaking provides the woman with a highly stimulating, but ultimately impossible fantasy:

> Because the object of desire, perfect rooms, mirrors an illusion of her more powerful self. How silently drives the engine of its contradictions. She can never achieve this standard she measures herself against. She visualizes making the perfect home for herself and her family. But perfect rooms, standing in for the perfect home, do not accommodate the household's people. (8)

Despite her control over the household—a control that is waning—Ana, confronted by an abysmal absence, can only describe her life in terms of "Nada, absolutamente nada. Nada de nada" (77) where she cannot even undertake basic activities of human sustenance: "Comer y dormir. Comer poco y dormir menos aún. Cuidar de mi marido y de mi niño. Cuidarles poco" (77). Ana's body as a text of femininity depicts the glaring contradictions legislated by mass culture. Susan Bordo argues:

> On the one hand, our culture still widely advertises domestic conceptions of femininity, the ideological moorings for a rigorously dualistic sexual division of labor that casts women as chief emotional and physical nurturer. The rules for this construction of femininity (and I speak here in a language both symbolic and literal) require that women learn to feed others, not the self, and to construe any desires for self-nurturance and self-feeding as greedy and excessive. (171)

As a result, women are encouraged to develop an emotional economy that is totally based on the other. To make it through her day Ana submits her body to a regimen of chemical warfare, taking "tranxilium" to sleep and "Dicel" in the morning to awaken her and overcome the sedative effects of her nighttime drug; these are interchanged with a medley of other mood-altering chemicals such as "donormil," "minilip," "adofén," lexatín." As Ana herself admits: "creo que no hay pastilla que cambia el ánimo que yo no haya probado" (229).

Ana's existence has been consumed with achieving and exemplifiying the dictates of the patriarchal system. Throughout her life Ana had been informed by the patriarchal economy, the church, and her family (mother) that women were to incarnate the proverbial "good girl" image. This further extended into adulthood by becoming subservient, passive wives and mothers. This sister, referred to as "la dulce," "la estable," "el epítome de la cordura," proclaims to have it all: "tengo un marido maravilloso y un niño guapísimo y una casa que podría salir fotografiada en el *Elle* decoración" (118); yet feels completely empty, "el caso es que las horas y los días se me pasan sin hacer nada, como una sucesión inacable de hojas en el calendario, y yo no paro de llorar, la vida se me escapa por los ojos brillantes" (157–58). Her subjectivity, contingent upon her consumption of high-end goods and rhetoric, is not so much destabilized by consumption of the goods that denote upper class. This is illustrated by her fantasy of constructing her identity similar to that of her sister Rosa; while she may evolve in terms of profession, she still displays a desire for high-end goods. After having dedicated her life to adhering to the naturalized model of woman, taking extreme caution so as to fit the mold, Ana looks with eyes of resignation at the power paradigm: "Lo único que importaba, lo único que ha importado siempre, era limpiar una mancha. Pero eso tampoco importa ya. Al fin y al cabo, ya no me obsesiona la limpieza" (193–94). Powerless and desperate, the oldest Gaena sister feels floating and disconnected, as if she were a speck of dust, mucking the surrounding environment that she herself created: "Ana duerme ahora con un extraño, confinada en una casa que ha demostrado no necesitarla, recluida en un calabozo que ella misma ha decorado. Y yo me siento vacía como una mujer burbuja" (194). As López argues, her illness elucidates the notion that Betty Friedan treats in *The Feminine Mystique* as "the problem that has no name" (López, 3). This powerful book addresses the social lived reality of the housewife in the 1950s uncovering the maladies suffered by stay-at-home women such as oppression, psychological damage resulting from isolation, and severely constrained options. Ana demonstrates cogently the problem facing housewives: the yearning to desire properly and appropriately.

Living according to the dominant precepts, Ana finds herself miserable and seeks to erase those feelings through the consumption of prescription drugs. Indeed she increases her doses to the point where she is constantly "atiborrada de pastillas" (227) and the only way—she believes—to feel the full effect of the drugs is to down them with alcohol. Faced with arrested development, the oldest Gaena sister is unable to express her emotions to her family and the only mode that gives her the exit she needs is making anonymous phone calls to her sister Rosa in which she plays Purcell's *La hora fatal*. Through playing this song for her sister, it lends to Ana the voice she cannot summon of her own.

> Como no sé como decir estoy sola, estoy desesperada, quiero ser como tú y necesito ayuda. Me limitaré a hacerle escuchar *La hora fatal*, convencida de que el desgarro de la canción expresa perfectamente el estado en que me siento y transmite cómo la idea de la muerte no me abandona en ningún momento, cómo vivo en una agonía opaca e ingrata, encenagada en el tedio. (231)

Ironically Ana believes that if she were in Rosa's position—a self-made woman—her life would not be the chaos that it currently is. She dreams about being an unmarried businesswoman replete with the briefcase. Even her body language—in her dream—embodies the certainty and efficiency of the business world: "Me veo como una mujer eficiente y segura, vestida con un elegante traje de chaqueta oscuro, que se mueve como un pez en un mar de pasillos y despachos, enarbolando un attaché negro lleno de valiosos documentos" (230). As a consumer of television, she yearns to be the protagonist of *Ley de Los Angeles*, a woman that men admire and other women envy.

Upon waking one morning, Ana confronted her husband, Borja, and announced to him that she desired a divorce; this action elicited two phone calls. First Borja called Ana's mother who replied to him that this was quite deviant of Ana and the second phone call was made to a psychologist to validate their collective claim that this, indeed, was abnormal. Much to the surprise of everyone, Ana was admitted into a detoxification center for her clandestine chemical dependency and specifically requested that her mother be prohibited from visiting her. Cristina comments: "desde que tengo uso de razón Anita siempre ha sido la niña de los ojos de mi madre y en la vida ha dado un paso sin consultarla y no me cabía en la cabeza que la propia Anita hubiera dado instrucciones semejantes" (257). Upon reuniting with Ana at the center, the oldest Gaena sister solemnly explained to her two younger sisters that she wanted a divorce and, furthermore, she solicited her sister Rosa's help. This decision, in particular, recalls Braidotti's theory. To approximate the nomadic subjectivity, one must *work through* personal experiences, calling upon history, while questioning the dualities upon which the power structure is centered. Through her choices and actions, Ana becomes an active agent, cognizant of her life options and possibilities; upon recognizing the futility of her dreams for salvation, Ana works with the present and strives for her survival. Whereas she was fabricated as a lack by the binary system of hierarchical dualities, an opposition that she internalized and thus as a result felt inferior and contemptible, Ana transgresses the dominant economy through her contemplation of a new conceptual space and subsequent metamorphoses of self. While she does not imagine a blueprint for a perfect location, she is dynamic in her unending process to find the truth. In light of this journey Lucy Sargisson suggests: "The future cannot be programmed in terms of the present, as constructed by the past. It must be dreamt and imagined according to desire . . . to subvert and exploit the ways in which our perceptions of reality . . . are constructed" (225).

Conclusions

"No os lo he dicho todavía: mi madre se llama Eva.
Pero espero que nosotras seamos hijas de Lilith."
(267)

In the novel *Amor, curiosidad, prozac y dudas* Lucía Etxebarria portrays three divergent representations of femininity in contemporary Spanish society.

While they are descendents of Eva Gaena, their embodiment reveals they are daughters of Lilith.[18] As perhaps suggested by their affinity with Lilith, the common factor among Cristina, Rosa, and Ana is that they represent models of identities that negotiate subjectivity by a complex set of resistances and choices through consumption. Explicit in the examples of identity is the questioning of current gender relationships and naturalized identities. The three Gaena sisters pursue distinct paths of consumption by which they forge identity and embody consumption affectually; each woman is intent to pursue identity and either directly or indirectly questions hierarchies of knowledge. Each of the Gaena sisters is cognizant of her unique character, which she verbalizes through discerning her self from the other two women, and their respective imagined communities. For instance, Cristina quickly labels her older sister Ana as a "maruja" (21) while admitting that her sister would render her a "putón" (21). Ana, on the other hand, embodies a paradox; she sports upper-class contemporary name brands, and at the same time, she mixes this desire with the tradition of upkeeping her home and family. By way of these choices, she separates herself from what she deems "Cristina tan moderna" (149) and Rosa "todo el día con su carrera y su trabajo" (149) Rosa, in contrast to the representation of her sisters, is completely absorbed in her mutant technological world, effectively blocked off from emotion. Albeit in a dissimilar fashion, these three women—consciouslessly or not—radicalize the concept of difference. Hélène Cixous tells us:

> If woman has always functioned "within" the discourse of man, a signifier that has always referred back to the opposite signifier which annihilates its specific energy and diminishes or stifles its very different sounds, it is time for her to dislocate this "within," to explode it, turn it around, seize it; to make it hers, containing it, taking it into her own mouth, biting that tongue with her very own teeth to invent for herself a language to get inside of. And you'll see with what ease she will spring forth from that "within"—the "within" where she once so drowsily crouched—to overflow at the lips she will cover with foam. (257)

This narrative, via the spectrum of models of identities portrayed and their respective nomadic wanderings, critiques assigned gender roles, and in doing so, produces a breach in conventional thinking. As Cixous suggests, the three sisters engage in transgressive contemplation; they bring their body into the language through various economies not to invoke closure or salvation. Each comes to the realization vis-à-vis working through their experiences that the symbolic order and their relationship within and to this structure must change. I read this as resisting the construction or adherence to any rigid code. Moreover, through their refusal to define the essence of woman, these sisters have come to foster disorder; the instability portrayed is not a simple inversion of patriarchal values but an attempt to approach the world in a new mode: "a utopian gesturing toward an alternative imaginary beyond the constraints of patriarchal thought" (Felski 120). In this way, the main function of the literary production of Etxebarria is to question social and cultural practices of the patriarchy with the hope of inspiring change through contemplation. While Etxebarria offers no image of the perfect society, by way of her novel she gives voice to her intolerance for the perpetuation of an absolutist paradigm and aspires to provide on an imaginary level a radically other world beyond what exists. This is achieved through the spaces for speculation, subversion, and expression of a desire for different ways of being.

Notes

1. In 2004, coinciding with the tenth anniversary of the suicide of Cobain, Etxebarria was asked to re-edit this book. Charged with this task, the author not only edited *Aguanta esto*, omitting outdated information, but also added a second part in which she elaborates upon the notion of society as spectacle (Debord, Baudrillard) whereby representation does not necessarily corroborate with reality.

2. In September of 2001, Lucía Etxebarria was accused of plagiarism by the magazine *Interviú* for her work, *Estación de Infierno*. According to *Interviú*, Etxebarria extracted many words and phrases of the Galician poet Antonio Colinas, for whom she has a special affinity, and made them her own. Colinas was also interviewed by the magazine and noted the striking correspondence among his work and that of Etxebarria, yet implored the reader to arrive at her own conclusion with respect to the intertextuality of the two works. For her part, Etxebarria professes a sincere admiration for the Galician that has only multiplied due to his comportment in this matter. For extra information, see the following web pages: http://www.el-mundo.es/2001/10/02/cultura/1054828-imp.html and http://www.5dias.com/especiales/especiales/2001/especiales2001/html/cul2.html.

3. It must be mentioned that alongside *Interviú's* accusation against Etxebarria for plagiarism of the Galician Antonio Colinas, the magazine suggested that the novel under discussion bears a striking similarity to *Prozac Nation* to the point of plagiarism. It was published in 1994 in English by the *Rolling Stone* journalist Elizabeth Wurtzel, and was translated into Spanish in 1995.

4. While the vocabulary utilized may be vulgar, it illustrates succinctly the social lived reality of Spain in the last decade of the twentieth century.

5. Cristina and Iain used to experiment with a number of S&M devices; likewise, the first time they were together sexually, Cristina allowed him to blindfold her to intensify their experience.

Amor, curiosidad, prozac y dudas: The Raver, the Cyborg, and the Housewife ~ 113

Cristina attempted suicide a handful of times via alternate methods. The first time she ingested Pacharán, which is a powerful and sweet liquor from the Basque region; interestingly, her mother—a take on Lorca's Bernarda Alba—also hails from this province. Hence in swilling Pacharán, she hoped to hurt her mother. The second time Cristina cut herself beginning at her waist and ending at her ankles, however, she was found just in time by her sister Ana.

6. Cristina continues on her diatribe against capitalism describing in detail the parallels among the office workers and a herd of cattle.

7. The manner in which Etxebarria describes the environment of the multinational alludes strongly to Douglas Coupland's *Generation X*. One can note parallels among the terminology utilized to describe today's info-laden culture and the resulting embodiment of these elements among the protagonists.

8. On Etxebarria's personal web page, http://teleline.terra.es/personal/luciaetx/mundo.htm, she unmasks the traditional concept of knowledge and the patriarchal institutions that are founded on these principles. Furthermore, she cites statistics on gender inequalities; concretely, she treats the unequal job practices reflected around the globe. She argues,

> Las mujeres representan la mitad de la población mundial, cubren cerca de dos tercios del total de horas de TRABAJO, reciben la décima parte de los INGRESOS y poseen menos del 1% de los BIENES. . . . En el mundo, solo el 2% de los EJECUTIVOS de alto nivel son mujeres, pero solo el 5% de los puestos de socio en los bufetes privados están ocupados por ellas…En la Real Academia de la Lengua Española hay 45 hombres y una mujer, Ana María Matute. La Academia indica en sus Estatutos que deberán figurar, obligatoriamente, como miembros, al menos un cardenal y un militar. (http://teleline.terra.es/personal/luciaetx/mundo.htm)

9. In her article "'Alternative' Music and the Oppositional Potential of Generation X Culture" Leslie Haynsworth notes that alienation and anomie are defining characteristics of Generation X as this particular culture locates itself outside of the mainstream.

10. While Rosa does take care of this situation, that is, stop the objectification of Cristina by a bar patron, does she not also further objectify her, calling more attention to Cristina through her perhaps possessive claims that they are lesbian partners?

11. While Cristina did walk out of the multinational, she did interchange one patriarchal structure for another, Planeta X. She is not really outside of the system, rather operates within it to her advantage, vis-à-vis her job at the bar.

12. To be feminized means to be subject to vulnerability, to be able to be "disassembled, reassembled, exploited as a reserve labour force" (Haraway 16).

13. Rosa feels that jeans are inappropriate for someone in her position. It is ironic to note, though, that she is quite jealous of her sister Cristina due to how good her body—in particular her derriere—looks in a pair of jeans. (42)

14. Henry Purcell (1658–1695) was an English composer who wrote and performed a wide variety of musical scores, ranging from sacred music to secular and

opera. The piece "The Fatal Hour Comes on Apace" is a baroque work saturated with emotion and affectation that employs the metaphor of death for a painful separation, perhaps between lovers. The following are the lyrics of the piece.

> The fatal hour comes on apace,
> Which I had rather die than see,
> For when fear calls you from this place,
> You go to certain misery.
> The thought does stab me to the heart,
> And gives me pangs no word can speak,
> It wracks me in each vital part,
> Sure when you go, my heart will break.
> Since I for you so much endure,
> May I not hope you will believe,
> 'Tis you alone these wounds can cure,
> Which are the fountains of my grief.

15. Her mother was quite bitter about her failed marriage and as a result believed the entire institution to be "una solemne tontería" (181).

16. Ana lost her virginity to Borja's close childhood friend, Antonio, who raped her fifteen years earlier. When she tried to confront him about what happened nearly two decades ago, his only response was "no sé de qué me hablas" (186).

17. The images disseminated by fashion and decoration magazines may be read as vehicles that perpetuate the binary oppositions and reinforce the naturalization of gendered identities.

18. The figure of Lilith is famed for being the first wife of Adam, created from earth, just like him. Rejecting Adam's desires, she flees from Eden and is replaced by a subservient Eve, a figure who does not have a claim to equality since she was created from a part of his body, his side. Lilith has been portrayed as the archetype of feminism through her willingness to sacrifice paradise for equality and autonomy.

CHAPTER FOUR

Veo, veo: Consumption and the Dazzling Diva of Image

Cultural Context

The author Gabriela Bustelo (1962) is both novelist and translator with a degree in English Philology.[1] Her novelistic production includes *Veo, veo* and *Planeta hembra*.[2] While born in Madrid, this author spent nearly the first decade of her life in Washington, D.C. Her family relocated to Madrid in the 1970s in the midst of the disintegration of the Franco regime. While their experiences and literary production are quite distinct, both Lucía Etxebarria and Gabriela Bustelo share the commonality of a trans-national perspective gleaned from shifts in location as well as physical distance from the social, political, and economic epicenter of Spain: Madrid. Much like Etxebarria, Bustelo—as a result of her dynamic social reality—dialogues with the international community through her work, evidenced by the use of English terminology, internationally recognized brand names, global pop music icons, and the mention of globalized tourist destinations.[3] The author herself acknowledges the tremendous power the inflow of cultures has had on Spain—a cultural phenomenon manifest in her writing: "Fue un recurso que usé en mi primera novela. La influencia del inglés es enorme" (Personal Interview 2003). As Bustelo dialogues with the international community through her work, she also maintains a local discourse in which she focuses on the numerous advancements realized in Spain within the last twenty-five years. Like Etxebarria, Bustelo spent her youth between opposing scopes of the political spectrum; she was born into the Franco dictatorship, resided for a decade in the States, beginning in the latter half of the 1960s—a period of instability stemming from the Vietnam War and the human rights struggle—only to return to her birth land, Spain, on the cusp of the collapse of the dictatorship. Consequently, she was witness, and perhaps more acutely sensitive, to the changing political dynamics in her country, in particular the effects these alterations had on the condition of women and the dynamics of conventional structures. During a personal interview Bustelo stated: "Históricamente, España ha avanzado en el último cuarto de siglo como no lo había hecho nunca. . . . Conviene recordar que hace veinticinco años una española no podía tener una cuenta bancaria sin permiso de su marido" (Personal Interview 2003).

With the imminent collapse of the Franco dictatorship in 1975 and the installation of the new Constitution in 1978, the Spanish society found itself in a position to be spectator and participator in international events via the television and other media communications (Riquer i Permanyer 265). Indeed, this political transformation, which sparked a reverberation of changes far beyond the scope of the political sphere, altered the very concept of Spanish identity both individually and collectively. Likewise, advances in technology communications have led to the acceleration of the influx of globalization of cultures, reconstructing the very notion of identity and social reality in this country. Bustelo affirms:

> Siendo estrictos, todo es consumo. Hoy en día el consumismo y el mercantilismo han invadido terrenos donde nunca debieron entrar, que aun si somos sinceros, probablemente el amor, el matrimonio e incluso la amistad han sido siempre utilitaristas en mayor o menor grado. (Personal Interview 2003)

Her revelation about the proliferation of consumption in the Spanish society—as well as on an international level—further suggests its significance as a fundamental constituent of personal and collective identity. Additionally, it hints at the ambivalence about consumption and the various readings that it may yield.

Alongside the piecemeal effacement of the old order and the infiltration of mass consumer society, reality transformed into signs and time fragmented into a series of present sites (Fuat Firat 83). As a consequence of the reification of a new order, one in which consumerism is at the nucleus, consumers began to learn and adopt new codes stemming from the close proximity and intimate relationships fabricated with meaning-laden objects. By means of acquiring and consuming goods, a subject associates the self with the meanings embedded in those materials; these adopted messages, then, coalesce with the self. Hence the consumption of goods is an integral part of postmodern identity both social and personal, as attested by Bustelo. In this context, Robert Dunn elaborates: "sources of identity have shifted historically from the internalization and integration of social roles to the appropriation of disposable commodities, images, and techniques, selected and discarded at will from the extensive repertoire for consumer culture" (114). The posing of such possibilities afforded by consumerism can be read as a pluralization of social realities, differentiating and articulating new vocabularies for personal identification. Dunn affirms: "Contrary to the critics of mass culture and consumerism, then, contemporary consumer culture has thus in a sense made it possible to contemplate the commodity as a vehicle for a more fully and creatively developed self" (114). Following Dunn's argument, cultures of consumption inflect personal identity with new accents and provide the self with the freedom of identity election. Bustelo similarly avows: "Es verdad que el consumo puede ser liberador y es verdad que la liberación de la mujer ha acabado con muchos valores tradicionales" (Personal Interview 2003). This writer acknowledges the potential autonomy that the realm of consumption can offer an individual, especially the woman, as it may be a site for active self-formation. In this way, women have the agency to subvert as well as resist the organic and essentialized notion of woman. "El cuerpo propio es una realidad mucho más presente para una mujer que para un hombre" (Personal Interview 2003). As she highlights, historically there has existed a connection between woman and nature and woman and body. Throughout history, woman has been defined as man's opposite; he is the subject and she, consequently, is the other. The mind has been associated with the masculine, and as such, rationality and logic are posited as superior; the construction of Woman is akin to nature, associated with the body, sex, and irrationality. Hence, the very concept of Woman cannot be separated from her body, but rather it is intimately associated with her subject and identity. While acknowledging the potential liberation offered by the realm of consumption, the author cautiously mentions the seductive powers of the material world and the potential contradictory reality that it yields. She states: "la asociación entre consumo y feminidad es peligrosa" (Personal Interview 2003). While acknowledging the potential gains offered by consumerism, Bustelo likewise advises caution: "La mujer tiene la posibilidad de modelar y transformar su cuerpo, pero esto siempre tiene consecuencias, a veces negativas, sobre su vida. Vania está experimentando para ver qué sucede en función de que su imagen sea una o otra" (Personal Interview 2004). These transformations effected through varying cultures of consumption as well as the resulting embodiment are poignantly illustrated through the socially lived experiences of the protagonists in both of her novels, *Veo, veo* and *Planeta hembra*.

Stemming perhaps from her personal narratives and experiences, consistent among the work of Gabriela Bustelo is a probing critique of dominant cultural symbols and language. Her work is a creative forum that questions and subverts the symbolic order by toying with it via her usage of parody, irony, fresh language, and a play on gender performance. Through her employment of these resources, the author appropriates language for her own ends: to interrogate the supposedly organic nature of gender. The re-appropriation of the symbolic, as evidenced in this author's production, is dissonant because, as Judith Butler theorized, the act manipulates the underlying discourses within these symbols and thus alters the social order (Butler, *Bodies That Matter* 53). In this process, the power dynamics imbricated in cultural signs are transformed, and by re-signifying their meanings they become empowering. Vis-à-vis her critique of the hegemonic systems, Bustelo highlights the fluidity of identity in our postmodern era as well as proposes alternative spaces for becoming woman. In the study of this writer's novel *Veo, veo*, written in 1996, I analyze the portrayal of female subjectivity through the optic of consumption, focusing on various cultures such as fashion, music, drugs, and the female gaze. Concomitantly, this chapter explores the resulting embodiment that emerges as a result of the personal election of the female consumer.

Veo, veo plays back a particular version of reality that suggests an active registering of social alterations—especially with respect to the role of the woman—occurring in Spain in the last two decades of the twentieth century. Gabriela Bustelo navigates a rich and complicated landscape of social change in Spain, and by way of her work, she engages with dynamic modes of femininity that consequently tells us something of real significance about society. The novel, peppered with cinematographic techniques, reflects the last years of the "movida madrileña," roughly equivalent to the "movement" or the "scene" in English. In her meditation on this time period, Gabriela elaborates:

> "La movida" como corriente artística y cultural afectó a personas de la clase acomodada, aunque también fue un despertar de la capital de España tras cuarenta años de letargo. Paradójicamente, la libertad era mucho mayor en la España de los ochenta que en la de hoy. Los horarios españoles se han adaptado a los europeos, está prohibido el consumo de alcohol en la calle y las ciudades son peligrosas de noche. "La movida" ya es sólo una anécdota histórica. (Personal Interview 2003)

After the death of Franco in 1975 "la movida" emerged as a pop cultural scene that embodied a cocktail of humor, wild eccentricity, and passion. At its nucleus radiated cultural reawakening, creativity, and intellectualism. The late mayor-poet-professor Tierno Galvan was significant to the upstart of this atmosphere; his efforts—creations of parks and renovation of public and private spaces—catalyzed this explosion of artistic, intellectual and social life which translated into a new-found freedom intimately linked with and exercised through cultures of consumption.[4] The social background—the collapse of the suffocating dictatorship—was propitious for the consumer boom in the 1980s, as it permitted new concepts to be imported into the country.

The "movida," a period roughly encompassing 1977 to 1985, can be considered the confluence of a series of changes occurring in Madrid on various levels: politics, culture, and economy. It manifests as an underground phenomena among an intellectually curious and artistically inclined group of youths who espoused a punk ideology; it represented a breach from the hegemonic power structure as those that participated backlashed against social conformism. This was realized in a number of ways through various artists. For instance, through the medium of cinema Almodóvar celebrated sexual desire that was repressed for forty years under the dictatorship. Another artist that surfaced during the "movida," Ouka Lele, toyed with evocative representations via the camera lens. Operating against the grain like the aforementioned masters, Gabriela Bustelo glorifies this newly acquired sexual freedom vis-à-vis the protagonist Vania and the mode that she experiences her body-in-use. This transgressive ideology is reflected in the novel *Veo, veo* on a medley of levels. To begin with, bearing striking similarity to a film, the novel resembles the genre of film noir.[5] Yet, it transcends this genre and its authorial presence through parody and irony. Likewise, the novel reflects the detective genre in that at its essence, it is the investigation of a puzzle: the search for Truth. The backlash against authority and linearity is acknowledged through the absence of a singular tightly woven plot; one that is mediated by a variety of discourses such as pop-psychology, detective literature, and popular media and culture. Furthermore, the defiance embodied in this transgression is influenced by three factors: the temporal, the spatial, and the affectual.

The novel *Veo, veo* consistently interrogates universality, at the same time that it unveils the possibility for multiplicity: things are not what they seem, people change identities, and there are unforeseen twists and turns along the journey. The nucleus of the work is Madrid in the 1980s, a society intensely affected by globalization of cultures and media technologies, reflected in the opening chapter of the novel, which bears the name of an American icon. "Mickey Rourke," chapter one, details the central conflict of the novel and the protagonist Vania: a persecutory neurosis that someone is watching her every move. After her consultation with a psychiatrist, who bore a striking similarity in appearance to American icon Mickey Rourke, she arrived at multiple realizations. With respect to her concerns regarding her mental health, she concluded that she was not crazy. Moreover, she felt unable to confide in or trust the commodified image of her psychiatrist. He was: "sospechosamente alto y guapo," and his office space: "una habitación pequeña, con una ventana que debía dar a un patio interior, por la poca luz que había. Los muebles eran de esos de pino lechoso y para colmo de desgracias, estaba todo abarrotado de almohadones con floripondios Liberty" (9). Indeed, his appearance did not correspond with her preconceived conception: "lo que yo esperaba era una especie de vejete judío con barba, firme y paternal a la vez. Y por supuesto, que tuviera muebles de caoba y butacas de esas de cuero que se amoldan a la nalga. Y un reloj de mesa inglés" (10). In selecting a therapist, she is consuming not only his advice but also the commodified image that he displays. After his trite recommendation to take a vacation, Vania leaves his office—confirming her trust in packaged images and feeling her stalker at her heels—and seeks out a detective whose image and surroundings coincide with his profession. In this vein, chapter two "El Cejas" succinctly describes the detective hired by Vania to help her solve her troubles:

> El barrio era de bastante peor tono, la puerta más sucia y desvencijada, harta de hacer de umbral cutre. El hombre que salió a abrir en esta ocasión no me defraudó para nada. Chaparreta, cejijunto y con un Ducados en la boca. El perfecto detective hispánico. (11)

His rough-around-the-edges appearance coupled with less than flashy location render him the perfect person to get to the bottom of her dilemma. The remaining chapters of the novel (sixty-five in total) revolve around humorous and ironic escapades to uncover the root of Vania's neurosis: a stalker who has gained access to her surroundings, both apartment and car, and planted several secret microphones and video cameras disguised as two-way mirrors to record her in her most vulnerable moments. In her narration, Bustelo portrays the journey of the protagonist on her quest for the Truth; along the way, she awakens to a consciousness that there is not one but a multiplicity of truths. As such, Bustelo toys with the hegemonic discourse through her use of irony and unveils a protagonist who actively constructs herself vis-à-vis her relationship with space and material goods such as fashion, music, and the gaze.

Throughout the novel, the reader witnesses the many trials that confront the protagonist. From the most prosaic to the more spectacular, the reader maintains a vantage point to observe: from the mystery caller who asks to speak with Soledad to the protagonist's own discovery of a "cilindro diminuto. Era un micrófono" (21) in her lavish Gastón and Daniela sheets. Yet despite the numerous insidious tribulations, we attest to a female subject who is an adept consumer, from brand names and luxury goods to marijuana and cocaine, she possesses equal knowledge of high-end clothing and home goods as she does of the underground space of the "movida" nightlife and the accoutrements that accompany these particular locations. Each of the various aforementioned components—brand names, drugs, music, and underground venues—in conjunction with an atmosphere of sexual freedom serve as articulation points that work upon and produce, in Foucauldian terms, the selfhood of Vania.

The modus operandi of Peláez, also known as "El cejas" due to his unibrow, is to find and apprehend whoever is spying on the protagonist: "un hombre con un bigote en forma de manillar de bici" (13). The best way, he proposes, to achieve this is to flesh out her personal history and also follow Vania inconspicuously to her usual hangouts to stake out from a distance whoever it is that is spying on her. As an observer of the narrative, the reader learns that Vania is a twenty-six-year-old scriptwriter working in "una productora de audiovisuales" (12). While she is not "forrada" with cash, she earns a decent income, which permits her to own a Mazda, rent an apartment in a reformed palace on calle Pez, and purchase a myriad of material goods. As the story unfolds revealing a number of intrigues, the reader finds out that the protagonist takes great pleasure in conspicuous consumption as she represents relative wealth, is in a position to participate in the multiplication of material goods, and takes pride in this fact.[6] For instance, after her initial meeting with Peláez she states: "El psiquiatra me había despertado ligeramente la líbido y el detective me había servido de psiquiatra. Lo malo era que Peláez, mi recién contratado sabueso, se había quedado absolutamente convencido de que yo era una tronada paranoica" (14). Feeling static—after her meetings there had been no advancement in the resolution of her conflict—she turns to the material world to ease her concerns. "Me bajé en el Vips y en un arrebato masoca cogí el video *Orquídea salvaje*. Debía ser aún peor que *Nueve semanas y media*, pero como mi ex psiquiatra se parecía a Mickey Rourke, ver la película era la forma de exorcizarles a los dos juntos" (14). Through consumption of imported North American movies and icons,

Vania not only participates in a fluid international dialogue, interacting with cultural knowledge, but also channels and alleviates her preoccupations via consumption of the cinema; that is, she mediates her supposed "neurosis" (10) through her consumption practices.

Writing subversion, Bustelo opens closures that destroy, or otherwise contain the protagonist, as well as her imagined community, which threatens patriarchal control and its symbolic order. The transgressions that form part of the architecture of the plot are embodied on various planes: temporal, spatial, and affectual. The novel set amongst the backdrop of the "movida" diverges in two opposing temporalities. Bustelo skillfully creates two separate yet convergent worlds in which the protagonist, Vania, maneuvers: the day—hours spent at the "productora" (24) or home full of concern and plotting to figure out the puzzle of her "manía persecutoria" (21)—and the night—a world of glamour heightened by scenes of expression involving the consumption of myriad elements. With respect to the two temporal planes, it is interesting to note the spatial confines Vania negotiates. She largely interacts with the consumer society within specific territories of the Spanish capital—Malasaña and Chueca—locales historically associated with bacchanalian pleasures. Devoid of numerous historic monuments and palaces that characterize the majority of Madrid, the labyrinthine streets of Malasaña and Chueca house countless sites such as Pachá, Archys, El Café, and Via Láctea to name a few. Likewise, these districts are hailed as the cradle of the "movida" movement, which by night bristle with Madrid's alternative scene. These spaces represent contingents of experiential consumption by which Vania articulates her subversive identity, as the practices associated with them intimately affect Vania's conception of identity and belonging. Ben Malbon elaborates upon the formation of the individual within the contemporary postmodern location:

> As the site of a multitude of 'social spaces' of varying levels of sociality the city intensely stimulates our emotions and senses, at times to the brink of sensory overload, but also offers sites and spaces of relief from this intensity, if only through bounding these experiences in certain spaces and at certain times. (267)

After the walls of Franco's gerontocracy fell, Spanish society experimented a flourished surge, profoundly influenced by the globalization of mass consumer culture. This translated into the importation of new concepts and paradigms such as advances in technology and media communications that altered the notions of time and space, self and nation. In sum, these sweeping societal transformations consequently resulted in the acceleration and intensity of socially lived experience that created a complex, dense environment in which identity began to be informed by globalized cultural knowledge (Malbon); in partaking in diverse cultures of consumption, subjects forged dynamic multiple subjectivities.

Madonna Reincarnate: A New Look, a New You

In *Veo, veo*, Gabriela Bustelo interrogates conventional gender paradigms in a manner that raises the difficulty of knowing anything at all, especially when we can articulate that knowing only through language. As the story begins to unravel, the spectator witnesses the bouts of paranoia and doubt that plague the protagonist. She confesses: "Cada vez me sentía más marciana. No tenía claro en quién podía confiar y en quién no" (31). Stemming from the effect of her stalker, Vania feels alien and does not know whom to trust, this disbelief extending to her network of friendships. Given this, Vania channels her energy into the realm of consumerism whereby she articulates her identity. In so doing, she removes herself from an absence of power, if not actively empower herself. From the label on her tube of lipstick "«Escarlata Ojalá»" (28) to her brand name clothing attire "Hechter" (39) Vania freely manufactures a multi-textured self composed of a plethora of elements: the seductive, alluring red lipstick called "Wanting Scarlet" juxtaposed with the chic but conservative uptown style of Hechter clothing. By way of inscribing her body with commodities that send contrasting messages, each however carefully chosen, Vania fabricates her desired paradoxical representation. The construction of her hybrid identity is buttressed by her consumption of women's magazines: "Siempre que me daba por comprar las revistillas de turno, acababa con la nostalgia de un futuro en el que yo vivía a lo grande. Como Angelica Huston, mismamente. Leer, tocar el piano y montar a caballo" (47). In the spirit of glamour, Vania has complete license and freedom to create herself, even if it is fugacious.

In an accelerated world that cannot adequately represent truth claims through language, consumer goods and images not only offer solace, but also, in the age of information, are heralded as primary vehicles of communication (Lury) as evidenced in the dedicatory page of the novel. Bustelo includes verses from a popular Lou Reed song, "I'll be your mirror" (1977), that emphasized the significant pervasiveness of material representation in conjunction with the gaze in consumer society; the chosen verses state: "I'll be your mirror. Reflect what you are in case you don't know." The idea of the mirror projecting one's image in totality recalls an important component in Lacan's critical reinterpretation of the work of Freud, namely that of the "mirror stage." Elaborating upon investigations previously undertaken in the fields of physiology and animal psychology, Lacan developed the concept of the "mirror stage," a period in which an external portrait of the body (reflected in a mirror) yields a germane response; it is from this elicited response that a mental representation of "I" surges. As Lacan affirms, the mirror stage is akin to a drama, in which the individual immerse in the process of self-formation conceives of an aggregate selfhood, perceived formerly in fragments. It is also noted as a phase of development in which the infant experiences feelings of alienation, stemming from the recognition that it is a separate entity.[7] The image reflected is recognized to be, at the same time, representative of the self yet different. This split recognition makes desire and lack fundamental forces in our lives: lack stemming from the recognition that the subject is a separate entity from the mother and desire surfacing from the longing to achieve that previous totality. As Silverman affirms, "the mirror stage as imaginary mapping, suggesting that it is no more possible to be seen than to see ourselves without intervention of representation" (107), and consequently, it is "through this mediation of asks that the masculine and the feminine meet in the most acute, most intense way" (107). The citing of Reed's songs "I'll be your mirror" is not innocuous, but rather Bustelo alludes to an important moment in self-formation. This occurs when the subject, upon looking at her mirror image, recognizes that the reflected equivalent is the projection of her corporeality into a representation, and as a result, recognizes the margins of her subjectivity: the identification of self. In sum, as Bustelo hints in her dedicatory page, consciousness is not inherent but rather created. The human subject arrives into this world experimenting a fragmented reality; it is not until the subject recognizes and accepts the image of herself in the mirror—one that provides unity and stability—that she creates a totalizing notion of her very subjectivity. One potential for the construction of the conscious remains the consumer realm. Via the consumption of particular objects, goods, or people, the subject—through appropriating the good—merges with the world of matter, and as such becomes an extension of its qualities with a defined identity. Laura Oswald states: "The subject of consumption is nothing if not an actor in search of an identity. . . . Lacking a basic core identity, the post-modern subject constructs itself around the image it projects for others in consumer culture. 'I am what you perceive me to be.' Consumption enables people to change hats as the occasion demands" (49). Taking into consideration the theories of Lacan through the optic of consumption, the subject vacillates in the attempt to locate a fixed identity, to make the self stable. This achievement is contingent upon positioning ourselves into the discourse of the image in the mirror. The discourse, or signifying system, is that which endows meaning to the signifier, or material good; the mélange of images that we interplay with daily is embedded in the power dynamics of the societies in which we live. Within this dance, the subject finds personal meaning from the signifier and then may locate herself and her identity, albeit fleetingly.

What characterizes consumption as a mode of significance is that these goods or commodities no longer exist in and of themselves, but circulate as signs within a system of differences, or as Baudrillard states: "the object is no longer referred to in relation to a specific utility, but as a collection of objects in their total meaning" (Baudrillard, *Simulacra and Simulation* 31). Thus it is within this differential sign-value that the commodity in question has any meaning at all; cultural commodities structure meaning for the consumer in specific contexts and constitute the horizon of possibilities within which the consumer can structure meaning for herself. In the context of Vania, preparing to go out is not just a matter of collecting pertinent belongings such as keys, purse, etc., rather it entails the complex process of self fabrication, which includes the conversion of her body into a legible text. On one occasion Vania notes "Me acicalé a lo Versace con vaqueros y en vista de que no tenía espejo, decidí ir de cara lavada y recién peiná" (93). Her clothing choice is not innocent; rather as Alison Lurie observes in her book *El lenguaje de la Moda*:

> Incluso cuando no decimos nada, nuestra ropa habla a voces a cualquiera que nos ve. Llevar lo mismo que todo el mundo no es una solución al problema, no más que lo sería decir lo mismo que dice todo el mundo. Podemos mentir en el lenguaje de la vestimenta, o intentar decir la verdad; pero a menos que estemos desnudos y calvos es imposible guardar el silencio. (2)

As manifest in her clothing, her body text incarnates a hybrid mixture of aesthetics. While sporting imported Versace jeans, she ironically maintains the traditional Spanish "cara lavada y recién peiná." The protagonist sends a clear message that she is above trying to look good, above conforming to social expectations. It can be said that she is a contradiction of the aesthetic she embodies: a dissonant that flaunts femininity yet transgresses these regulations going sans coiffure and makeup. One of the most salient characteristics of visual culture in postmodernity is the disassemblage and heteroglossia of tastes and attitudes regarding attire: "the wide range and quality of fabrics, trims, colors, silhouettes, and particularly stylistic modes as well as the broad array of accessories spanning the spectrum from footwear and headdress to jewelry and hair style display an unprecedented openness and fragmentation in the history of post-Enlightenment Western clothing conventions" (Leitch 111). Clothing, as a form of dress, has the ability to communicate for the masses and the individual that which they cannot express verbally and that which they would like to make obvious about themselves. Body dressing, furthermore, is imbricated in the dynamics of cultural capital; it mediates between patriarchal norms and domination as well as serves as a prescription for conformity yet also resistance, as illustrated in the aforementioned description of Vania's attire (Leitch). In assuming a particular fad or aesthetic, one also is subsumed within a specific milieu; however, identity formation as manifest through clothing is a function of multiple subject positions that cohere in contradiction.

The formation of identity, in conjunction with fashion, does not erect itself in a vacuum, but rather it is a process that is embedded in the mirroring effects afforded by other spectators. In a world of gazing and being gazed upon, body attire systematically submits to inscription and re-inscription vis-à-vis complex operations of social interaction. The body is dressed and its spectacle submitted to critical cultural inventories and praxis, and as a result subjectivity unfolds in a play of images (Entwistle). The dialogue between the material realm and spectator initiates with the fascination of look or the gaze. According to Patrizia Calefato: "la mirada permite acceder a situaciones irreversibles, marca el paso hacia un estado en que todo parece haberse cumplido. Mirar es, a la vez, modificar el mundo y a los otros que se miran, y ser modificado por la mirada de los otros" (129). Looking, then, is not simply an innocent action, but rather a process mediated by our own experiences, thoughts, and cultural knowledge. In the context of the novel, it is significant to note that Vania had always preferred to be the "mirona"(93), in possession of the gaze and by association, power, rather than the "mirada" (93), a traditional female position historically relegated as passive. Nevertheless, along her journey, the protagonist problematizes this binary structure of one/other through her subversion—intimately linked to her active self-formation—of the paradox. In her meditation on body dressing Iris Marion Young sustains: "female imagination has liberating possibilities. . . . The unreal that wells up through imagination always creates the space for a negation of what is, and thus the possibility of alternatives" (209). In this vein, we can consider such liberatory phenomena as resistance of styles, voguing, parody, masquerade, and anti-hegemonic dress. Thus, fashion serves as an instrument to aid and abet gender constraints and display Vania's assertiveness.

Fashion and its coding of the body is not a new concept. It has served to mark and textualize the bodies of both the masculine and the feminine for centuries according to supposedly organic gender prescriptions. Nevertheless, it may be considered in a positive light due to the ability to select and confect one's selfhood. Fashion codes and denotes that which Vania is: her subject. As a system of signs, body dressing constitutes a popular cultural form of communication, capable of reproducing and reinventing itself. The value of Vania's fashion consumption lies not in the usage of the clothes but rather in their highly effective manner of writing the body so that the body enters into the realm of circulation as currency. Similar to music, fashion articulates how an individual perceives space, time, and her body. According to Calefato: "Lo que tienen en común el lenguaje del cuerpo revestido y el lenguaje musical, de forma peculiar, es el elemento de sensorialidad: traje y música son formas mediante las cuales el cuerpo parece 'sentir' el mundo circunstante de manera completa y amplificada" (175). Hence fashion and music articulate in a more penetrating and excited mode that which we may know or feel. Vania's self illuminates this affectuality evidenced by her selection of body dressing as well as her transformation through dress. Regularly in the process of altering her bodily text, her clothes, style, and body images range from evening dresses to bedroom wear and flashy garb to techno-futuristic fashion. Not infrequently, though, clothing functions ironically with Vania, for instance the galactic part-woman, part-machinic image she sports with the lime green lycra dress, a mix between "Star Trek y Barbarella" (113), paired with "botas blancas de media pierna tipo Courréges" (113). It is noteworthy that her look—a hybrid—is grounded in North American popular media references: *Barbarella* and *Star Trek*. Ironic in particular, *Barbarella* is a 1968 Jane Fonda camp classic, as it depicts the story of a stunningly beautiful woman charged with leading a revolution to save planet Earth. Vania is also on a mission: to question and play with convention. Through the use of strongly sexualized images and the futuristic, Bustelo reconceptualizes the notion of woman as sex object. Daniel Harris affirms: "The futuristic creates its imagery through willful disobedience, an almost bratty, aesthetic misbehavior, rather than through a genuine spirit of inventiveness, of artistic prescience about the appearance of tomorrow" (129). As Harris confirms, the employment of the futuristic aesthetic does not portend the creation of a new order, rather: "an ever-clearer sense of the obsolescence of the past which, through a crotchety series of negations and disavowals, it seeks to cancel out" (129–30). By way of the combination of feminine consciousness and pleasurable playfulness Bustelo toys with tradition to create a potentially liberating female subject.

While the clothing Vania consumes reproduces gender conventions, it is also open to subversion through her usage of irony. That is, it can be described as "campy" in the aesthetic sense. Susan Sontag in "Notes on Camp" elaborates that camp is located in a "seriousness that fails" (2) as it is premised on irony and it prizes style over content. The trademark of camp is a love of the exaggerated and is the most patent example of the metaphor: life is a theater, as it responds to the roles one assumes and plays in life. Moreover, camp can also be employed to satirize; for instance, by presenting people and/or objects as exaggerated, camp signals and interrogates the prolific stereotypes in society. To this extent, the look Vania cultivates is not innocuous; her (re)presentation can be read as "campy." For example, one occasion, Vania reveals: "Para ir a cenar a Archy quería estar atómica. Me puse un traje negro de Hechter que consistía en una falda stretch y una chaqueta entallada con cremallera y escote en pico. Así contado no parece nada del otro mundo, pero con unos zapatos altos causaba sensación" (39). Her choice in attire is interesting in that the stretch skirt and zippered, fitted coat serve to mold and shape her body, and consequently her self. To test the impact her body dressing would have, she consulted with two male friends to solicit their opinion; their response was precisely what she had hoped to elicit. "Los hombres siempre cambian de comportamiento en cuanto ven una falda, un tacón y un trozo de pierna. No pueden remediarlo. Perfecto. Se me quedaron mirando como si fuera otra distinta de la que acababa de abrirles la puerta. Justo lo que yo quería" (39). This example exposes the complexity of gender constraints. While it appears to reinforce traditional notions of patriarchy, it can also be read as a parody of the dominant structure. Vania fabricates a highly sexually charged image, yet she is not an object. Rather, through the commodification of her body, she wields power over the men, and also parodies supposed, inherent 'natural' structures. At the same time, she produces a subject that conforms in every way to the denigration of content for style. That is, the two men are portrayed as pitiful, simpletons, incapacitated by the erotically charged image she wields. Additionally, via the communication of their body language, she understands the type of power her body, a commodity, possesses. I view her choice of dress as an important investment in subject formation—one which opens up the potential for Vania and other women to use clothing/fashion for their own purposes and experience pleasures that are the reverse of dominant ones. Through her fashion choices, she communicates to her self and the world the pleasure she gleans from exercising her sexuality. Vania affirms: "Esta noche le tocaba el turno al vestido verde lima. Como estaba muy morena, el contraste tela con piel era perfecto. Cuando yo misma me deseaba, sabía que estaba deseable" (135). This superfeminine figure defines and exceeds the boundaries of what it means to be a Woman; she is an icon that is meant to be desired, envied, and emulated. Likewise, the protagonist plays off cultural anxieties surrounding female sexuality with a special zeal, in a manner that represents a direct attack on hegemonic ideas of women incarnating the binary opposition of a Madonna or a prostitute. It must be noted that some feminists read tight sexual clothing as garments that set out to discipline and regulate the female body, rendering her docile and subservient (Bordo, Dworkin); yet Vania is in no way subservient. Consistent with Braidotti's theory of becoming-woman and the nomadic figuration, Vania experiences multiple pleasures derived from fashion and the power it gives to her as seen through shifts in her identity. Furthermore, she uses this to her advantage within the hegemonic power structure.

As the detective teases out the various intrigues of the conundrum and puzzle pieces slowly come together vis-à-vis multiple discoveries, the enigma of Vania's stalker becomes shrouded in mystery. Peláez, in conjunction with his friends Federico and Samperio, scour her apartment and car, which prove to be an enormous success as they expose numerous secret microphones, video cameras placed in the most intimate rooms of her apartment, and to top it off, multiple two-way mirrors mascarading as walls. As Vania puts it, her home is "cuajada de micros" (60) and as a result of the secret cameras and two-way mirrors she was observed during "las escenas más comprometidas que le pueden ocurrir a alguien en el cuarto de baño, en el dormitorio y en el salón de su casa" (84). Perhaps the culminating point of the infiltration of her privacy arrives with the discovery of the videotapes, revealing extremely vulnerable moments in her day. Watching the tapes, to validate their footing, Vania remained completely stunned:

> Primera toma. Yo despatarrada en el sofa aún sin agujeros, desnuda de cintura para abajo y viendo la tele con cara de zombi. Segunda toma. Yo en el cuarto de baño, sentada en el retrete, en plena tarea. Tercera toma. Yo, en el sofa otra vez, de tiros largos y con ojos de lunática, dándome la paliza total con un tipo trajeado. Cuarta toma. Yo mirándome en el espejo del cuarto de baño, haciendo muecas circenses y limpiándome los oídos con un bastoncillo de algodón. Quinta toma. Yo, el el salon otra vez, hablando sola con gran convencimiento y atizándome vodkas a saco. Sexta toma. Yo en mi habitación, guardando a cámara rápida un burruño de ropa en el armario mientras entraba un tío por la puerta. Séptima toma. Yo con un body negro tipo Dallas, haciendo un despliegue de posturitas provo encima del taburete de cuarto de baño. Octava toma. Yo devorando sin piedad sobre mi cama a un elemento que estaba como un tren. (82)

The camera, as the omnipotent eye, has captured from the mundane and prosaic to the more spectacular and devious of Vania's daily activities. Upon watching the different takes, the protagonist is at once in the position of observing and being observed. Dealing with the situation, she had to confront herself with a dual identity and two different roles. This realization—perhaps always known to Vania but never felt so acutely—endows her with power. That is to say, the way of looking defines people and things as the subject or the object, and vacillating between the two positions is a propitious space to describe, interpret, and redefine these roles. It is through this experience that the protagonist, as viewer, confronts herself with the varying identities connected with viewing. The act of looking is fundamental to our notion of being. Quoting John Berger: "It is seeing which establishes our place in the surrounding world" (5). Watching the video montage, Vania's subject enters the realm of exhibition—a peep show depicting her intimate moments—as she witnesses her own prohibited pleasure. It is interesting to note that whether being listened to, video-taped, or watched, Vania's body converts into a commodity, an object of masculine desire and an object she creates for her own pleasure. While the intent can be read to subdue and render passive Vania's subject, the impact of this melee on her lived reality is not that clear-cut.

As Vania experiences the insidious invasion of her personal territory, her self undergoes a transformation vis-à-vis her participation in the consumer realm. From the inception of the novel, the protagonist reveals to the reader the importance of seeing and being seen. "Lo fundamental era el juego ver-ser visto" (19). An integral part of this game, which mediates communication between the various players, is the spectacle; Vania notes: "Poco a poco había ido descubriendo una forma completamente distinta de relacionarse con lo real. La imagen. Otro mundo en el que la rapidez y el instante concreto eran lo que contaba" (64). Unlike the deterministic tendencies associated with the modern era, in postmodernity identity is malleable and a subject acts as her own master sculptor. In this way, Vania is in control of her image, not trapped by it; the proof lies in her ironic and chameleon-like approach to the construction of her subjectivity, her keen ability to slip into and out of character at will, to defy definition and keep them guessing. It is curious that the protagonist cites Madonna, the postmodern material girl par excellence, as queen of self-manufactured images.[8] Much like this "campy" global pop icon, Vania has invented herself to excess as a mutable being and container for a multiplicity of images: she can be anything. "Eran cerca de las diez de la noche. Puse la tele y vi en «Informe Semanal» un reportaje sobre Madonna, la reina del escándalo prefabricado. Esa si que sabía montarse bien la vida" (58–59). Like the global pop star Madonna, Vania is a multi-talented dazzler that never gets bogged in a fixed mold. This grammar conjoins concepts such as power and control to autonomous invention so as to deviate from static fixity. It is, then, the interface between material subjection to hegemonic discourses on beauty and its re-appropriation through masquerade—as will be elaborated in the following section—that Vania activates her female subjectivity through erotically charged images, all the while enjoying her own exhibitionist self-display.

Music, Dance, Drugs, and Female Subjectivity

As John Berger argues in *Ways of Seeing*: "according to the usage and conventions which are at last being questioned but have by no means been overcome—men act and women appear. Men look at women. Women watch themselves being looked at" (45). He contends that in European art from the Renaissance and beyond women were depicted as being "aware of being seen by a [male] spectator" (49). Furthermore, Berger states that from the seventeenth century, paintings of female nudes reflected the woman's subjugation to "the owner of both woman and painting" (52), a submission that, he argues, continues to be depicted present-day in color photography and other mediums. His theory—grounded in principles of the Enlightenment—maintains that women were and are still "depicted in a different way to men because the 'ideal' spectator is always assumed to be male and the image of woman is designed to flatter him" (64). Gabriela Bustelo in her novel *Veo, veo* fools with the traditional conceptions of the gaze (specifically within the territory of the movida nightlife), and in particular utilizes the technique of irony to subvert and parody these antiquated conventions.

As the story unravels, it becomes patently clear to the reader the pleasure Vania receives from her deliberate and carefully chosen commodification of body and self. Upon validation that Vania is not suffering from 'neurosis,' the existence of the protagonist is akin to an exhibition devoted to the extreme state of watching and being watched. Vania knows that she is under surveillance; not only is she being followed by an unknown but also within the confines of her personal space—her home—the placement of the hidden cameras and video recorders have converted her daily intimate activity into a peep show, public and visible for others, yet she maintains: "Lo que no pensaba hacer era abandonar mis costumbres" (60). This knowledge propels Vania to experience her life as if it were a quasi-performance; that is, she channels her energy into consumerism, one of high end goods, and thus, actively manufactures the type of self that she wants to be peeped on, both inside and outside of the home. And moreover, not only does Vania experience intense personal pleasure from the attention she dotes on herself in the process of her subject formation, but also the production of her very subjectivity serves to reproduce the mystery of the surveillance gaze.

In order to unveil the mystery and expose the stalker, detective Peláez in conjunction with his cronies propose to follow the protagonist to her regular locales, and from a distance, observe her interactions within those environments. In this situation, with the looker-on, the assumption that the gaze is always male and always omnipotent is questioned. There are numerous instances in the novel in which the woman turns the gaze on men and still others that challenge the hierarchical positioning of male and female that the gendered gaze entails. In this vein, the gaze on the part of Vania can serve to destabilize the spectator as well as confer mastery to the protagonist over her own subject formation. Although under constant surveillance by known and unknown individuals, the space of the "movida" nightlife affords Vania a distinct opportunity to freely create her self—a subject mediated by material goods, assemblage of the club, and drugs. That is, knowing full well she is being observed, the protagonist does not allow the mysterious stalker nor her paranoia to control, manipulate, or render docile her subjectivity. Instead, through her assertion of power and female sexuality she can be seen as the embodiment of the subversive nomad. Through the mode in which she experiences this location, "very much an encounter of mind *and* body" (Malbon 270), the protagonist forges a space and identity of her own. According to Bauman, in our postmodern era, physical social spaces are constructed so "that meetings which are not actively sought may be avoided" (157). This suggests that public locations are denominated as spaces to pass through rather than interact among. "Potential meetings become 'mismeetings' in which the point is to see whilst pretending that one is not looking—scrutiny disguised as indifference" (Malbon 267). The suffocating abundance of different bodies and faces in the city intensifies feelings of unease, experienced as citizens negotiate various social territories (Malbon). To manage these feelings of otherness, a number of strategies are utilized, one being what Simmel denominates the 'blasé outlook,' which entails projecting an indifference, which paradoxically is another form of sociality. Yet, as witnessed vis-à-vis the socially lived experience of our protagonist, these tactics which provide temporal relief from these "civilising influences" (Malbon 269) or "ceremonial codes" (Goffman 55) are redirected as she seeks on a temporal and spatial level enjoyment from experiences of close proximity to others in a more positive and liberating form than she experiences in the streets. While exposed social spaces offer a thrill to those negotiating its location, according to Malbon this excitement is coupled with a feeling of ease or belonging: "others are driven by the urge to feel at ease in space, even if only fleetingly" (269). This desire to express affinity with a community even among strangers—to identify with a place, people, and social circumstances, can be read as fundamental to the experience of social situations. There exists many possibilities where this unity and becoming might be experienced, and the underground nightlife of the movida, as seen through the actions of the protagonist, can be considered one of these territories.

Through participating and consuming this underground environment, Vania feels empowered to pursue a distinctive lifestyle and develop an autonomous sense of self. Regarding a particular venue, Pachá, that she frequents the protagonist expounds on the relationship of her self to the other bodies and objects-in-use.

> Pachá, según se entraba por la puerta después de pasar por el guardarropa, estaba dividido en dos sectores. El lado de la derecha era donde se instalaban los niños bien de toda la vida, con botella a su nombre y apellidos rimbombantes como Funster y Funiga. Y el lado izquierdo, el auténtico, era donde iba la ralea de incondicionales que todas las noches se ponían exactamente en el mismo sitio y pedían exactamente la misma copa. Mi esquina preferida estaba en un extremo de la zona auténtica, enfrente de la cabina de pinchas. Durante un tiempo había cogido la costumbre de ir a Pachá simplemente a pensar con música a tope. (32)

Vania's testimony underlines the importance of location or proxemics in connection with the concept of self-formation or as Braidotti states becoming-woman. The right hand side of Pachá, populated by a yuppified crowd, chose libations that reflected their cultural capital. On the other hand, the left side of Pachá was inhabited by customers that regularly frequented the club. The most authentic and valid space of Pachá, nevertheless, was the space she herself occupied, in front of the DJ booth. It is interesting to note that the territory she denominates as her own is one of high-profile and, above all, authentic; in club lingo, the DJ—synonymous with god—garners deity-like worship, as this person architects the sonic structure of the bar milieu, infusing the music with passion that translates to emotive ripples, caressing and working upon each patron. Her authentic space, regardless of venue, though, is one that maintains unobstructed visibility, placing her in a position of power: "controlando perfectamente quién entraba y salía" (107). Through the appropriation of that space as her own, she opens up a territory for the resistance of control and actively experiences libidinal pleasure. While the bar or club scene is predominantly a masculine site of experience—from levels of musical production, to drug distribution, profit making, and the appropriation of the male gaze—this location, the underground world of Pachá, can be read not only as a space of auto-erotic pleasure but also can be read as a challenge to heterosexual masculinity's traditional centrality. This is achieved via the deconstruction of the traditional notion of the unified subject with finite ego boundaries. Within this ambience, there are many elements and praxis working to erase the bodily frontiers: dancing, ornamentation, lighting, music, and drugs. The experiences of the protagonist demonstrate the various ways of constituting identities that refuse stability, that remain fluid, and that resist definition. As Susan Rubin Suleiman signals, women must surpass the notion of validation of historically suppressed values and instead, elaborating upon Derrida's idea of "incalculable choreographies" (Derrida 76), opt for a "dizzying accumulation of narratives" (Suleiman 24) to capture the fluidity inherent in postmodern female subjectivity. This tendency on the part of Vania becomes increasingly pronounced after the realization of the existence of a stalker. Instead of waging war on feminine sexuality and objectification, she strategically uses her body to challenge the fixed, stable notions of gender. According to Malbon, the atmosphere of a club is a space:

> Of identification, with its rituals and customs, its intensive sociality, its overwhelmingly sensuous and emotional ethos, its re-citing and re-fusing of musical histories, boundaries and cultures and its seeming dislocation from the binds of a life which appears increasingly uncertain, the club situation offers clubbers opportunities to inscribe their own creativities upon a shared space, to create a space of their own making of which they are also the consumers. (279)

In the context of Vania, there is more of the self in this new vocabulary of femininity that translates to more self-esteem, and more autonomy; her self becomes unbound and released from the supposedly natural, organic notion of Woman. There is also a redefinition of the female self that is endlessly constructed and reconstructed. No longer lavishing her attention on a male figure, the protagonist, Vania, is free to lavish attention on herself and is aided in doing so by the world of consumer goods. I view her actions as consistent with the theorist of sexual difference Rosi Braidotti's desire to create positive categories for becoming-woman.

The nocturnal world Bustelo depicts in her novel can be said to encourage a particular subjectivity through a medley of accoutrements that operate molding and texturizing one's subjecthood. In his essay "Techniques of the Body," Marcel Mauss elaborates upon the learning the body undergoes as it acquires certain techniques specific to the culture in which it is inscribed; he delineates the mode in which the reproduction of the spatial realm is manifest through the corporeal, arguing for the mimetic nature of the transmission of techniques from one body to another. He contends: "The individual borrows the series of movements of which he is composed from the action executed in front of him, or with him, by others" (459). The sort of apprenticeship he names can be exemplified in Vania's experience of movement within the club; in time, her body meshes with the location so that the very accoutrements become extensions of her body, blurring the frontier between flesh and material good (Fuat Firat 96). This notion debunks the Cartesian theory of a division among objects and subjects into distinct units; this re-signification highlights a new relationship, as well as clouds the distinction, between space and self. Foucault, likewise, elaborates upon a similar theory of corporeal apprenticeship in which he discusses the positive power endowed in a body in the contemporary setting. That is to say, whereby power in former regimes functioned via the infliction of power upon the corporeal, denying the body, and in some cases, taking life, his notion of body-power focuses on molding the material in accord with society, sans denial. While not believing in the existence of a stable human nature, Foucault postulated that via power, one may shape the body and its dispositions in the desired manner. For Foucault the body is not a self-contained system, rather: "The body is broken down by a great many distinct regimes; it is broken down by the rhythms of work, rest and holidays; it is poisoned by food or values, through eating habits or moral laws; it constructs resistances" (*Power/Knowledge: Selected Interviews and Other Writings* 153). In this context, "the body is . . . directly involved in the political field; power relations have an immediate hold upon it; they invest it, mark it, train it, torture it, force it to carry out tasks, to perform ceremonies, to emit signs . . . " (*Discipline and Punishment: The Birth of the Prison* 25). Furthermore, he maintains that the mastery we enjoy over our own bodies and the awareness, the self-consciousness, which reflexively circuits us back to them are each effects of the investment on our bodies by power:

> Mastery and awareness of one's own body can be acquired only through the effect of an investment of power in the body; gymnastics, exercises, muscle building, glorification of the body beautiful. All of this belongs to the pathway leading to the desire of one's own body, by way of the insistent, persistent, meticulous work of power on the bodies of children or soldiers, the healthy bodies. But once power produces this effect, there inevitably emerge corresponding claims and affirmations, those of one's own body against power, of health against the economic system, of pleasure against the moral norms of sexuality, marriage, decency. Suddenly what had made power strong becomes used to attack it. Power, after investing itself in the body, finds itself exposed to counter-attack by the same body. (*Power/Knowledge* 56)

Within this underground world of clubbing the feminine self is no longer a passive neatly bounded entity, rather it is the primary target to be worked, relished, chemically enhanced and taken higher, and in Foucauldian terms, 'produced.' Participation and enjoyment are experienced in terms of connections between the self and others and between the self and the machine or technology. Describing the scene of one of her frequented venues, Vania observes:

> Pachá estaba en plena apoteosis. Era uno de esos domingos en que la concurrencia había decidido curarse la resaca en la calle. Estaba todo dios. Modernos y auténticos conviviendo en fraternidad. Me aposenté con Tono, que me invitó a una serie de rayas más. Ben estaba también, con el Manel famoso, dando conversación a diestro y siniestro, como si Pachá fuera el salón de su casa. A mí lo que más me apetecía era moverme. Salí a la pista y me olvidé del mundo, entrando en ese estado de letargo eléctrico que es la danza. Imitar chiclosamente el ritmo de una canción es dejar que el alma, savia sabia, nos recorra por dentro, de arriba abajo, hasta la punta de los dedos. (75–76)

Located within the territory of the nocturnal, Vania undergoes a conversion to the malleable and the sociable through the almost addictive pleasure of dance by which she enters into a different relationship with her own body, one which is more tactile and more sensuous (Pini). Through her testimony, it becomes patent the connection among her self, drugs, and music. Along the lines of a sybaritic encounter, the experiences within this location can be read: "as a performance, where the lights (or darkness), the sounds, the possible use of drugs, the practices (and rituals) of dancing and the proximity of the 'audience' all add to its intensity" (Malbon 271). In this context, as she confesses, her experience within this realm is intimately dependent upon aural stimulation; the music works upon the space of Pachá and her body intertwining the two via emotional infusion and re-creating the self and ambience for her consumption. She affirms:

> La música era muy instrumentada, envolvente como un túnel musgoso. «Vamos hacia el misterio. Déjate llevar. No hay mejor lugar. Lo sé» Hay canciones que se oyen una vez y se recuerdan siempre. A mí me ocurrió con aquella. Me parecía una especie de mensaje de los cielos, codificado y sólo entendible para mí. El hilo invisible de melodía, letra y voz me producía ese cosquilleo eléctrico en la nuca que me paralizaba de puro placer. (72)

This example demonstrates the transformation that transpires by way of the conjugation of elements. Placing at the forefront female sexuality, the imagery utilized by the protagonist "túnel musgoso" to describe how the music affects her self-formation can be interpreted as a vaginal womb, from which Vania experiences not so much transcendental rebirth but a regeneration of the multiplicity of her subject. The music, the heart and motor of the club, articulates a language that engenders a spiral sensation of libidinal pleasure that continues ascending, opening up a fresh space for the exploration of new forms of feminine identity and pleasure. In other instances, Vania reveals the rush she receives from the musical vibes; this exciting, driving force channels her soul, body, and mind into new directions. Interestingly, though, the majority of music that she consumes—be it in the club or elsewhere—is imported North American and British hits such as "Crazy River" (133), "Change My Mind" (134), "Cigarette of a Single Man" (135), and "Little Red Corvette" (32). Likewise, some of her favorite artists are also imported chart toppers: the Mamas and the Papas, Prince, Teddy Pendergrass, Steve Miller, and the Rolling Stones; this selection unveils not only the proliferation of globalization of cultures within Spain, but also how individual identity is to a much less extent nationally grounded, rather nurtured through a fluid navigation among cultures. Bustelo agrees noting: "La música pop nació en Inglaterra . . . y en España hemos tenido una enorme influencia del pop inglés. En los años ochenta uno no era 'moderno' si no había ido a Londres" (Personal Interview 2004). Through consuming global products, Vania also consumes experiences. With respect to her affinity for music, she admits:

> Teniendo un buen punto, poner música era un placer. Cada canción me llevaba a otra, guiada unas veces por la melodía, otras por la letra, otras por los recuerdos, otras por la intrepidez o la curiosidad, como los diyeis profesionales. Al dejarme llevar, había un momento en que lograba una conexión tan sublime entre un tema y otro, que era como estar creando una obra propia, arte sobre arte. (134)

As evidenced by her words, there exists a special relationship among music and its perceiver. The music, much like an artist, works upon the body and retains the ability to transform and re-create subjectivities. Likewise, her confession highlights another capability of the sonic architecture: "the total nature of the sound present in some club experiences can effect the obliteration of the aural *outside* of the music. This notion of 'losing it' or 'losing yourself' appears to be at the heart of many clubbing experiences" (Malbon 274). Malbon, in his article, highlights that the music affords subjects the ability to move beyond the laborious burdens of daily existence, and delve into a situation of "inward emigration" (Goffman 69). This is patent in

Vania's confession regarding the grip music possesses on her. "Yo pongo una canción de Guy Beart y no sé bien qué me pasa, pero no estoy con todos mi átomos en Madrid, en la calle del Pez. Dejo de ser un pastiche compacto y me diluyo en no sé qué lugares remotos del espacio" (134). Freed from a lifeless imitation or pastiche, which according to Jameson transpires from radical fragmentation that manifests in "nothing but stylistic diversity and heterogeneity" (Bertens 114), the music conjoins with Vania's subject to produce new narratives that are not merely recycled affiliations. In this vein, one can construct a new identity, albeit temporary, crossing boundaries and opening up new possibilities for experiencing liberation.[9]

In the context of clubbing, dancing—a highly visible reaction to sonic stimulation—qualifies as the most recognizable bodily practices. Whereas traditionally the act of dancing has been utilized to showcase the female body for the delectation of the male, Vania uses it to signify fun, self-indulgence, and non-conformity. "Bailar es volverse puro cuerpo, cada nota un hilo de la marioneta en que nos convierte la música" (76). Likewise, her dancing appears to validate her pure physical abandon in the company of others without requiring the narrative of sex or romance. Describing an evening at Archy, a venue where her friend Leo is a DJ, she states:

> La pista estaba a tope. Estaba pinchando Leo, y me acerqué a pedirle el tema ese que dice «¿Cómo puedes bailar cuando nuestras camas están ardiendo?» Venía muy a cuento, o eso pensaba yo. Nos desmadramos bastante. Cuando yo cogía el ritmo de la música, me daba la sensación de ir al compás de la mismísima Tierra Madre. Me dejaba llevar de tal manera que perdía la noción de todo. (62–63)

Evanescing and fleeting, her body moves with the beats and her dancing can be read as an embodied verbalization that she will not be constrained by tensions of daily existence. Grooving to the alternative beat of "Midnight Oil," Vania's body joins the sonic anti-establishment protest. The song bears a strong message; it is a plight for the return of land to the marginalized: the aboriginal people of Australia. In the same way, Vania's dancing may be read as a testimony of re-possession. The rhythmic succession of steps endows Vania with active agency, and the freedom experienced signifies power, energy and vitality, rather than passivity. Among the crowd, the protagonist partakes collectively in the ecstatic fluid celebration yet can be read individually, as Vania brings her own personal history and experience, and therefore incarnates her own "figuration"—in Braidotti's terms—of the nomadic subject.

Vania's experiences—both in and out of the nightclub venue—are enhanced by way of the consumption of recreational drugs, employed to intensify the emotive texture of her experience. Collin asserts that the use of chemical enhancements serves to heighten a feeling of euphoria, bolster self-assurance, delectate and, on a prosaic level, buttress energy. By way of its relentless dynamism and perpetual self-invention, the drug experience is intensely personal as it conjugates sounds, chemicals, the pleasure of dancing and the intoxication of release on the body and brain (Collin). This culture of consumption provides its consumers with options as opposed to rigid rules. Fundamentally, the pharmacological enhancements flow through the consumers' cortex and tinker with body chemistry, constructing a reciprocal corroboration between the sonic architecture and the chemically enhanced brain. Devoid of dogma, this scene is subject to individual interpretation; that is, it offers a forum to which people can bring narratives about sex, class, or whatever they desire. In an analogous manner, chemical enhancements play with one's state of mind vis-à-vis breaking with the establishment, going off into the uncharted and devising a plan as one proceeds. Not only is an emotional break made with known reality but also a physical one. In light of Vania, an array of chemical accompaniments flows through and acts upon her subject such as "alcohol," "coca," "porros," "éxtasis," and from time to time, an "espidbol." It is significant to note how these substances act upon and produce subjectivity. For instance, one evening Vania was offered "un tiro" (71) from her DJ friend Leo; after graciously accepting his offer she notes: "Después de la raya, todo era nítido. A los objetos se les afilaban las aristas, como en un gigantesco cuadro de Antonio López. Lo real se volvía casi hiriente" (71). Noteworthy again, the comparison between her experiences and perception and the visual arena: a chemical high akin to a work of Antonio López, best known for collaging disparate realist vignettes in disjointed compositions. In consuming, the cocaine erases the fixed bodily borders and un-hinges Vania's self to the point that she maintain a dual identification: one constrained by norms and another liberated through subversion. Hence, the use of drugs attests to a special time when traditional conventions are deferred, opening up a zone for an idealized, apex of utopic fancy. With respect to the prolific use of drugs within the space of the club, Malbon affirms:

> In clubbing they find a unique blend of pleasures (musical, tactile, sensual, emotional, sexual, chemical, bodily), a potential for illicit activities, the stimulation experienced through proximity to difference (and in particular of being so close to what in other contexts they would regard as 'strangers' and thus potentially a 'danger') and an escape route (albeit an ephemeral one) from the

rigours and stresses of an ever quicker society which offers no guarantees and provides few opportunities for the release of deep seated emotions and desires in close proximity to others. (280)

The consumption of drugs heightens transitorily the sociality within the space of identification. Partaking in the chemical celebration with friends, Vania identifies her subject with those contexts and forms of sociality within them. For example, after meeting up one evening with her friend Mota, "una asesora de imagen de una agencia de modelos" (108), she was invited to a series of lines which was carefully balanced with alcohol: "Pedimos una copa para bajar la raya, luego nos metimos una raya para subir la copa, y otro copazo para equilibrar el peligroso tentetieso coca-copa" (121). These rituals not only provide sheer escapism, but also a resistance found through losing your self, to contrarily find your self. Chambers argues that within the space of the club the dynamics of power are manipulated and re-appropriated; reality is exploited and consequently "produces an unexpected, sometimes magical, space. . . . It is dwelling in this mutable space, inhabiting its languages, cultivating and building on them and thereby transforming them into particular places, that engenders our very sense of existence and discloses its possibilities" (16). To partake in these codes—dancing, pharmaceutical enhancements, sonic narratives—Vania journeys across experiences and erases the notion of finite limits. She manifests the nomadic figuration via the generation of alternative values and subsequently, an alternative self, as she encounters the notion of home—a physical, emotional and psychical space—through her direct participation in cultures of consumption, contingencies for the appropriation of the female subject.

Now You See Me, Now You Don't!
Re-appropriation of the Gaze

As indicated in the title, the motif of the eye and its gaze proliferates throughout the novel *Veo, veo*. The term gaze is complex. To begin with, it refers to the act of looking or staring with desire; however, through the optic of psychoanalysis, it characterizes not only the act but also the viewing relationship within specific social circumstances. Both the symbolic and literal attention to the ocular function and the ubiquity of the gaze underlines the complexity and instability of seeing. Within this context, the protagonist critiques identity-based politics as the method for achieving female emancipation. She exposes and de-rationalizes the social power systems that construct norms regarding the organic gender identities of men and women as well as the logic of heterosexuality. As Butler suggests, through subversion of identity, the constructs of the continuity among sex, gender, and desire will destroy its normative status and allow "cultural configurations of sex and gender to proliferate" (Butler 190) and become knowable rather than deviant. Due to the fact that Vania parodies traditional female stereotypes and adopts at will identities that contradict the notion of a unified female subject, she exposes Butler's concept of the potential for a 'variable construction of identity' beyond the conventional binary oppositions. Furthermore, she elucidates the notion that women are not restricted to one fixed identity, but rather there exists a range of possibilities. Indeed, Vania has demonstrated fluidity and ambiguity in the negotiation of her identity—notably in chapter 43 entitled "Fiambre y Niu Look." This chapter opens with an inventory of the detective's legwork. Upon relaying a major discovery—not only did one of her stalkers, "Bigotes," mysteriously die in a hotel room the night before, but also the detective's side-kick was able to slyly remove a bag of video tapes from that room after his death—the protagonist delves deeper into her contemplation of the gaze. This breakthrough also determines their next course of action, "Seguir con la misma técnica, usarla a usted como anzuelo a ver qué peces pican" (117) as neither the detective nor the protagonist desired to speak with the police regarding the issue. The protagonist greets this proposal with both relief and slight excitement, as it channels her into the consumption realm. She reveals: "Decidí no pensar en peligros pistoleros y concentrarme en el atavío para la ocasión. De la ropa nueva, elegí el vestido rojo, el más cantoso, para ponerme. Si se va de anzuelo por la vida, se va de anzuelo por la vida" (117). As the testimony exposes, her paranoia is displaced by the opportunity to freely create her self vis-à-vis the material world. It can be said that through her consumption choices, the emotive red dress, she manufactures a very particular commodity, the femme fatale, and recognizes the implications of this choice—that she is bait. To complete the package, she carefully chooses her perfume Chanel Cristalle: "Un buen perfume es un buen embozo. Además, según cuál se elija, las noches funcionan de una manera o de otra. Y Cristalle, como todos los perfumes Chanel, es un chiticalla temerario" (117). Indeed, Vania carefully crafts her subject-formation choosing not only high-end products, but also those that architect an intense, sexually charged image, yet not a victim. In overplaying her feminine identity, the protagonist places at the forefront a masquerade, which through its expression of excessive femininity goes against the grain of traditional conventions. Judith Butler postulates that if the gender sequences of man and woman are fictive constructs—that is, "Socially instituted and maintained norms of intelligibility" (23)—"gender as substance, the viability of man and woman as nouns, is called into question by the dissonant play of attributes that fail to conform to sequential or causal models of intelligibility" (32). In this vein, gender ceases to function as a noun; it is performative. "Gender is always a doing, though not a doing by a subject who might be said to preexist the deed. . . . There is no gender identity behind the expressions of gender; that identity is performatively constituted by the very expressions that are said to be its results"[10] (33). The masquerade is, then, a type of expression that threatens the symbolic order: "watching a woman demonstrate the representation of a woman's body" (Bovenschen 129). Corresponding with the representation of the femme fatale, this species of masquerade is deemed by the masculine economy as contrary to virtue. Montrelay elaborates: "It is this evil which scandalizes whenever woman plays out her sex in order to evade the word and the law. Each time she subverts a law or a word which relies on the predominantly masculine structure of the look" (93). Thus, the masquerade problematizes the symbolic order of the gaze via re-appropriating Woman and endowing the sign with multiple narratives.

After actively composing her self vis-à-vis a myriad of material goods in order to perform as "bait," Vania decided that she wanted to try something different: "La verdad es que no me apetecía nada triscarme los bares sola en plan pidiendo guerra. De repente se me ocurrió una idea" (117). She proposed that they go together, instead of her going alone and him observing from a distance. The only way he would accept this plan was under the condition of disguising their identity, so as to not jeopardize the stake-out. Peláez disguises himself with "una barba falsa y unas gafas" (118), meanwhile Vania decides that she prefers a disguise that would allow her to know "cómo se porta un tío si no sabe que yo estoy delante" (118). The process of converting to "otra" (118) also requires the assemblage of carefully chosen material goods. This conversion entails:

> Una peluca castaña con rizos y me la puse encima de mi espesa melena negra. Me quité el vestido y lo sustituí por un traje de chaqueta de mi abuela con unos zapatos bajos. Me pinté mucho y mal, coronándolo todo con unas gafas alargadas de cristales ahumados liláceos. (118)

The results of this performance were quite dramatic. Through her fabrication of a distinct identity Vania highlights the instability of supposedly organic yet contrived notions of gender. As Butler argues, the imitation of gender exposes "the imitative structure of gender itself—as well as its contingency" (175). Moreover, the manner in which Vania parodies gender is in itself a parody of that which is natural and original. As a result of gender performativity, there is "subversive laughter" (186) "in the realization that all along the original was derived" (176). The displacement of identities on Vania's behalf highlights a "fluidity of identities that is open to resignification and recontextualisation" (176).

It is interesting to note that depending upon the image she actively constructs, Vania's relationship with the bodies and objects-in-use differs. For instance, in consuming the necessary accoutrements to perform the identity of the older, provincial woman, Vania noticed that not only was she not an object of the gaze, but rather she appeared invisible to people that identified with her other packaged identity. She comments to herself:

> Lo divertido era que Leo no sólo no miraba hacia nosotros, sino que miraba a través de nosotros cuando quería concentrarse en algún famoso fundamental, como la actriz Sisi Silicon, que estaba con un grupo de gente de la onda abanico-pendiente-morro-tacón. El luk que Fedor Lamodorra exportaba bien. (119)[11]

In light of her impersonation, she highlights the commodification of the female image, as well as the consequence of a less marketable look: invisibility. Not only did she receive this treatment from her acquaintances, but the entire staff of the establishment, Archy. A central element to Vania's subjectivity, though, is the freedom she appropriates to construct variable and fluid identity constructions. After disguising as a stranger to ascertain how she would be treated, the protagonist decides to return to the same establishment after having replaced her disguise with her initial outfit, the 'cantoso' red dress. Upon her return to the venue, the dynamics of the sociality of the bar were distinct. She comments:

> Esta vez los de la puerta estuvieron suaves como un guante y en el restaurante me hicieron toda clase de agasajos. Una vez sentada en la mesa, fumando a lo Sara Montiel en la chaise lonje, me percaté de que el brasileño parecía mucho más animado que antes. Se había convertido de repente en el gracioso de su mesa, soltando lindezas a todas las nenas, que respondían como teclas de piano. Cosa curiosa, con lo desanimado que se le veía hace media horita. (120)

With cigarette in hand, exuding eroticism and intrigue, Vania assumes a posture reminiscent of Sara Montiel, a Spanish film icon and Hollywood celebrity who embodied the aesthetic of glamour.[12] The overt display of sexuality and the desire for control in women are typically labeled as unchaste and manipulative by hegemonic narratives. Yet the actions of Vania deliver these conventional notions back at men by over-emphasizing female sexuality.

In contrast to being a passive sex object, she communicates her authority via manipulating the femme fatale image as well as mocking femininity as a quasi-masquerade. That is, the image she creates and presents wields much power evidenced by the reactions of the male patrons who behave in a pathetic, silly and desperate mode. Here, Bustelo's writing can be seen to mock male power and identity by reducing gender and sex to the level of fashion and style or camp, as she exposes gender as something one puts on and takes off at will.

Through her campy attire, Vania manipulates gender codes, and in the process, unveils the fallacies of these supposedly organic structures. According to Judith Butler, camp is located at the nucleus of a radical agenda for metamorphosing consciousness. Due to its ability to satire received ideas by inverting notions and by emphasizing the "unnaturalness" of what the patriarchy believes to be "organic," camp has a central part to play in sexual politics. By disrupting notions of the naturalness of gender, camp liberates one to perform according to desire. In contrast to theories of Butler, Andrew Ross believes that camp reconciles people to their powerlessness. Ross contends that camp compensates for failure and a sort of nostalgia for the past. As a result, Ross maintains that camp is problematic in mass culture because it attempts to prohibit society from becoming aware of its oppression. Furthermore, he contends that camp is part of the controlling mechanism of late capitalism. To an extent, participants of camp are reconciled to their oppression, yet that does mean that they believe it to be "natural." This investigation places importance on Butler's argument as Ross's theories render the subject as victim, unable to escape the capitalist cycle. Nevertheless, as Butler argues, camp has the power to open up dimension after dimension of ambiguity, and furthermore, lend agency to marginalized subject through the re-appropriation of hegemonic codes and norms. Camp, then, provides another space or territory within which a subject may not only access power, but also toy with conventions via the re-appropriation and transmission of code.

In a variety of modes, the protagonist Vania re-appropriates mechanisms which have served to control women and their bodies. Aware of her precarious stalker situation, Vania arrives at the realization that nothing is as it seems and that those surrounding her possess ulterior motives.

> Valco quería usarme como carnaza de reportaje barato, Ortuño se había esnobizado por las buenas, Mota era todo lo contrario de una amiga caballerosa, Franny jugaba a la frivolona etérea porque creía que eso molaba, mi abuela me consideraba una niña a la que hay que proteger incluso de su propia herencia. Y Ben quería llevarme al huerto después de haberme torturado lentamente. (110)

In a stupor, these doubts provoke the protagonist to question herself and her surroundings. Fleshing through experiences entailing the stalker and other dubious characters in her world, Vania is propelled to challenge the dominant hierarchy that has been attempting to encroach upon her private domain. "Me levanté y fui al cuarto de baño. Arranqué la sábana que había clavado delante del espejo. Miré hacia el interior del mercurio reluciente, como si fuera cuestión de conseguir ver algo en el azogue del crystal. Lerda. Que tú no puedes ver nada. Los que te ven son ellos" (111). When this attempt at confrontation proves futile, Vania emerges as the ultimate sexual voyeur and prepares to offer the observing eyes exactly what they want: a soft-porn performance, only with a twist. "Pues les voy a enseñar cosas . . . Si quieren ver tanto, pues que miren. No tengo nada de que avergonzarme" (111). And with this declaration, she asserts control over her body, self, and domain. That is, she looks, and then asks that she be looked at. The gaze is a concept imbricated in desire and control. Numerous theories, stemming from film studies and art history, have explored the complicated and slippery power relations that are part and parcel of the act of looking and that of being looked at. With respect to traditional psychoanalytic theory, Freud pioneered the study of the gaze, later updated by Lacan who placed the look at the forefront of his approach to how the individual handles desire (mirror phase). In the 1970s, film theory expounded upon the psychoanalytic theories of Freud and Lacan and posited that in film, the gaze of the spectator upon an object was an implicitly male one, structured by the patriarchal unconscious, which positioned women as objects in cinema. Derived from Laura Mulvey's seminal article "Visual Pleasure and Narrative Cinema," Jonathan Schroeder elaborates "Film has been called an instrument of the male gaze, producing representations of women, the good life, and sexual fantasy from a male point of view" (208). Studies of spectatorship have focused on the mode in which subjectivities are constructed via subject positions. Mulvey, in her article, notes how Freud referred to scopophilia—the pleasure involved in looking at other people's bodies as sexual objects, and further argues that various techniques of cinema facilitate the voyeuristic process of objectification of female characters, declaring that within the patriarchal paradigm "pleasure in looking has been split between active/male and passive/female" (27). That is, traditionally men are portrayed as controlling, active subjects and consequently treat women as inert, desirous goods available for male consumption. Nevertheless, while women may be relegated to the position of sex object, it is never for their pleasure rather for the "controlling male gaze" (33), which Mulvey distinguishes in two modes: voyeuristic and fetishistic.[13] Per Mulvey, the camera functions as a tool of voyeurism and sadism while disempowering those before its gaze. It is important to note that contemporary theories of the gaze have made more complex the original model delivered by the Lacan and Freud. Nevertheless, Mulvey's article generated considerable controversy amongst film theorists. Many objected to the essentialist discourse of the alignment of passivity with femininity and activity with masculinity. Furthermore, there was criticism of her failure to account for the female spectator. A fundamental protest underlying many critical responses has been that Mulvey's argument is essentialist: spectator and male are treated as homogenous. According to Mulvey, one type of spectator exists (male) and one norm for sexuality (heterosexual). In response to Mulvey's articles, Silverman (1980) contends that the gaze may be appropriated by male and female subjects. The male is not always the controlling subject nor is the female always the passive object. Indeed, Mulvey's theory centers on a unitary spectator position while she overlooks other potential readings or possibilities.

Working against the grain, the protagonist, however, is involved in what Teresa de Lauretis deems a double-identification with both the passive and active subjects. Within the location of her bathroom, Vania re-creates the ambience of a soft-porn film; she turns on soul music, fills the bathtub with hot water, and then begins to undress "de la manera más provocativa posible" (111). These actions—through the disruption of the male gaze—establish a rejection of the self-monitoring of female sexuality, whereby "Men act and women appear" (Berger 47). Instead, Vania subjects the on-looking male gaze to the scrutiny of her gaze, confronting the camera eye directly. As Skeggs affirms: "looking at men is treated as something to be blatant and positive about" (69) as opposed to the traditional dynamics in which "women often avert their eyes in modesty and submission to the gaze of the male audience" (Van Zoonen 101). Conscious of her gender performance, Vania experiences libidinal pleasure: "un placer especial al pensar que estaba desnuda y que alguien me estaba mirando sin tomar cartas en el asunto" (111). This pleasure becomes heightened "me hacía disfrutar aún más" (112) by the explicit knowledge that she is not alone. Her radicalism lies in the fact that she consistently interrogates cultural premises of femininity and masculinity and continues to construct for herself her own version of femininity, highlighting its dynamic nature. Furthermore, according to Lury, the "projection of the gaze offers women a passionate return on their investment that supercedes the pleasure they receive as a potential object of the male gaze" (148). Hence, she utilizes the currency of pornography to challenge the idea of women as passive sex objects. Here it can be read that Vania recognizes that she is a sex symbol, and appropriates this position to her advantage.

Not only does Vania challenge the patriarchal discourse vis-à-vis her re-creation of soft-porn in her bathroom, she parodies the same paradigm manifest in her concern regarding the validity of her home-made movie. Reflecting on her role as the star performer Vania relates:

> Pero ya metida en mi papel de protagonista de mi película, procuraba no mirar a la cámara nunca. No hay cosa que más jorobe un plano. Esta escena tenía que salir bien a la primera. Cogí el peta de encima del borde del lavabo y, mierda, me había dejado el mechero fuera. Corten, que ahora mismo vuelvo. (112)

The ambiguity of the previous scene emphasizes the de-centering of the masculine economy by way of the gratuitous use of elements such as parody and play. The customary kinship of power between the object and the voyeuristic male gaze is destabilized by the portrayal of the (unseen) male on-lookers as leering and pathetic; she makes it clear that she is being watched and breaches the process of fetishization by facetiously playing to the eye of the camera. At the same time the portrayal of Vania as a porn star is deconstructed at the end of the bath through invoking a parody of the popular refrain: "Si no puedes contra ellos, únete a ellos" (112). Moreover, in this scene, Vania confronts a pernicious stereotype and intends to channel it into a distinct realm: a space where the female need not be the object of the patriarchal gaze, where its energy impulses play and non-sexual pleasure.[14] Upon finishing her bath and concomitantly her rendition of soft-porn, she ironically remarks: "Salí de mi fragante concha, una Venus terrena y dopada. Me puse un camisón solo por sentir el tacto de la seda en la piel" (112). Reenacting Botticelli's *Birth of Venus*, Vania stages her own interpretation of the Renaissance painting depicting a beautiful, modest woman being birthed from a conch shell; while infused with emotion, she toys with the concept of divine love and submitting to hierarchies through her drug-induced rendition. Favoring irony and ambiguity, Vania is an artistic alchemist who is able to blend creativity and controversy in equal measure so as to entertain herself and out of a desire to toy with the masculine paradigm.

In chapter 59, "La pipa," the enigma surrounding the mysterious stalkers who observe and follow Vania begins to dissipate. Following a series of deaths—one of her stalkers and Ben Ganza, a former love interest of the protagonist who orchestrated the game—the pieces of the puzzle began to fall into place.[15] Vania comes to recognize that the existence of the stalker was real yet imaginary; that is, it was contrived by her former love interest who had "una necesidad absoluta de saber en todo momento lo que estaba haciendo aquella mujer" (153). In conjunction with the psychiatrist, dubbed

Mickey Rourke, and detective Peláez, the bitter Ganza formulated a plan to "acabar con ese libre albedrío que ella tanto buscaba, en otras palabras, convertirse en amo y señor de cada uno de sus movimientos, jugar a ser una forma terrena de ese Dios omnipresente que posiblemente exista para todo el resto de los seres humanos" (153). Espousing a new identity, the sexy Brazilian accustomed to having all women who "caían rendidas a sus pies" (155) did not calculate correctly the manner in which his dubious scheme would affect Vania's subjectivity; indeed Ben represented irresistible eye candy for women, that is "todas las mujeres, menos una" (155). Armed with his grandiose, inferiority driven contrivance, not only was he was unable to get the girl, but his overabundance of efforts toward his primary goal—possession of Vania—was thwarted: Vania received much pleasure from re-appropriating the gaze, parading her self, and delving into the consumer realm. Clearly, male spectatorship is not without limitations, nor consequences. A key scene in this chapter indicating the botched plan was her playful peep-show performance. Armed with a pistol,[16] Vania enters into the bathroom and decides to give the ever-present eye a taste of his own medicine, and at the same time, finalize the boyish shenanigans: "El final. El final lo iban a ver ahora mismo, hombre. Me metí la pistola en el bolsillo de la bata y fui al cuarto de baño. Me iba a volar la tapa de los sesos delante de ellos. Ese si que iba a ser un buen video, hombre. Suicidio en directo, tíos" (160). Before completing her staged suicide, Vania sets the ambience (bathroom) for her performance, "un numerito pour monsieur Le Voyeur" (160), by selecting appropriate music: *The End* by the Doors. Her choice of music is not innocent; with its entrancing sound, chilling imagery, and Oedipal fury, the melody revolves around the theme of journey, both physical and emotional. Opening with revelations of incumbent instability and ending with death, the song expresses a profound desire and search for freedom, symbolically realized at the close. The consumption of this particular song, embedded with the Oedipal pretext, is subversive as it serves as a metaphor of arriving at the truth and breaking free of the structure of ideas enforced and instilled by the dominant paradigm. Even more dissonant, though, is her manipulation of the codes. After assembling the accoutrements, Vania exchanges her bathrobe for a towel and begins her seduction "me lo monté de peep-show, jugueteando con una toalla. Ahora lo ves, ahora no lo ves. Cómo lo ves" (160). She continued her montage, parading like a Playboy Bunny Girl and then while taking out her pistol, changes her mind on the intended recipient of the bullet. "Giré de golpe, poniéndome cara al espejo, y sujetando la pistola con las dos manos, disparé hacia el mercurio, que clin-clin-clin se hizo añicos dejando el descubierto el espacio negro que había al otro lado" (160). Peering through the hole in the wall, the body that lay on the floor belonged to her detective, Peláez. Without panic or much emotion, Vania returned to her side of the two-way mirror and ironically felt relieved and also grateful that she could consume: "Tenía caballo" (160) and "la botella de Dewar's" (160). This example highlights the complexity of spectatorship. The notion of Peeping Tom literalizes the idea that the camera function as a weapon of male gaze. Traditionally, the spectator was perceived to wield more power than the object of the gaze, the landscape of images in Bustelo's novel demonstrates that this is not always the case. Like a contemporary reincarnation of the Lady Godiva myth, Vania utilizes her charm and sex appeal to influence the behavior of others, as well as work to her advantage; like the legendary Peeping Tom, Peláez is blinded, Ganza, the modern reincarnation of Leofric, gets burned and she regenerates and carries on.[17]

Patriarchal society considers there to be one sex—the masculine—that remains at the forefront. The Other as Irigaray postulates is the feminine, positioned as the opposite of men: "They've left us only lacks, deficiencies, to designate ourselves. They've left us their negative(s)" (*The Sex Which is Not One* 207). Male domination is systemic and consequently, women's worth is their "use-value" for men and they are treated as commodities (Irigaray 31), which is illustrated by the games and strategies of the stalkers. In accord with Irigaray's tenets, Vania escapes gender oppression by way of her subversion of the hierarchical framework. That is, via the invention of her own strategies and language, she expresses and realizes her desires that do not necessarily coincide with the norms dictated by the masculine economy: she holds her own, does not render herself passive, and most importantly, thinks for herself.

Conclusions

"Feminist women have a long history of dancing through a variety of potential lethal mine-fields in their pursuit of socio-symbolic justice,"

—Braidotti, www.let.uu.nl/womens_studies/rosi/cyberfem.htm

With the advent of the age of information, communications technologies have accelerated, cultures have become globalized, and consumption has become an outlet through which citizens, as consumers, may shape and mold identities. As evidenced through the multiplicity of representations of the protagonist, the realm of consumption can potentially offer new areas of authority and expertise, and a new sense of consumer right. One of the consequences of these developments has been a heightened awareness of entitlement outside the sphere of consumption. In light of this, the realm of consumption is understood in two dimensions: as a space in which to negotiate and resist the inert, absent feminine identity, as assigned through sex roles, and furthermore as the ongoing process of the creation of identity that embodies the nomadic subject. In Vania's situation in *Veo, veo*, the cultures of consumption—fashion, music, drugs, and the gaze—provide a basis for becoming-woman as these arising cultures afford a libidinal return on her investment that is experienced as liberating and is seen as positive in feminist terms. Her actions highlight the social construction of gender codes in fashion, as they operate against the conservative view that gender is biologically constructed. Likewise, her overt sexual behavior defies the patriarchal double standard in which women are the objects of sexual desire but only heterosexual men are permitted to express desire. In this vein, she makes the process of sexual objectification of women visible by producing it in an exaggerated and comic form. Vania shamelessly packages and repackages herself, and in the process presents a vision of freedom, a daring to transgress sexist boundaries and a presentation of a complex, invigorating, evolving subject. Her life, peppered with extreme outcomes and mixed results, is not free from reactionary throwbacks and constricting hegemonic conventions, yet through the adoption of complex and contradictory codes, she embodies new types of creativity and unveils spaces for the liberation of female subjectivity.

Notes

1. Gabriela Bustelo has translated a wide range of works by Edgar Allan Poe, Beverly Cleary, Oscar Wilde, and Rudyard Kipling.

2. Similar to *Veo, veo,* the theme of consumption also appears and weighs heavily in *Planeta hembra*. According to the author, the protagonist of *Veo, veo,* Vania, "es un germen de lo que son las protagonistas de *Planeta hembra*" (Interview 2004). This provocative novel takes place at the end of the second millennium, and depicts a world controlled by the X Party, composed solely of women. The X Party only permits lesbian love, controls all aspects of information technology, and intends to erase all evidence of the existence (influences, achievements, and social conventions) of Man. Furthermore, the novel radically highlights the communication difficulties prolific among the sexes, the dangers associated with advancing technologies, as well as the manipulation of information. Curiously, however, this group of women spends enormous amounts of money on their appearance; while they are leaders of the world, they are also ridiculously obsessed with their coiffure and clothing.

3. For further information regarding the mode in which Peninsular authors' writing in the final decade of the second millennium have been informed by the influx of global cultures see the article written by José María Izquierdo: "Narradores es-

pañoles novísimos de los años noventa" http://www.hf.uio.no/kri/spansk/emne/spa1301/textos/sem/ultimanarrativaespizquierdo.pdf.

4. For further information, see the following web site: http://www.uclm.es/area/constitucional/18-97.htm as well as *Sólo se vive una vez* (1991), a foundational book that treats theoretical and historical accents of the movida, written by José Luis Gallero.

5. Film noir is the French term for the "black film" genre that peaked in the forties and fifties. This genre has roots in detective novels produced during the 1920s and 1930s by Dashiell Hammett and Raymond Chandler. In general, the plots of this genre portray a contemporary world that has been corrupted by exterior forces, and consequently lost its moral certainty. Furthermore, the prevailing cynicism of the characters reflected the reality of the atomic bomb, Cold War, totalitarianism, propaganda, and the devious power of the government and press.

6. Resulting from multiple discoveries, the reader and the protagonist arrive at the following knowledge: Vania is an heiress of a considerable sum of money, a fact that she was not privy to due to her grandmother's over-protective nature.

7. Per Lacan, infants begin to pass through this stage around eighteen months, a time when, concurrently, their ego begins to establish. The process is initiated by way of the look, either viewing their reflected image in a mirror or their mother (does not have to necessarily be a mirror image of their own body).

8. Throughout her career, it appears that Madonna's fundamental goal has been to attract viewers' attention vis-à-vis pushing the envelope and surprising people. While admitting that she is not the best dancer nor singer, this star acknowledges that she is not hesitant to go to extremes or make a spectacle.

9. It must be noted that Malbon contends that "losing oneself" in music affords the possibility for individual identities to: "become (temporarily) less significant than the nature of the social situation of which they are a part" (275). Nevertheless, it is my position, especially in the case of female subjectivity, that this location offers the female clubber an opportunity to exercise elements of the self such as sexuality and assertiveness that would be unacceptable outside of this paradigm. The act of "losing oneself" illustrates the unbinding of traditional parallels among dancing, drugs, and women. As such, it opens up a new territory, previously vilified, to explore female subjectivity and pleasure.

10. In this instance Butler is drawing upon theories utilized by Nietzsche that "there is no 'being' behind doing, effecting, becoming; 'the doer' is merely a fiction added to the deed—the deed is everything."

11. The mention of the look that Fedor Lamodorra exports can be read as a take on Pedro Almodóvar. The inclusion of this name is not innocent, but rather it demonstrates the prolific commodification of Spanish culture in the global media market.

12. Among the Hispanic culture, due to her beauty and talent, she was deemed a mythical persona. Terenci Moix states: "Sara Montiel—nuestra Mae West—representa la inspiración de un erotismo tranquilizador, donde la agresividad de la

súperhembra viene suavizada tanto por sus extravagancias externas—vestuario, fraselogía, simpatía, canciones—como por lo absolutamente increíble de los temas en que reina" (http://pagina.de/saritisima).

13. The voyeuristic mode of looking entails a controlling gaze which Mulvey contends bears associations with sadism, "pleasure lies in ascertaining guilt—asserting control and subjecting the guilty person through punishment or forgiveness" (29). The fetishistic gaze, in contrast, deals with "the substitution of a fetish object or turning the represented figure itself into a fetish so that it becomes reassuring rather than dangerous. This builds up the physical beauty of the object, transforming it into something satisfying in itself. The erotic instinct is focused on the look alone" (29).

14. Some feminists confuse enjoyment of sexuality with sexual objectifications. Vania's enjoyment of her sexuality can be seen as providing a healthy correction to those feminists who situate women's abilities to nurture at the forefront of subjectivity.

15. A decade earlier, Ben Ganza, dubbed "el brasileño," and Vania Barcia were passionately in love and quite content, until one day things abruptly changed and the relationship ended. Ganza, however, maintained his unrequited love for the protagonist, observing her and her dalliances from afar—Brazil—planning the day he would return and enter, once again, into her life. Through a carefully contrived plan, Ben dedicated himself to observing and controlling every move of Vania's vis-à-vis the construction of the stalker operation.

16. An element of the contrived plot, the pistol was given to her by Peláez for protection against the supposed stalkers.

17. While many versions of the Godiva legend exist, most historians accord that she was an Anglo-Saxon woman that lived during the period 1040–1080 A.D. and was married to Leofric, Earl of Mercia. A woman inspired by arts and social justice, she had deep hopes to aid the poor townspeople. This became increasingly difficult as her husband, Leofric, began imposing broad taxes on society on goods ranging from food to manure. Realizing the impoverishment already plaguing the villagers, Godiva moved her art interests to the back seat while she patronized important considerations such as water and basic supplies. After much haranguing, Leofric agreed to reduce the taxes upon one condition: Godiva had to offer the villagers an example of artistic and glorious beauty by riding a horse naked one late August afternoon through the market of the town from one end to the other, with the villagers present. Upon her return, she would be granted the tax relief. Expecting his wife to withdraw, Leofric was shocked when she agreed. As the legend goes, she commanded the common folk to turn their heads as she passed; a tailor named Tom disobeyed her command and after peeking at her was miraculously struck blind. The justly punished voyeur was the original "Peeping Tom."

CHAPTER FIVE

Alivio rápido: Traversing the Techno Terrain to the Multinational

Cultural Context

Journalist and author Silvia Grijalba was born in Madrid, and shortly afterward relocated to the southern Spanish city of Torremolinos. From a very tender age, the world of music attracted this author, such that while as a student at secondary school, she collaborated with a fanzine titled *Imágenes alteradas*. While this was a small-scale project with very limited dissemination that she created with a few of her friends in Malaga, her participation in this endeavor is nevertheless noteworthy. There is a double significance: it planted the seed for her future career in journalism and gave her a reason to interact and dialogue with her musical idols. After nurturing her passion for writing via the fanzine, Grijalba traveled to Madrid to begin a degree in journalism at the Universidad Complutense. Aside from the knowledge imparted at the University, her writing has also been influenced by the work of the Canadian writer Douglas Coupland. In 1989, with the advent of the newspaper *El Mundo*, Silvia Grijalba initiated her professional career as a journalist for a literature column. Within six months she was contracted by the same newspaper to collaborate on musical reviews, projects, and interviews ranging from rock-and-roll to punk and techno variations. Since that time, Grijalba has been a regular columnist for *El Mundo* and its supplement *La Luna*, only taking leave of absence to write her first novel, *Alivio rápido* (2002). Aside from her post with the periodical, Grijalba also writes columns for *Glamour*, *Vogue*, *Rolling Stones*, *Marie Claire*, and *MTV Magazine*, while giving seminars on electronic music in Gijón, Alicante, the Canary Islands, and Barcelona. Currently, she is also involved with the writing of a second novel, managing her bar, El Alivio, in the Malasaña zone, and playing/producing electronic music with her group.

Due to her profession—music journalist—Grijalba has traversed the globe to attend and report on musical festivals. From the twenty-fifth anniversary of Woodstock to Glastonbury and a range of national festivals including Espárrago Rock and Festimad, Grijalba has participated in international dialogue and accumulated a wealth of knowledge regarding the constructs and components of the music business, as she was a first-hand spectator and participator in the dynamics. In conjunction with the newspaper, this writer has also secured a number of interviews with global music icons such as David Bowie, Mick Jagger, Stockhausen, and John Cage. Aside from her work with *El Mundo*, Grijalba has published a series of monographs treating the internationally recognized music groups Depeche Mode and Dire Straits. Moreover, within the past decade—illustrating further her affinity for sonic narrative—this writer entered the music circuit as a disk jockey and "theremíndista," the first electronic instrument, under the pseudonym Morgana.[1] It is significant to note that her participation in this fashion—as an orchestrator of music (DJ or instrument player)—Grijalba enters and achieves success in a domain inscribed and reified by hegemonic norms. In an interview regarding her location in this space she affirms: "Pues sí [la mujer dj] tiene que luchar más que un hombre para entrar en la cabina como en casi todo en la vida, excepto para ser azafata, prostituta o ama de casa" (www.el-mundo.es/encuentros/invitados/2002/09/508). Further evidence of her success and transgression of boundaries, Grijalba had the opportunity to disk jockey at major Spanish music festivals: Benicassim, Doctor Music, Festimad, and Espárrago Rock.

Vis-à-vis direct and indirect participation in the international alternative music scene, this writer has gained a perspective on the multiplicity of identities that proliferate the sonic landscape. Likewise, as observer and participator Grijalba possesses profound knowledge on what it means to be a woman living in contemporary Spain as well as the experience of the female subject within the music scene, as she has had the opportunity to cross many 'naturalized' gender barriers. The shifts in international and national locations afforded this writer the opportunity to be immersed in a myriad of cultures around the globe, and subsequently interact in the global economy as well as be transformed by it. As manifest in her journal and novelistic work, Grijalba participates in dialogue with the global community exploring and reporting upon the transformations in the music scene, and detailing various subjectivities encouraged and produced within the respective space. According to this author, the rise of cultures of consumption in Spain is "cada vez mayor" (Personal Interview 2004), and while it is a paradoxical phenomenon, Grijalba maintains that consumption can be read as a recuperation of spaces reflecting new societal needs: "determinados núcleos culturales que sí se están separando un poco de la cultura masiva y se están creando grupos underground" (Personal Interview 2004) of various types. This, in fact, is reflected at the end of the novel; she includes a dictionary of neo-tribes in which she gives name to and describes multiple identities that participate in this location. For instance, some of the terms she unpacks are: *chandalista desdentado*, *laly*, and *noctámbulos acreditados*. The creation of this terminology stemmed from her experiences observing diverse bodies-in-use, as she states: "el cuerpo femenino y el masculino son para la producción de significado" (Personal Interview 2004). In her opinion, that which adorns the body (brand names, hair styles, tattoos, etc.): "explica como es el personaje" (Personal Interview 2004). Due to her experiences in the social realm, she herself can be read as a representation of Donna Haraway's "cyborg," as she is a hybrid product of culture negotiations, traversing the musical landscape, which is in itself a product of technological processes.

The novel *Alivio rápido* emerges as a distinct narrative that traces the path to self-knowledge and self-discovery within masculine-defined economies; concomitantly, it articulates the possibility of individual liberation from existing ideological and social constraints toward a degree of self-determination. While it retains a certain nihilistic texture, *Alivio rápido* is a powerful and ambitious novel that embarks upon the negotiation of identity—both individual and collective—of youth culture in the musical terrain. The depth and power of its investigation into the process of construction of self in conjunction with the other in a capitalist society, and the way in which the individual relates, or fails to relate with the other, endows the novel with both artistic merit and profound social insight. The architecture of the narrative reflects postmodern socialities through its continuous weaving of dialogue, monologue, and streams of consciousness. Likewise, paying homage to her journalistic career, the novel displays an onus for detail, no doubt stemming from her familiarity with current events in the musical arena and mastery of conveying this knowledge in a succinct manner. While it may considered a progressive narrative due to Alba's fluid journey, it is important to not gloss over details that Grijalba injects into the novel such as the increase of violence against women and the rise of "chistes machistas." These elements juxtaposed with the molecular wanderings of Alba serve to highlight the paradox not only of consumption, but also the advancements of the notion of Woman within contemporary Spanish society.

The novel is divided into three parts and each section depicts a distinct sociality. The plot of *Alivio rápido* revolves around a well-known techno music group, Asian Vibes, and its five contingents: Fernando, the star of the band, Alba, his girlfriend and sitar player in the group, Pablo and Manolo, members of the band, and Marcos, the manager of the group. Likewise, in its examination of the techno scene in which Asian Vibes is immersed, the narrative takes into consideration the dynamics of Alba's parents—Sofia and Alberto—and how they relate in this space as well as the subjectivities produced through their negotiation of this musical landscape. As stated, the novel diverges into three time/space divisions: the music festival in Zaragoza, various Spanish penitentiaries, and the location of the multinational, including the international destinations of London and Morocco to which Alba is required to travel. The work can be read as a journey of the nomadic self, which dazzles across boundaries and transforms through multiple experiences to arise at a higher understanding of one's subject. While this revelation may be valid for a number of the characters, this chapter primarily explores the subjectivity of Alba; at the opening of the novel her selfhood can be described as unhealthy and static, yet transforms through multiple experiences and realizations that affect profoundly the conception and construction of her identity.

This chapter analyzes the formation and evolution of the protagonist's identity vis-à-vis her interaction with the material realm. It is significant to note that consumption is understood not as an economic phenomenon but as a "particular means of creating identity, one that is realized in a material reorganization of time and space, as the instrument of self-construction which is itself dependent on high-order modes of channeling available objects into a specific relation to a person or persons" (Friedman 151). Hence the cultural examination of consumption points to the analysis of consumer identity, ways and causes of self-construction and presentation to the other. In agreement, Grijalba affirms: "para el mundo la imagen es muy importante, que uno demuestra al mundo como es por dentro por su imagen . . . es una forma de crear una identidad" (Personal Interview 2004). As the task is to examine cultures of consumption as illustrated in the novel *Alivio rápido*, it is essential to trace any differences in the process of consumption among various players in the novel. In this vein, D. Miller affirms:

> Mass consumption goods often come to stand for the new superordinate point of identity that subsumes and suppresses cultural difference and creates drastic global homogenization . . . there is another source of difference, which might be called posteriori difference, that is more rarely acknowledged or theorized.

> This is the sense of quite unprecedented diversity created by the differential consumption of what had once been thought to be global and homogenizing institutions. (2–3)

While cultural phenomena such as the techno/rave scene can be treated as a globally circulating product of culture, as noted by D. Miller, that does not necessarily endow the commodity with a globalized meaning, rather the consumer via her relationship with the product, forms her own meaning: "people do specific things and they attribute specific meanings, also a practice of a specific sort" (Friedman 204). As such this chapter explores the consumption of specific locations—techno/rave and the foreign multinational—to ascertain the type of subjectivity cultivated within the respective confines as well as the embodied content. Thus, the aim is to analyze the basis of subjectivity within this youth culture, considering the various contingencies that compose it: presentation of the self to the self and others, behavior, and the relation of the self with the surrounding environment.

Traversing the Techno Terrain: Music, Ritual, and Commodification

> Our generation is the best mass movement in history—experimenting with anything in our search for love and peace. Our temple is sound, we fight our battles with music, drums like thunder, cymbals like lightning, banks of electronic equipment like nuclear missiles of sound. (qtd. in Collin 185)

Written by Phil Russel in 1974, this manifesto, utilizing the philosophy of techno as its foundation, intended to reclaim collective and individual freedoms, embodied in the celebratory rites of music and dance, jettisoned by the hegemonic economy.[2] Creators of this sonic architecture maintain that this particular genre of music is analogous to a revolt against the "dictatorship" of rock-n-roll. The sonic rebellion of techno was understood not only as the appropriation of a new kind of music, but also an assumption of a radically distinct life ideology. This style of music, a blend of technological elements, began as a revolution in consciousness. The participants, both creators and listeners, reacted to the power of the multinational music recording business through their musical creativity, one that resists the trend of pop. As such, this music culture—in the eyes of the participants—became a new rite that visibly eclipsed the old.[3] With the imminent decadence of the rock era, the rise of techno portended a new sociality. This sociality resists hegemonic norms by the subversive manifestation of the dynamic relationship among the human and machine. Donskis affirms: "we are living in the period of the death of rock. It became the part of mass culture and of earlier so much despised establishment . . . it became successfully integrated into the system of cultural industry, which it tried to resist and negate so much" (12). Unlike the commodified mainstream rock-n-roll, whose motto revolved around the trilogy of sex, drugs, and music, the roots of techno music served as a platform for introspection into the self and an escape from the rigors of institutionalized constraining norms. In this way, techno was heralded as a "new folk music" (Collin 203), speaking for the "culturally dispossessed" (203) through its gripping, tenuating sonic narratives. Innovative, the confection of this hypnotic, expressive music depended upon electronical means; this technology-based music, according to H. Kumagai, offers many possibilities through the interplay of its various accoutrements: "the key ingredients for techno maestros include a couple direct-drive turntables . . . a sampling synthesizer, a computer" (321). Since its emergence, this culture organized around ritual festivity, orgiastic celebration and Saturnalian explosion, reminiscent of a tribal era. Its most salient feature, the music, subsumes the subject in a harmony of blissful sensations. Sound waves circulate, penetrating the bodies of participants, arousing sensations of rapture, ravishment, being engulfed and overwhelmed.

Techno, an eternally evolving musical style, can be described as progressive and cosmopolitan. That is, as it espouses a counterculture mentality, this manifests through its continual changing, experimental nature. Likewise, this subculture is to a large degree global. United by an aesthetic that prizes rhythm over words (yet not to their absence), techno has branched way beyond its disco, hip-hop and synth-pop roots into the musical traditions of just about every country. Laid over bass or trance-like drums, Indian classical music is now as in vogue as scratching, and vibes from India, Morocco, and Spain all thump together on the same records (Collin). The best examples of this internationalist underground present an exuberant sonic dream of the world as a musical bazaar, overflowing with exotic melodies and multifarious lyrics. This scene presents itself as culture with concerns of a global nature being voiced from within local environments; likewise, its aim is a spiritual experience (Collin). At its best, this music can offer the jaded something genuinely innovative, something that is exotic and also that gives electronic music an emotional depth, generally lacking in club music. Beyond that, Western dilettantes—as evidenced by Sofía, Alba's mother—in search of Eastern wisdom have looked for spiritual solace in the traditional music of far less affluent countries. As the world becomes condensed due to the processes of globalization, it is also expanding as via music, one arrives at an understanding of another culture.

Continuing with an analysis of this location, a techno event is a total concept (Collin). As well as music, there is the décor, the lighting, and the performances: the way it is choreographed and staged. Additionally, this subculture possesses its own language and codes riff with specialized knowledge, tribal identities, idiolects and subcultures (Collin). Grijalba succinctly portrays her knowledge of techno terminology through her addition of the "diccionario de nuevas tribus urbanas"; many of the words she coined herself after observing various groupings of people and their commonalities as well as their differences from other collectivities at diverse music venues. At its foundation, there is an informal philosophy which values experience over words. It is not so much a question of opposing society but rather of demanding new social relationships based on emotive accord. Within the location of techno, events—parties or festivals—represented "shamanic rites which, using the new musical technologies in combination with certain chemicals and long periods of dancing, preferably in settings with spiritual significance" (Collin 203) that provided a forum for reconnection and recombination of energies. The scene, a community composed of a variety of ingredients such as festive-like gatherings, dancing, and drugs, subverts the hegemonic system in oblique manners (Collin). Its radical potential grounds itself in the usage of advanced technologies that serve as a protest in a traditional sense against the dominant economy. As such this scene occupies a position that combines experimentalism with criticism as it contrasts the ceaseless and unquestioning euphoria that has historically plagued the progress of musical technology.

The discourse of techno, as manifest in Asian Vibes, intertwines with that of the Hippie movement, making manifest a number of commonalities. The similarities between these discourses are not just a matter of surface style, but rather signal more profound kinship. The 1960s was an epoch of revolution across the spectrum: politics, art, music, technology, and lifestyles. Experimentation challenged convention. In the late 1960s and the early 1970s, the East witnessed an influx of "tourists" from First World nations. In general, these "tourists" were not yearning for a luxury experience, but rather were pilgrims in search of an "authentic" Eastern experience, as they admired the purportedly superior spirituality of the East. The inflow of Western foreigners attracted to the spiritual life of the East led to the exoticization of the other (and all that constitutes that space), which Edward Said attributes to the creation of unequal power dynamics between the East and the West. In *Orientalism*, Said stresses that the East (Orient) does not merely exist as a geographical territory inhabited by a population of particular religion or cultures (Said 322). The East remains an imagined construction, erected by the West as a result of the West's interest (imaginary and political) in the other.

By way of the exoticization of the Orient, the West was able to create an image of the East that stood in stark opposition to Occidental sovereignty. Said maintains that the notions of the Orient does not simply signal "an airy European fantasy" (6), but rather a "created body of theory and practice in which, for many generations, there has been a considerable material investment" (6). Given this, the Orient reflected the binary opposition of the rational West: passion and pacification.[4] *Orientalism* provides a critical account of the development of this dichotomy in multiple discourses, political, scientific, and a product of the arts.

The hippie mecca, India, and in particular Goa, acquired special notoriety during the late 1960s and early 1970s for numerous reasons.[5] Imagined as the nucleus of free-thinking and looser morals, First World pilgrims arrived to exercise their free agency, and partake in the "exotic" through their consumption of the territory and its accoutrements: an articulation of music, dance, drugs, internationalism, and pilgrimage. Flash forward three decades, this spirit of resistance and experimentation manifests within the techno community of Asian Vibes. The techno culture, similar to the old time hippies, is bound by a common sense of tolerance and desire to form opinions independent of authority or tradition. The eclectic beat of techno music initiated a new scene that integrated a hippie approach to life via the sonic. This style of music is molded to reflect anti-hegemonic feelings and beliefs, culminating in a mèlange of eclectic, electronic beats. The threads that intertwine the hippie and techno communities—music, drugs, internationalism, and pilgrimage—are rooted in the mission of repossessing consciousness in opposition to dominant conformity (Collin).

Since its emergence into the sonic scene this subculture, appearing within specific social and cultural contexts, has often been evaluated as counterculture against the patriarchy. Nevertheless, similar to other musical genres, the techno/rave scene is being commodified and marketed; however, it remains a prominent form of new production in music and youth cultures. Similar to the styles of rock-n-roll and punk that began as diatribes against hegemonic norms, techno, in a sense, has lost some of its original meaning because like the other musical cultures, it became recognized as an established genre by the dominant culture. In this respect, the music and culture cannot escape from the systematic constraint of capitalism insofar as they depend upon commodities in the expression of self-identity. This notion is highlighted in the thoughts of the protagonist, Alba, as she meditates upon the ideological structure of the music scene: "Los esquemas burgueses trasladados al rock . . . el rock era el ambiente más machista de cuantos conocía" (21).

As culture is not liberated from hegemonic norms or capitalism, the multiple constituents that compose culture are prone to commodification. This process owes itself, in large part, to the prolific media technologies, which aid and encourage the creation of celebrity. The notion of fame and celebrity is not a new concept. From the Ancient Greek and early Christian cultures there existed people of renowned who were admired and worshiped for their many achievements. However, as Rojek notes, it was not until the birth of mass media that celebrity culture emerged and flourished; he states, "I believe that mass-media representation is the key principle in the formation of celebrity culture" (13). Due to advancements in information technologies, images circulate and are converted into commodities. In contemporary culture, people no longer achieve fame for their achievements, but rather for packaged personality, as celebrities are "cultural fabrications" (Rojek 13) that have transformed into commodities as goods to be marketed in their own right or utilized to market other commodities. "The celebrity's ultimate power is to sell the commodity that is themselves" (Turner, Bonner, Marshall 12). Forming part of this economy, Fernando enters into the realm of commodification as the lead singer. This is evidenced by the number of female groupies that follow and pursue Fernando, much to his delight, throughout the music festivals, daring even to attain access to the personal territory of Asian Vibes—their van—which Alba dubs "las furgonetas son el peor patio de vecinas" (21). While Fernando and his body can be read as a commodity, it is significant to note that he also enters as a player into this game, in particular commodifying women. For instance, no matter which music festival he attends, there is always a number of "fijas"(19) happy to gratify him sexually. Likewise, the star singer of the band Las Monaguillash, Mónica, is an important and highly desirable commodity to Fernando as she is "una bomba sexual" (30). His meditations on her comportment in conjunction with her raw beauty illustrate her value as a sign:

> Mónica hablaba sin parar. Siempre. Aunque Fernando había follado—¿tres? ¿cuatro veces?—con ella, solo habían dormido juntos una noche. El despertar había sido horrible. Hablaba, hablaba, hablaba. A Fernando le hubiera gustado tener un mando a distancia y bajarle el volumen. (30)

As he is unable to tolerate her incessant chit-chat, the idea of being able to turn-on and turn-off this woman, as if she were a machinic doll, is a striking option; or at least, it is much more appealing than "echarla de la cama" (30) given her sexually charged fabricated representation. In consuming women and sex, Fernando commodifies the two, as he himself represents a commodity to them.

Rojek states that celebrity and success have become synonymous in a culture that judges by how rich, seductive, and riveting the image. This new less durable fame, the kind refracted through images, proves in this case to be especially corrosive to the self, (Rojek) as Fernando deals with it through his consumption of drugs, which ultimately leads to his demise, as well as his selling of drugs to his fans, something he particularly enjoys doing because it lets him adopt the role of "antiestrella consciente" (62). Indeed, Fernando appears to find it difficult to cope with fame. That is, his actions ranging from indiscriminately selling drugs to not taking responsibility for his decisions suggest that he is suffering from a messiah-like complex. Certainly he believed he was untouchable: "Coño, soy un músico más o menos conocido, llevo una vida normal, tengo uno de los mejores abogados del país . . . no voy a ir a la cárcel" (62). While his ability to generate collective efferverscence in audiences is undeniable, perhaps even legendary, Fernando is emphatically mortal, an imperfect human being. In other words, although fans may worship him to the point of idolizing him, Fernando is not exempt from the human realm or his responsibilities.

The celebrity as a commodity is essentially culturally manufactured. In light of this, Rojek contends:

> Celebrities are cultural fabrications. [. . .] In fact, celebrities are carefully mediated through what might be termed chains of attraction. No celebrity now acquires public recognition without the assistance of cultural intermediaries who operate to stage-manage celebrity presence in the eyes of the public. [. . .] Their task is to concoct the public presentation of celebrity personalities that will result in enduring appeal for the audience of fans. (51)

Thus the image dictates how the self is perceived by the other, as well as the comportment of others towards the subject. An important element in the analysis of the celebrity image is the phenomenon of the fan. The fan is, in fact, an integral feature in the creation process of the image as she has the power to choose of a plethora of images, the ones to which she will give attention. The images floating freely as signs have the potential to provide compelling ideas of perfection. Likewise, they have the potential to convey the promise that such beauty remains within reach via consumption of commodified images. The fan, then, responds to a celebrity figure via speculative desire. This desire, not static as it evolves according to commodity innovations, propels the fan to want to control, even own, her icon.

> The boundaries of attachment between the public face and the fan are not clearly delineated. Consuming celebrity products, and generally reinforcing the image of the public face in ordinary social interaction, are merely the out-

ward manifestations of attachment. At deeper psychic levels, fans may adopt the values and style of the public face, and in some cases, develop unmanageable obsessions. . . . Isolation may produce over-identification with the public face and engender the desire to possess the celebrity or deprive the public face of volition. (Rojek 47)

Thus, this "cult of celebrity" encourages bodies to be viewed as a commodity in the construction of power, beauty, and desire. These images, consequently, possess gripping power as fans aspire to resemble images of celebrities despite awareness of their unreality.

The sociologist Jean Baudrillard suggests that the "cult of celebrity" grounds itself in a larger trend towards living in the "ecstasy of communication" (*The Consumer Society* 2). That is, we are barraged by a succession of topical images in the media that do not necessarily cohere with reality. Consequently, the distinction between that which is real and its converse, the imaginary, dissolves. In effect, images of celebrities become "more real than real" in our consumer culture. Fiske echoes this idea stating: "fantasy can be as 'real' an experience as any other" (10). In accord with this line of argument, we are trying to imitate the people we admire when we use them as models for ourselves. In consuming a specific milieu, participants are also marking their identity to the self and others. One identifies with celebrity because these renowned people seem to possess qualities that are lacking in common daily life. Rojek affirms: "Celebrities offer peculiarly powerful affirmations of belonging, recognition and meaning in the midst of the lives of their audiences, lives that may otherwise be poignantly experienced as under-performing, anti-climatic or sub-clinically depressing. . . . Celebrities are thought to possess God-like qualities by some fans" (52–53). Hence, be it through adoption of fashion or physical proximity, the celebrity intrigues the fan as the perceived socially lived reality contrasts sharply with everyday experiences, and so encourage consumption, escapism, and identification. Indeed, fans attach glamorous excitement and even deity-status to their icons.

Proxemics of Techno and Portraits of Female Subjectivity

She suddenly began again. "Then it really *has* happened, after all! And now, who am I? I *will* remember, if I can! I'm determined to do it!" But being determined didn't help her much, and all she could say, after a great deal of puzzling, was: "L, I *know* it begins with L." (*Through the Looking Glass* 157)

Alba is the twenty-seven-year-old sitar player in the group Asian Vibes and, more importantly, girlfriend to the well-known singer of the group who has a reputation for drug- and alcohol-fuelled impropriety. As the novel opens, Alba's meditations about the band and her connection to it are significant as they foreground her identity. She contemplates: "Llevaba dos meses de gira con un grupo del que sería fan si no formara parte de él; era la novia oficial de cantante más deseado del panorama indie nacional" (14). Her testimony elucidates that which she consumes and is consequently consumed by: a series of commodified images revolving around her proximity and relationship to a celebrity within the techno music scene. Consequently, the most fundamental component (and also the most destructive) to her identity construction emerges from her status of official girlfriend and group member, the former surpassing in significance: Alba is obsessively in love with Fernando.

From the inception of the novel emerges the contradictory reality of Alba in the formation of her subjectivity juxtaposed with the complexity of consumption practices. The contingencies that form part of her subject formation—girlfriend of a famous rock star—signal the manner in which she consciously elects to construct her identity and her life. Her choice of consumption, Fernando, points to her desire to consume celebrity, which is interwoven with images and signs that incarnate basic values and display desires. In a culture saturated by a bricolage of images, these very images are heralded as primary vehicles for expression and communication and serve as factors for identity construction. Nevertheless, it would be negligent to consider that identity construction via consumption practices always yields an active liberated subject. Rather in the case of Alba, her consumption of Fernando and the space that it (celebrity) entails proves to be unhealthy and transpose her to an inert state. This is patently clear in the attitudes and actions of Alba as she is on a never-ending vigilant mission of Fernando, for without him, she feels lost. She relates:

> Era la misma sensación que sentía de pequeña cuando en unos grandes almacenes, en el parque de atracciones o en la calle, se soltaba de la mano de su madre y dejaba de verla durante más de un minuto: la ansiedad de estar perdida. Lo malo era que, de niña el agobio duraba como mucho tres minutos . . . con Fernando . . . tres o cuatro horas. (42)

As evidenced by her admissions, her boyfriend is not simply her romantic partner, but rather ironically she classifies him within the same category as she does her mother—an image of a nurturer who paradoxically denies her that. Unlike the protagonist of *Veo, veo* or Cristina within the proxemics of Planeta X in *Amor, curiosidad, prozac y dudas*—both of which experience libidinal pleasure from their consumption of various accoutrements such as music, dance, and drugs, which act upon and produce an active subjectivity—

Alba maintains a distinct approach evidenced through the subtleties of her consumption. While frustrated and depressed, she, in part, is able to share in the celebrity—albeit in an nonresistant mode—through her determinate consumption of Fernando.

Within the proxemics of the techno/rave scene, Alba, indeed, is a consumer of the musical assemblage to an extent; however, she is most consumed by presenting a certain image—her status as official girlfriend of Fernando. In this mode, her consumption grounds itself in pure spectacle. The narrative voice reveals:

> Estaba angustiada. Aparentaba divertirse, se emborrachaba como todos y parecía que disfrutaba, pero se pasaba el día vigilando: persiguiendo con la mirada a Fernando. A Fernando hablando con alguna bakalaera que se empeñaba en enseñarle el piercing de su ombligo; Fernando mirando con cara de embeleso a alguna laly sorprendentemente guapa a la que el pelo al uno pegado a la cara, el jersey de cuello alto y los pantalones mal cortados le sentaban como si fueran de Prada, o Fernando abriendo mucho la boca, mientras alguna techno hippie medio desnuda le metía una pastilla en la boca, con la esperanza de que la química le hiciera abalanzarse sobre ella. (14)

While feigning interest in consuming the accoutrements of a bacchanalian festival, Alba appropriates her gaze to exercise surveillance of Fernando and deconstruct the different types of eye-candy that willingly offer themselves to him. Alba is so consumed by maintaining her relationship, not with just any man but in particular this rock star, that she willingly goes to extremes to protect the image she consumes. As the novel opens, the protagonist reveals her alchemic dabblings which have yielded a modern day version "la Poción Mágica: el remedio para amortiguar los efectos del alcohol y acentuar la acción de cualquier droga estimulante" (13). What she failed to mention prior to administering this medicine to Fernando was a secret ingredient, "un valium 10" (13) that was completely dissolved. Justifying the creation of this potion, Alba affirms:

> En circunstancias normales no lo habría hecho, pero estaba en una situación de emergencia. Llevaba tres días de vigilia con las que intentaba conseguir, por medio del control exhaustivo y de no quitarle el ojo encima, que Fernando no terminara compartiendo saco de dormir y fluidos corporales con cualquiera de las lalys que pululaban por el festival. (13)

In her role as chemical alchemist, Alba feels no remorse, but rather she takes pride in the power that this act endows her: "La idea de convertirse en una especie de Charles Manson involuntaria le hacía cierta gracias" (15).

Moreover, while her actions may seem extreme, within the music industry, the kind of lifestyle she endures is not out of the ordinary for "«esposas de rock»" (20), women who were perhaps former groupies and are pathologically in love with their significant other as well as the image. The prolific privileging of the image has led to the creation of a new parlance: "seductive spectacles fascinate the denizens of the media and consumer society and involve them in the semiotics of a new world of entertainment, information, and drama, which deeply influence thought and action" (Kellner 2). Undoubtedly, Alba is enchanted with the free-floating display of images that surround the celebrity of Fernando and, by association, endow her with the experience of prestige, albeit as a shadow. Within this territory of the techno scene and given her relationship to a celebrity, Alba does not actively produce her self, rather vis-à-vis her passive consumption of celebrity image (her pathological love of Fernando), she is separated from actively producing her subjectivity and her life. For her, Fernando is not simply a boyfriend but also he represents a name. "Celebrity itself is thus commodified; notoriety becomes a type of capital. Famous people are widely referred to within the entertainment industry simply as 'names'" (Gamson 62). Intent on maintaining her relationship at all costs as well as the cultural capital it endows, Alba is caught in a maze of power constantly trying to please Fernando yet also control him.

Consumption practices and their relationship with subjectivity are clearly slippery concepts. While formation of identity occurs by way of consumption of goods and practices, this process does not always yield liberating healthy results, as is the case of Alba. Since her aim is to maintain the status quo, the protagonist tolerates all types of abuse and exploitation and she lacks the confidence and the ability to establish personal boundaries. For instance, Alba was implicitly aware of Fernando's indiscretions. Nonetheless, she resigned herself to this fact; she ascertained that, more likely than not, his sexual rendezvous would not come to an end. In light of this, not only does she try to normalize his infidelity, but also bolster herself, to an extent, by associating herself with the "imagined community" of girlfriends and wives of rock stars. As her affirmation hints, belonging to this small but "prestigious" group of women forms the foundation of her identity, and differentiates her from others.

> Con el tiempo Alba dejó de hacer predicciones. Él [Pablo] pensó que era porque se daba cuenta de que cuando le decía que Fernando era un santo fidelísimo, ella sabía que mentía. Pero no, Alba se había resignado, tenía la certeza de que cada vez que Fernando salía de gira, la caja de condones se iba

vaciando y algo le decía que eso no iba a cambiar nunca. Al principio pensó en dejarle. Pero se dio cuenta de que había pasado a formar parte de lo que ella definía como las «esposas del rock»: chicas modernas, más o menos cultas, patológicamente enamoradas y muchas de las veces con un pasado como groupies que aplicaban con un estoicismo natural la teoría del «ojos que no ven, corazón que no siente». (20)

In consuming the image of music star, Alba (consciously or otherwise) relinquishes her rights of independence and freedom (of speech), yet all the while she resents those she empowers. As Rojek contends, "Public acclaim answers to a deep psychological need in all of us for recognition. Acclaim carries the sensual pleasure of being acknowledged as an object of desire and approval" (95). True to the goal of advertising and mass media, Fernando functions as a fantasy object. As a commodity, he is an image of impossible perfection tantalizing the public with the lure of a fully achieved selfhood; Alba buys into this image.

Via her choices in consumption, the protagonist negotiates a unique situation as she forms part of the packaged image that is Asian Vibes, yet she still remains on the outside as she is marginalized within that position. In the group, Alba forms part of the texture of the sonic narrative as she plays the sitar. Nevertheless, her boyfriend Fernando wishes she did not participate and subsequently desires to disassociate her and her presence from his public image. He contemplates:

> Mi madre no acompañaba a mi padre al estudio de arquitectura, ni iba con él a los viajes de trabajo. ¿Por qué soy así de débil, coño? ¿Será posible que otra vez me haya dejado convencer por Alba para que toque el sitar durante la gira? Joder, Pablo consigue unos samplers mucho mejores. No nos hacía falta un sitar en directo . . . hombre, sí necesito a Alba, pero no durante las giras. (29)

The comparison he draws between the role of his mother and that of Alba is noteworthy as it mirrors the patriarchal model whereby the woman is represented as an absence. Furthermore, it elucidates how he views Alba as a sexual commodity with a use-value, however, only valuable to him outside of the territory of the techno scene. Within this musical landscape, the attention he desires is that of his numerous female fans who consume not only his music, but also his celebrity and sexually charged physical aspect. Alba does not fit within this plan; indeed, he compares her appearance at musical events to that of his mother's presence. Nevertheless, within the territory of home when he is off-stage and the fans are not mobbing him with their desire, the presence of Alba suffices.

As significant other to a celebrity, it is interesting to note the connections Alba establishes—due principally to her experiences—between musical stars and their girlfriends. From the inception of their relationship, Alba was confronted with the reality about relationships and the meaning of fidelity among musical stars and their significant others. At the beginning of their relationship three years earlier, Alba traveled to the town of Marbella in order to meet up with a popular singer for the purpose of collaborating on the compilation of a disc that included his singing and her playing the sitar. While there, she had the opportunity to accompany him around the southern towns of Marbella and Estepona; in both locations: "terminaban asediados por toda una avalancha de chicas locas por ligar con él. Cada mañana tenían a una distinta en la mesa del desayuno" (20–21). In the position of observer, Alba witnessed the interactions between the celebrity and the plethora of women, each perhaps as replaceable as the next. Her last day in Marbella she had the privilege to meet the singer's girlfriend who "llegó para recogerle e irse de vacaciones a Calcuta" (21). Before the couple left, Alba had the opportunity to have an insightful chat alone with the girlfriend of the musical star, in which "la química femenina funcionó y empezaron las confidencias" (21). Their conversation is significant as it uncovers a commonality amongst them: their function as girlfriend of highly desirable celebrities. The girlfriend explained to Alba:

> Algo que a Alba entonces le horrorizó, pero que entendería con el tiempo. La novia no intentó sonsacarla, averiguar si el músico había estado con otras, ni nada parecido. Como para salvar su honor, le explicó que entendía que era muy difícil vencer la tentación de acabar la noche con chicas guapísimas, que te admiran ciegamente y no piden nada a cambio. Que ella entendía que su novio se fuera con ellas y que no le importaba demasiado. Intentaba no pensar en el asunto, jamás investigaba ningún indicio y decía que lo importante era que siempre volvía. «Cuando estamos juntos, me hace feliz», se conformaba. (21)

This anecdote of shared commonalities among the two women highlights Irigaray's claim that woman—within the masculine economy—does not cease to function as a commodity.

> For woman is traditionally a use-value for man, an exchange value among men; in other words, a commodity. As such, she remains the guardian of material substance, whose price will be established, in terms of the standard of their work and of their need/desire, by "subjects": workers, merchants, consumers. Women are marked phallicly by their fathers, husbands, procurers. And this branding determines their value in sexual commerce. Woman is never any-

thing but the locus of a more or less competitive exchange between two men. (*This Sex Which is Not One* 31)

Many people are curious as to the allure of a man like Fernando, which indeed, extends to the reality behind the public perception of his way of living. The press and his groupies dub him a sexy and desirable commodity and considered him to be the "cantante más deseado del panorama indie nacional" (14). Hence these festivals and events attended by music icons spawn a backstage culture in which groupies thrive. In this vein, Asian Vibes would not be complete without a shoal of young females clamoring to gain entry to the hallowed vans in order to gain a glimpse of their object of desire—Fernando. Much like these groupies, Alba consumes celebrity; she consumes the items that she imagines will help create and sustain her idea of herself, image, and identity. Alba's actions reaffirm Bocock's theory that consumers buy commodities in hopes that the goods fulfill their desire to internalize the symbolic identities of the commodities (68). In her pursuit and much desired possession of Fernando, Alba, too, selects goods—rhetorical and material items—that align with her quest. While remaining unfulfilled, via her enduring dedication and consumption of this scene, the protagonist aspires to be the one and only woman in Fernando's life as well as garner the eminence that emanates from this rock star. Similar to stalker fans who relentlessly tail the object of their obsession and attach a personal meaning to their every word and gesture, Alba borders on a dangerously fixated fan who came close to harming Fernando, in order to control him. Many people are attracted to marrying/dating a rock star without having given due consideration to what the person may actually be like. This manifests in Alba's thoughts as it angered her that Fernando "encajara tan perfectamente en sus cánones estéticos. Estaba convencida de que ésa era la raíz de todas sus desgracias" (64). As evidenced through her admission, she consumes the spectacle of Fernando without regard to his interior qualities. Although it has crossed her mind an exponential number of times, she was incapable of leaving him: "Una vez salvados los escollos de la costumbre; el prestigio social que daba estar con el cantante de Asian Vibes; la complicidad y una vida sexual infrecuente pero intensa . . . al tenerlo delante no podía" (64). From Alba's perspective, the idea of her relationship with Fernando is quite glamorous, as he incarnates her notion of the aesthetically perfect man and reminds her of the many international musical idols she fantasized about as a youth—Miguel Bosé, Peter Murphy, Julian Cope, Richard Butler, and Jeremy Irons; the difference, though, lies in the fact that those men represented a dream and for her, while Fernando is tangible, her own personal idol worthy of deity-like worship: "Al mirarle se producía una especial de hechizo por el que le resultaba imposible pronunciar la frase que llevaba días resonando en su cabeza: «Hemos terminado, estoy harta de tu egoísmo y tus infidelidades, lo nuestro no funciona»" (64). As her thoughts highlight, reality with Fernando does not corroborate with her dreams of glamour and glitz. What happens to Alba is that she forms a relationship with a person who is so desirable in the eyes of his fans, his record companies, his groupies and his peers that she veers dangerously close to believing that Fernando is as wonderful as his packaged image. Furthermore, not only does she consume Fernando and his celebrity in the music landscape to bolster her own self-esteem and worth, but also she justifies his infidelity through what she believes to be her own personal deficiencies:

> «Si yo estuviera tan buena como él y fuera consciente de que cualquier persona que se me acerque estaría dispuesta a follar conmigo, creo que actuaría igual que sospecho que actúa él» . . . la infidelidad para Alba, no era cuestión de ética sino más bien de oportunidades. «Si tienes la ocasión de ser infiel con alguien que no merece la pena demasiado, pues a lo mejor vences la tentación. Pero si se te acerca gente estupenda: extraordinariamente guapa, simpática, inteligente . . . que además te admira y te lo dice . . . muy pocos quieren resistirse.» (65)

Alba maintains that if she were aesthetically on par with her lover, she too would possess the cultural capital with which he is endowed. This also hints at her perspective on relationships as she nearly likens them to an impulsive shopping spree in a store full of eye-candy; it is easier to resist that which does not stimulate the senses, yet exceedingly more difficult to not buy into the allure of a marketable beauty. Thus beauty is intimately linked to power. Expanding upon her theories, she admits that she was not "guapa de nacimiento" (64) and consequently she was impulsed to turn to the world of consumer goods in the attempt to acquire this highly prized and elusive commodity: beauty. Through stringent means such as diets, coloring her hair, and applying makeup, Alba molded and shaped her body with the hope of becoming an aesthetic equal of Fernando. Likewise, she reveals that this has not been a recent phenomena but something that has gained momentum since her childhood:

> De pequeña, le había dado por tomar litros y litros de vinagre. Le dijeron que destruía los globulos rojos, producía anemia y uno se quedaba pálido y flaco. Pero nada, los lingotazos del vino agrio que bebía para parecerse a La Dama del Lago, a Siouxie o incluso a Clarita (Alba pertenecía más bien al fenotipo de Heidi), no le hicieron efecto. (15)

Significantly, Alba cites renowned women portrayed in various media of popular iconography—posters, punk rock music, and television—disseminated by the mass media. In this instance, her body begs to be read as the body is a means over and through which relations of power are created, driven, and thwarted. Her revelations expose her profound yearning to incarnate the impractical and perhaps even inaccessible qualities of this "imagined community" of women: to have an attenuated figure similar to that of the aforementioned women. In light of this, the statements that the body makes take on increasingly more importance, as the notion of "thinness" and "paleness" bestows cultural capital. These two qualities signal a romanticized image of the decadent, explicitly associated with the rock and roll lifestyle. In the attempt to attain the beauty and stature of international icons prized by mass culture, Alba resorted to extraordinary means to fabricate the desired commodity. While she was able to "mantener los michelines bajo control" (15), she continued to envy those blessed with a genetics whom "estaban siempre demacrados" (15). Her standards for measuring beauty are noteworthy as they reflect the privileging of the slender, prepubescent body, exemplified by the figures from mass culture she mentioned earlier.

A contingent of the identity formation of Alba is her days spent in constant vigilance of Fernando—her appropriation of the gaze. Nevertheless, the task of surveillance becomes progressively more insurmountable and the prospect of finding happiness less likely. Yet along the way, Alba comforts herself with thoughts of other brave women who have sacrificed themselves on behalf of their famous significant others. Meditating on her relationship, Alba remembers the words of Juana, an ex-girlfriend of Fernando who "afirmaba que se había hecho yonqui por culpa de él" (88). When she first heard this, Alba believed it to be foolish but in hindsight it made more sense to her: "La única forma de soportar el ritmo de Fernando, su costumbre de tenerla siempre en vilo era, en opinión de Alba, o bien practicando durante años algún sistema de control mental o con ayuda de algún producto químico que hiciera soportar mejor el paso del tiempo, es decir, la espera. La heroína era la solución perfecta" (88). For Alba the use of drugs provides a respite from her continual self-doubts and paranoia about the rendezvous of her boyfriend. Within the proxemics of the techno scene, Alba occupies the position of girlfriend to a celebrity controlled by his impulses. As such, the subjectivity of the protagonist is marginalized by the infantile desires of Fernando. Alba is excluded and in the "position of experiencing herself only fragmentarily, in the little-structure margins of a dominant ideology, as waste, or excess, what is left of a mirror invested by the (masculine) 'subject' to reflect himself, to copy himself" (Irigaray *This Sex Which is Not One* 30). Not only is this evidenced through her use of drugs as an escape, but furthermore vis-à-vis her adoption of patriarchal discourse, whereby she silences her own voice. As the band travels to various festivals, often Alba is in the position to listen to the sexual trysts of her cohorts. On numerous occasions—due to physical proximity with the group—Alba was witness to locker room talk which detailed a ménage a trois had by Marcos, various rendezvous of Manolo, as well as "cómo los miembros de distintos grupos intercambiaban teléfonos de las fan de tal o cual ciudad para tener un polvo amarrado a su llegada" (42). Likewise she was privy to the sexual specialties of various women such as "la camarera del bar La Luna" (42), anxious to perform a variety of sexual acts on the music stars. Upon hearing these anecdotes, Alba participated enthusiastically in the banter of her cohorts, qualifying them as masculine comments that she would never repeat among her female friends. In this context, Alba herself appropriated a masculine discourse, treating other women as simple sexual commodities with specific use-values. To be accepted, she was unable to cultivate her true self, posing instead to garner attention and approval from the predominantly male band. Yet, she believed that this type of attitude was fundamental to her survival in the music world: "Era un mecanismo de supervivencia. Ella había aprendido que para ser aceptada en ese mundo más bien misógino y casi siempre cuartelero era necesario renunciar (hasta cierto punto) a algunos principios" (42). The question is, though, to what degree. In this environment, Alba constantly compares herself to other women and devalues other women for various reasons, viewing them and herself as commodities in competition for the position of girlfriend to a highly desired person. To this end, she appropriates a masculine discourse that depreciates and essentializes women, positioning them in constant combat amongst themselves. Yet, she maintains the romantic fantasy that perhaps, just maybe, change may occur.

Within this location, it is interesting to note the role of fashion in the construction of self-image. According to P. Willis: "clothes, like musical tastes, are indication of the cultural identities and leisure orientations of different groups of young people. Young people are very adept at the symbolic work of developing their own styles and also at 'reading off' and decoding the dress styles of others and relating them to musical, political, and social orientations" (88). In this way, body dressing should not simply be read as an amalgamation of mere commodities, but as a representation of ideas, values, and identity. This notion can be strengthened through Alba's choice of fashion, which projects a rebellious style that downplays feminine sexuality via her choice of sporting camouflage and a T-shirt.

> Imbécil, imbécil. Me he tenido que poner estos pantalones de camuflaje y la camiseta. ¿No había nada que me sentara peor? Con esta pinta mejor que ni salga. ¿Me daría tiempo de ponerme el biquini con el traje de plástico encima? Ni de coña. Debo tener la cara como un flotador y esa zorra ahí: perfecta, con las pestañas postizas a la una del mediodía. De verdad que para ser sex symbol hay que nacer. ¿Dónde se teñirá el pelo mientras está de gira? Yo llevo mes y medio y ya tengo unas raíces que ni Kurt Cobain. (30)

Nevertheless, it is noteworthy that upon gazing at Mónica and her highly sexualized image, Alba chastises herself for not fabricating a more seductive look by donning a bikini and plastic cover-up. Furthermore, she recognizes the commodification involved in the process of fashion and beauty. By virtue of beauty products and body dressing, Mónica creates an alluring image fabricated through her consumption of myriad consumer goods: hair dye, artificial eyelashes, and sensual clothing. Alba's image is sharply contrasted with that of Mónica, the star singer of Monaguillash.

> Aquel día el espectáculo visual que le ofrecía Mónica le había parecido impresionante . . . aquel cuerpo de adolescente con unas tetas ¿operadas? perfectas: mechones de pelo azul cubriendo las dos tiras de tela finísima y transparente; piel blanquísima decorada con un tatuaje de un tulipán rosa sobre el estómago, con un tallo que bajaba hasta el pubis; el coxis llenos de estrellitas y corazones; una Campanilla con su barita mágica sobre el brazo y un minishort vaquero minúsculo para tapar solo a medias un culo respingón. (30)

In consideration of the band name, Monaguillash, and her choice of body dressing there exists a double irony. First, the term 'monaguillo' is utilized to refer to male assistants that facilitate in the rituals of the Catholic mass, and here it is re-appropriated in its feminized form. Sexy and striking, Mónica incarnates a dangerous yet transgressive representation of the femme-fatale, as her dark blue hair contrasts with her fair complexion and her choice of clothing reveals a body emblazoned by provocative tattoos. Through her choice of clothing and skin decorations, she participates in a game of symbols, appropriating and revising while creating the image—one that is highly sexual—she desires to present. Alba, within the location of techno, functions more or less as raw material (Irigaray) for the authorization of the masculine fantasy. She solely bases her existence on being the girlfriend of a famous and highly desirable musician. By association, as the "official girlfriend" of Fernando, her body converts to currency, as she occupies an enviable position. That she receives gratification from her resulting commodification is undoubtedly true, but in the words of Irigaray, this type of enjoyment and its resulting embodiment "is above all a masochistic prostitution of her body to a desire that is not her own, and it leaves her in a familiar state of dependency upon man. Not knowing what she wants, ready for anything, even asking for more, so long as he will 'take' her as his 'object' when he seeks his own pleasure" (*Speculum* 250). At this stage in her journey, Alba does not access her voice nor know what she genuinely desires. Consequently, she is relegated to a state of passivity that impedes active self-formation.

While within the proxemics of the techno scene Alba does not actively construct her female subjectivity, it is interesting to compare how her mother, Sofía, negotiates this landscape as well as the type of subjectivity she exhibits. The mother of Alba manifests subjectivity distinct of her daughter's within this space of techno/rave culture, as she experiences this location in a sexually liberating mode. No strangers to the alternative scene, the parents of Alba, Sofia and Alberto, were members of the 1960s counterculture hippy movement that adopted a nomadic lifestyle at odds with traditional Western values. From their perspective, institutions such as government, industry, and traditional social mores embody a unified establishment lacking legitimacy. This ideology manifests in the dynamics of their family on various levels from the food they consume "el curry, el tofu y el seitán" (38) to their pilgrimages to San Francisco, a special place that reminds Sofia and Albert of "la época del love and peace, de las tardes tirados en el Golden Gate Park, los paseos por Haight Ashbury o los conciertos del Grateful Dead" (38), and from their own careers—both are artists—to their desire that Alba quit her job in public relations at the multinational and effectively "«abandonarlo todo por el arte, por la música»" (18). This type of artistic spirit cultivated among the parents of the protagonist is also embodied in the subjectivities of her brothers, Arturo and Zeus, albeit in distinct manners. Arturo, a vegetarian who studied ecological architecture, dedicates his energies to political activism, a devotion that was sparked at "las manifestaciones del 0,7" (40) and now travels to cities around the globe in order to "participar en las acciones en contra de la globalización y la condonación de la deuda externa de los países del Tercer Mundo" (40). Meanwhile, Zeus, who changed his name to Pedro much to the chagrin of his parents, followed a different path. Obsessively interested as a youth in math and computers, from an early age his goal in life was to become a "«Millonario»," which his parents believed to be akin to "la encarnación del diablo" (38), as this desire jettisoned their fundamental principles. After reaching his goal, attained by the creation and subsequent sale of "Videonet" (38) to Microsoft, he was plagued by his conscience that consequently led him to the role of benefactor of those less privileged. The narrative voice elaborates:

> Colaboraba activamente con Amnistía Internacional; había apadrinado a dieciséis niños indios; hizo una donación para construir un hospital en Mozambique; había financiado la construcción de una comunidad budista en Formentera (donde su madre impartía clases de meditación y yoga en verano) y, por fin, vivía reconciliado con sus padres, que ya veían con buenos ojos las prestaciones de internet. (39)

The consideration of his benevolence, however, is complicated if one gives thought to the tax deductions (capitalist gains) he receives in exchange for his goodwill. In sum, the dynamics of Alba's family illustrate the amalgamation of different identities informed and cultivated by international negotiations and models.

In contrast to her daughter, this environment and its accoutrements afford Sofía a libidinal return on her investment that is not possible for her offspring, due to her unhealthy consumption of celebrity. Sofía embodies hybrid subjectivity; she is "seductora y encantadora por naturaleza" (50), which belies her role as mother. Traditionally a patriarchal society defines the mother as a giving and available figure, one that downplays her own needs, ambitions, and desires. Occupying the position of mother, Sofía transgresses prescribed attributes and behaviors, interpreting herself as she thinks fit, and living her life according to her desires. Grijalba denominates this character as a "luchadora" (Personal Interview 2004), as she was reared during the Franco regime, yet chose to espouse counterculture progressive norms, an election reflected in her present day life as well. In contrast to the image offered by the mothers of her cohorts, Sofía embodies "la visión de una Madre vital, optimista, llena de una sensualidad natural" that one does not associate with maternity, but rather she commands admiration and entrances the members of the musical group, leaving them "hipnotizados" (51). Nevertheless, her image presents problems for Alba. That is, when she is present, Alba feels as if she does not exist: "ya empezaba a acostumbrarse a que cuando su madre estaba presente, ella no existiera" (50). For instance, on one occasion when her parents arrive bearing a gift for the members of Asian Vibes, "MDMA puro" (51), Alba feels the need to displace herself from the scene; she relates:

> En ese momento sabía que no existía. Fernando, Marcos y Manolo estaban embrujados por el encanto de esa mujer de cuarenta y pico años (que no aparentaba más de treinta y pocos) que, para más morbo, podía ser la madre de cualquiera de ellos no por la edad o por la apariencia, sino porque, de hecho, era la madre de uno de ellos: concretamente de Alba. (52)

It could be said that Sofia maintains a hybrid identity of a reprogrammer. That is, she views the techno/rave scene as a contemporary version of the ancient dance-drug rituals of tribal shamans. According to Grijalba, this is one of the positive aspects within this scene: "Lo ideal sería que la droga pueda efectuar una transformación shamánica" (Personal Interview 2004). Sofia possessed a romantic vision of this territory that is revitalized via the energies generated by the vibes in conjunction with drugs, yet not all drugs, but specifically MDMA.[6] This is evidenced by her participation in this space on the "carpa de dance" with Pablo, who accompanied her to avoid thinking and having to talk about his rocky long-distance relationship with his girlfriend, Ana.

As Grijalba accurately depicts in *Alivio rápido*, drugs such as Ecstasy are very often connected with the international techno/rave culture. While participants consume a palette of drugs, evidenced by the indulgences of Fernando, Manolo, and Marcos, Ecstasy is the drug most intimately linked with this culture. The salient effects of this chemical enhancement are "increased enjoyment of dancing, improved quality of life, greater ease of self expression, more caring for other people, increased spiritual awareness, greater happiness, increased closeness with lover" (Saunders 51). In *Ecstasy and the Dance Culture*, Saunders also affirms that "there have been various claims that Ecstasy facilitates spiritual practices including meditation, yoga, tai chi, guided imagery, psychosynthesis, shamanic journey work and rebirth"(39), and furthermore, "the combination of the drug with music and dancing can produce an exhilarating trancelike state, perhaps similar to that experienced in tribal rituals or religious ceremonies" (41). According to Sofia, who decides to consume pure MDMA, her main purpose for doing so is to feel free coupled with her desire to "A ver qué se siente tomándolo con tanta gente y para bailar" (52). Breaking through restraints, Ecstasy works upon her body to produce a more open, energized text. Likewise, as seen through her performance on the dance floor, the combination of drug-dance helps her to escape from the ordinary by providing possibilities for new experiences. In this context, it is significant to note that her use of drugs within the techno scene parallels the use of chemical enhancements by the hippie culture. According to P. Willis, in hippie culture, "the essence of the dialectical role of drugs is that they supplied the raw material of open and exceptional experience which could be interpreted in appropriate social and cultural ways to reflect and develop other aspects of consciousness and activity so as to further modify the drug experience" (135–36). Within the hippie culture, as the author notes, drugs were viewed as aids to "open up blocked experiential area" (139) as "there was a direct contact here with what was understood of Eastern religions and culture" (144). In a parallel manner, this corresponds with Sofía's socially lived experience and purpose for dabbling with chemical enhancements. In sum, the drugs work upon bodily texts encouraging a particular type of subjectivity; the act of indulging in alchemic intensifications represents the negotiation of new contingencies for the formation of subjectivity.

To understand how Sofía negotiates this territory and the subjectivity that it encourages, it is necessary to deconstruct the aspects of the dance floor. A sprawl of beings that resonates a collective energy, on the dance floor the bodies oscillate in unity forming concentric circles. The exterior is populated by "los mirones y los tímidos: los que solo movían el pie o, de vez en cuando, la cabeza" (56), whereas the participants at the nucleus heed the beats of the sonic narrative, opening up their selves to experience life as a dance, feeling a wholeness with the music: "A medida que uno se acercaba al núcleo era más nítida la sensación de calor, humedad, de roces viscosos y la necesidad de dejarse llevar por el sonido del bombo, palpitando en el vientre, y alguna línea de bajo para llevar el ritmo con los brazos" (56). Involvement within this particular location—the center of the "carpa de dance"—portrays a special kind of delirium, akin to a frenzy that borders on the religious and a total assault on the senses. Music is a fundamental experience of this territory as the electric vibes crash in visceral waves over the dancers, unleashing intense psychic energies and driving the audience further and further into trance (Collin). Sofía occupies the space at the center of the dance floor, dancing and pendulating "como una deidad hindú" (56). Significantly, there exists an association among the hippy counterculture surging from the Vietnam War and its revival (for Sofia) manifest in Asian Vibes. Part of the "baby-boom" generation, Sofía and Alberto were born into Francoism and came of age during the Vietnam War; they spent time in San Francisco and had a communion with the counterculture hippy community. This alternative community espoused oriental mysticism, radical political perspectives, very liberal ideas regading sexuality, the use of hallucinogenic drugs, communal living, and music. Within this territory Sofía is not only able to feel communion with a group through partaking in a collective ecstatic celebration, but also revive, if only temporarily, the connection between the past and the present.

> Sonidos repetidos una y otra vez, como mantras, un ritmo que iba aumentando de velocidad y obligaba al baile; hiperventilación y la consiguiente falta de anhídrido carbónico en la sangre (un truco que todas las religiones utilizan para llevar a la alucinación mística a sus feligreses); calor y comunión con el resto del grupo . . . los ingredientes que Sofía había aprendido que eran básicos para llegar al trance. (57)

Backlashing against conformism of dominant norms, there are no prescribed rules with regard to how to dance, which step one should take, or which direction to turn. As such her bodily text supports Haraway's concept of figuration of the cyborg; with the changing lights, her movements appear fluid, and in consuming the accoutrements of this scene, she explores new possibilities for the creation of female subjectivity.

> Todo le parecía perfecto: la música repetitiva que iba acelerándose al ritmo de los latidos de su corazón; aquella gente joven, tan guapa, tan feliz, que le contagiaba esa energía que hacía unos años salía de ella de forma natural y que con el tiempo tuvo que aprender a captar por medio de técnicas orientales y demás trucos alternativos. (57)

It seems that the dancing provides a means for her to reach her inner self, without turning to scripts or prescriptions. Likewise, her participation in this territory validates her escape of naturalized gender roles as she sheds the role of mother, instead opting for one of peer. In her negotiation of this location, Sofía asserts her sexuality; ever so gently, she provocatively touches a tattoo of a black star on the sternum of her dance partner Pablo: "A Sofía le hubiera gustado lamerla, quitarle la humedad mojándola más, pero se limitó a tocarla, muy suavemente, con el dedo índice muy estirado" (59). Instead of waiting for her dance partner Pablo to make an advance or even entertaining the idea that he maintained interest, Sofía enticingly caresses him, desiring though to do much more. In this context, Pini investigates the British rave scene in conjunction with the formation of female subjectivity and notes: "women involved in early British rave experienced this scene as sexually progressive in as much as it enabled an escape from the traditional associations between dancing, drugged-up women and sexual invitation" (117). Pini argues that this particular space, the rave, elucidates the unraveling of tradition; whereas throughout history the notion of woman has been neatly bound by patriarchal constrictions that control and shape textual body, these are eroded in the space of the rave. This is due to the "adventure" (154) that the territory of the rave permits women; it is a locale where the primary goal is to attain the utmost amout of pleasure and as such corporeal and cerebral delectation lie at the forefront. The rave can be considered an act of defiance to the patriarchy. The components of this space—the rave—are intimately linked to femininity and gay culture due to their close connection to dance, drugs, displays of emotion, and desire to heighten consciousness. Both of these groups remain on the margins in the dominant paradigm, yet challenge the power dynamics in a myriad of modes. This daring resistance to authority manifests in visual exhibitions of "happiness," auto-erotic pleasure, "friendliness," and the vigorous indulgence of dance (Dyer 101). In light of Sofía's experiences and Pini's argument, one can affirm that techno/rave liberates gender from traditional culturally prescribed norms and rules of dancing.

Kumagai emphasizes that the participants within this dance scene form a collectivity that partake and communicate to each other via the common language of dance. He contends that the dancers:

> Don't stand out as an individual. You are just part of the whole exhibition. The other troupe members include all the rave-happy dancers around you. Collective dancing ensures that no singular stars shine at raves. Instead, each dance-tranced raver shines equally as bright as all the others. As a result, dancing may form the most important bonding mechanism at a rave. A sense of commonality arises when hundreds or thousands of characters energetically stomp on common ground to a common groove. (318)

Not only is the commonality between participants evidenced through the sonic communion, but also Kumagai further alludes to an ongoing cosmic blending as the music nurtures the mind, body, and soul. According to Pini, this spiritual oneness that places "stress on 'wholeness' clearly echoes certain 'New Age' ideas about mind and body 'balance'" (121). Sofía exemplifies the mind-body connection not only by way of her participation in dance, but rather how she embodies and appropriates a harmonious combination of elements. The music—through its repetition—produces a transformation in states of consciousness, which precipitates a transcendental, whole-body experience. Enraptured by the repetitive beats that literally seize the body, heart, and mind, vis-à-vis her dancing experiences, Sofía arrives at a deeper understanding of her self, identity, and desires and at the same time sheds traditional gender constraints. This occurs via the relationship between the music and the vigor of her dancing, which penetrates her body as well as stimulates her mind, much like mantras and other practices she employed to arrive at a state of trance, communion with the group as well as a more profound communion with her self (something she notes that she has not experienced in years).

Worked upon by the sonic landscape and chemical enhancements, Pablo and Sofía share an intense sexual moment on the dance floor, which was initiated by her: "Sentía una mezcla entre una palpable excitación sexual y una ráfaga de calma, de protección que nunca antes había experimentado" (59–60). While the means to produce this style of music is technology, the end is to reach the human spirit, and indeed it does for the pair; the two describe this special time alluding to a literary reference: *The Island* by Aldous

Huxley. Their experience is reminiscent of "el Moshka" (61) in Huxley's novel, which in Sanskrit is akin to 'liberation' and also is the term utilized to refer to the drug taken by the residents of the island Pala; the ultimate goal of the drug is to arouse the idle mind so that it may begin to perceive and appreciate knowledge, and then strive toward liberation (Collin). Indeed, her experience—a complete contrast to that of her daughter—does reflect this philosophy as she does contemplate and experience new knowledge of her self. By way of her experiences within this musical realm she was able to shed traditional female stereotypes, realize pleasure stemming from alchemic play, and disconnect with establishment wandering into the unknown, making it up as she went along. In sum, this style of music calls attention to the evolving nature of our technological societies and to the global mélange of cultures that inform and conform them.

Nomadic Journey to Active Subjectivity

Albo, ba: . . . 3. Primera luz del día antes de salir el sol . . .
Amanecer (empezar a aparecer la luz del día).
Real Academia Española. *Diccionario de la Lengua Española. Vigésima Segunda Edición*. Real Academia Española, 2001, Tomo 1, 90.

Arising from circumstances outside of her direct control, the protagonist sets off on a journey that leads her through a variety of locations and experiences ultimately reaching a heightened awareness of her self. While traveling with the band to play at festivals, the tour is abruptly halted in Zaragoza due to the (unknown) incarceration of Fernando, the lead singer. While this proves to be a difficult and trying period for Alba, at the same time it is the much-needed blessing in disguise. She is propelled to actively take control of her needs and desires, while she negotiates her life, alone, both inside (during permitted visitation) and outside (in her professional life) of this patriarchal structured terrain.

The second part of the novel, weighing heavily on the informative as opposed to novelistic, depicts the life of Fernando in prison. This particular part of the novel is enriched by the fact that Grijalba was granted access to speak with prisoners incarcerated at the penitentiary on the outskirts of Mardrid, Navalcarnero. Her inquiry focused on their experiences and social reality within the space of the prison. Not only did she obtain the perspective of the male prisoners, but she was also able to interact with the female visitors, ranging from mothers to girlfriends.[7] Her primary research required that she travel from Madrid by the public bus "Centro Penitenciario Madrid II," the only bus that reaches that destination. Grijalba's experiences with the other women (both on the bus and within the space of the prison) are reflected in the narrative and lend the novel a sociological angle. This section, furthermore, describes the downfall of Fernando and his transformations, as he is dispossessed of his commodity value. His incarceration stems from a nocturnal rendezvous between himself and Mónica, the lead singer of the Monaguillash. While at the hotel—unbeknownst to his girlfriend Alba—not only does he indulge sexually, but also after consuming a plethora of drugs and alcohol he loses control and destroys property. Yet again he assumes no responsibility for his actions, citing again his fame, which relieves him from all culpability.

In consideration of the goods that Alba selects to consume and consequently form a basis for her subjectivity—image and celebrity of Fernando—it is significant to note the transformations in her desire. Whereas her boyfriend was a sexy well-known musical icon, within the proxemics of prison, this changes as he becomes enfeebled losing the vitalization and magnetic appeal of his former self. The romanticized rock and roll aspect of Fernando which attracted Alba has faded: "Le miró a la cara y vio que, de golpe, había envejecido. Miles de arrugas rodeaban sus ojos, las ojeras eran inmensas y estaba muy pálido, demacrado, pero no como a ella le gustaba, no tenía un ápice de glamour siniestro, sino más bien la cara de un anciano mal conservado" (117). As Fernando was not awarded a legal appeal, due to the negligence of his attorney, he was ordered to be confined for a minimum of one and half years. While imprisoned, Alba initiates the process of the reconfiguration of her life. Prior to the incarceration, Alba had toyed with the idea of perhaps leaving her day job and devoting her life to music with Asian Vibes. This, however, became an unreality as she begins to inundate herself with work: "De lunes a viernes tenía que lidiar con el universo jefe de telesushi, películas en version original, compactos de trip hop, Goran Begrovic y Kronos Quartet y ropa de Homeless, Amaya Arzuaga y, a veces, Prada, en el que vivían sumidos sus compañeros" (123). Finished sacrificing herself for Fernando, Alba is free to explore other contingencies for the basis of her identity. And most importantly, she does not displace these feelings onto another man, but rather she devotes her energies to her self-improvement. It is interesting to note Alba's position in the multinational: public relations agent. Working in this capacity, Alba is the person in charge of constructing images and marketing the goods. Through artful communication, she devises and disseminates the representation desired by her client.

The longer Fernando spends in prison, the more time Alba has to contemplate her situation and her feelings, or perhaps, change of sentiments towards her boyfriend. As time passes, the powerful image of him etched into her memory starkly clashes with reality: "Alba no le reconoció: estaba encorbado, arrastraba los pies. Sus andares que no tenían nada que ver con esa mezcla entre chulería y savoir faire de pasarela que tanto morbo le habían dado hacía solo unos meses. Estaba derrotado y aquello no había hecho más que empezar" (152). Upon the termination of her "vis a vis" (visitation with sexual privileges which they did not take advantage of) Alba exits the area in the company of other inmates' wives and girlfriends. However, before leaving the facility, she turns to glance at Fernando only to see him "mirando el culo de Samantha" (151), an action that under normal circumstances would have provoked intense jealousy. Within the proxemics of the prison, Alba's feelings mutate; she experiences "una ola de tranquilidad, de felicidad sin estridencias" (151), sentiments that have been foreign to her. The manifestation of these feelings leads her to an awakening: since Fernando has been incarcerated, she has felt liberated and "en general, mucho mejor" (152). Not only does she not have to concern herself with his philandering ways, but also, for the first time, their positions are ironically reversed:

> Alba tenía que reconocer ante sí misma (jamás lo haría ante los demás) que el hecho de que Fernando estuviera encerrado y dependiera totalmente de ella, le había dado la vida. Ya no tenía que estar alerta para que no se enrollara con otra; no hacía falta trasnochar, vigilar, maquinar estrategias para evitar que Fernando la sustituyera por una nueva. Pero lo mejor, pensaba Alba, era que su novio en ese momento dependía de ella para casi todo. (152)

While Alba still loved Fernando, she arrives at the realization that she does not need him "también le necesitaba cada vez menos" (171). He still remains one of her primary concerns, but in a different mode. "Ya no tenía esa ansiedad, ese temor insano a medio camino entre el miedo a perderle, la posibilidad de que encontrara a otra que le gustara más que ella o la certidumbre de que si salía de casa había muchas posibilidades de que regresara dos días después, sin dar demasiadas explicaciones" (166). Instead, Alba concerns herself with making her own life and discovering her own talents. While Fernando is incarcerated, Alba's existence transforms radically: "Había aceptado el pequeño ascenso que le habían ofrecido en la agencia y eso quería decir que ganaba más dinero pero también que tenía que trabajar muchos fines de semana, festivos y alargar su horario hasta lo inhumano. A Alba no le importaba demasiado" (166).

At the inception of the novel, Alba represented the traditional unspeaking subject. Yet, she assumes a new character by way of contemplation and making life choices. Whereas her subjectivity was emblematic of female processes and sentimentality, now her messages reflect her affirmed role as author of her life. Alba explicitly reveals herself as creator by way of thoughtful expressions of identity, authenticity, and self-ownership. In this vein, Alba generates a personal narrative that destabilizes the relationship between gender and identity. No longer passively consuming the celebrity of Fernando, she realizes that not only is life possible without her boyfriend but it is also more peaceful:

> Se daba cuenta de que la vida sin Fernando era posible y además mucho más tranquila. Incluso, cuando alguno de esos compañeros cercanos a los treinta y cinco, con zapatos de Prada, pantalon Levis Engineering Jeans, camisa Carthart, media melena, chalet en Las Rozas, Saab azul o negro y veraneo en Kenia la invitaba a cenar en el Nodo o en el Suntory y empezaba a pensar en la posibilidad de una vida acomodada. (172)

In this context, consumption is constitutive of identity (Campbell; McCracken) and possessions, thus, function as an extended sense of self. Alba as consumer uses goods to construct and communicate her identity, to relate to people and groups, to mark social differences, to seek comparative status, and to pursue emotional and aesthetic pleasures. Identity construction and expression rest on the quest for difference: "a need is not a need for a particular object as much as it is a 'need' for difference (the *desire for social meaning*)" (Baudrillard *The Consumer Society* 45). Without regard to the proxemics, Alba draws from all available global and local, new and old sources as she uses products to position herself in the local age, gender, and social class. In this process of identity construction she confronts tensions: to be like others (her *privileged* friends from work) yet also different. On one hand, Alba maneuvers within the proxemics of the Salamanca neighborhood, a wealthy, upper-class district. However, she differentiates herself from her privileged friends through her hippy body dressing and subversive dreadlocks.

Negotiation of Alba's identity through consumption rests on the meanings of objects and practices: exotic food, a luxury vehicle, and high-end fashion goods. Her identity-making process, then, is based on a double dynamic. On the one hand, objects and consumption practices express her identity in a positive manner as belonging to a certain social group: that of "acomodada" (172). On the other hand, they express identity in a negative manner as differences and distance (to other social groups or to other members of the same group). While some may comment that Alba is selling out to upper-middle class aspirations via her election of consumption habits, intimately connected to her transplantation, Alba's change in consumption practices marks an evolution in the production of a passive self to active self-formation. Of the options available to her, the protagonist voluntarily made the choice to enter the multinational (cognizant of its symbolic system) and, indeed, constructs a healthy, vigorous selfhood. Through consuming material goods of distinction—those that freely float in the social landscape of this "imagined community"—she aligns her identity and self with individuals negotiating that same landscape; in a similar way, she distances her subjectivity from her former reality including Fernando. Nevertheless, she maintains her coiffure of dreadlocks, an extreme stylistic contrast to the multinational norm.

The third and final part of the novel opens with Fernando's release from prison after a year and one-half stay.[8] While he had a strong desire to return to his former celebrity self, the only energy he could muster was directed towards domestic duties: "se pasaba el día entero en casa: limpiando (más o menos), viendo la televisión, jugando con Iggy (el gato) y esperando a que Alba llegara del trabajo estresadísima y harta de que él, Fernando, «no hiciera nada por solucionar su vida»" (183). Ironically, he now finds himself in a powerless position pendent of his girlfriend Alba. Instead of being surrounded by participants and players in the musical world, after his release from prison Fernando relies on Alba and her group of friends for company. Negotiating the barrio of Salamanca—one of the most posh neighborhoods in Madrid—the couple attends elegant soirees:

> Cenas en casas de decoración minimalista o abigarradas con elementos étnicos de mercadillos carísimos en las que gente vestida con zapatos de Prada, bolsos de Gucci, camisetas de mercadillo, faldas vintage y vaqueros desteñidos, comía sushi, cuscus biológico o pollo tandoori, bebía vinos carísimos, hablaba de viajes exóticos, problemas ecológicos, los vaivenes de la economía de las empresas de internet . . . y en cuyas estanterías había libros de diseño. (186–87)

In the past Fernando would never have conceived of attending a function of this sort, as this group represented his antithesis; nevertheless, since his ingression in prison, he remains a sad parody of his former self, which Alba points out to him.[9] Desiring to jump back into the music scene, Fernando composes a collection of what he believes to be top musical hits, only to hear: "—Cariño, pero esto es el «Love will tear us apart», de Joy Division, es una broma, ¿no?" (184). In the attempt to prove her wrong, Fernando performs a series of other songs, yet each time "resultaba que era una canción conocidísima que él no recordaba" (186). Feeling impotent and a poser, Fernando decided it was best to leave behind both the musical environment and its people. It is interesting to note that his passive attitude, in the past, would have represented paradise for Alba, "tres años atrás ésa era la idea que tenía Alba del Paraíso: un Fernando domesticado, que no la tuviera todo el día al borde del colapso nervioso" (195), but presently she just pitied Fernando and his unattractive state: "Efectivamente, Fernando estaba domesticado, se acercaba bastante a la idea general del compañero perfecto. Pero claro, con la doma, había perdido el brío que había hecho que Alba se enamorara (o se obsesionara, que lo mismo da) de él" (195). Returning from work to find him subsumed in MTV, (of course) without volume to avoid what he denominated "Síndrome del Plagio Inconsciente" (195), the admiration she once held for her former celebrity boyfriend was converted to compassion and pity. While Alba indeed constructs a subject formation in complete opposition of her former self, much like that of Fernando, her representation is not a parody of her past. This is due to two reasons: from the outset of the novel (although emphatically acknowledging her obsession for Fernando) she revealed various times her lack of desire to continue within the musical space, despite the overwhelming encouragement from her folks. Furthermore, when her existence was abruptly altered by the incarceration of Fernando, she opted to take active control of her life and the construction of her identity, instead of remaining inert. Indeed, she associates herself with the community of the multinational—one which has expensive tastes and frequents the Salamanca barrio—yet, she does not conform to this image, illustrated through her coif (dreadlocks) and the fact that she sports clothes that project an alternative, indie image.

The theorist Cixous, in "The Laugh of Medusa," calls for an end of silence instituted upon women when she proposes a feminine practice of writing that urges women to write themselves using the "white ink," the milk of the mother's breast (251). A plausible interpretation of this is that men cannot silence that which feeds their progeny so they are forced to let it flow in its own manner and design, be it the "white ink" of the breast or Alba's writing of her own narrative. From the time Fernando was incarcerated, Alba, as her name suggests, embarks upon a journey of reawakening. Diving into her work "como método de evasión" (192), Alba separated herself from the world of music that "nunca le había gustado demasiado y en el que, además, tenía que estar mintiendo constantemente sobre el paradero de Fernando" (192). Negotiating a new terrain, Alba also began to reconstruct her concept of self. Indeed she did not stop consuming images and symbols, but she did consume actively and use it to her advantage and further herself professionally: "se dio cuenta de que la cantidad de horas que invertía en aquella oficina y los esfuerzos que hacía servían de muy poco si no se acompañaban de una vida social activísima con sus superiores y algunos compañeros «elegidos»" (192). Aware of her surroundings and their inherent patriarchal structure, Alba took advantage of these parties to further her own desires; desires not based on being possessed by a man, but rather financially caring for herself: "Si Alba quería que su cuenta bancaria ascendiera todos los meses a doscientas mil pesetas daba igual cómo trabajara: lo importante era ganarse la confianza de sus superiores. Al fin y al cabo, los cargos de responsabilidad también se llamaban puestos de confianza, por algo sería" (193). Her nomadic negotiations through this location demonstrate the articulation of an active female subjectivity as well as the erection and appropriation of her own language; Grijalba concurs: "Alba sí podría ser un ejemplo de nómada. Yo creo que sí, va evolucionando" (Personal Interview 2004). While feminist critics continue to explore how to acquire language outside of the symbolic order, as Cixous suggests, this system of writing from the 'breast' allows for exclusivity among women that undermines patriarchal political agendas. For instance, while Alba did not particularly enjoy working "En realidad odiaba su trabajo: bueno, cualquier trabajo, incluido el de tocar el sitar de festival en festival" (193–94), she recognized that it was her means to independently establish herself and make possible future dreams: "ahorrar durante unos cinco años y después retirarse a vivir de las rentas y de algún trabajillo suelto" (194). To convert into reality these aspirations, Alba performed for her bosses—"Siempre decía que adoraba su trabajo, que la publicidad le parecía un arte y que los publicistas hacían una labor social muy importante" (194)—to the point of embodying a caricature of the traditional woman. When questioned about her future desire to have children with Fernando, Alba responded perfectly without hesitation: "la única que podía conducirle al ascenso rápido. Ponía cara de más confidencia aún y cierta desazón y decía: «Nos gustaría mucho, pero tengo un problema de esterilidad y no puedo. Pensé en adoptar un niño pero, no sé, no es lo mismo. No, estamos muy bien así y no necesitamos un hijo»" (194). In contrast to her location within the techno space, the power of the feminine makes a dramatic shift to the center within the space of the multinational. While some may read Alba's choices and resulting embodiment as an adoption of a masculine patriarchal paradigm, I do not believe that to be the case. Alba maintains and articulates a dual discourse to her benefit. She utilizes a "set of interrelated 'situated knowledges'" (Braidotti *Patterns of Dissonance* 278) or nomadism which leads her to ascertain and actively take control over her life, opening possibilities to achieve that which she truly desires yet "no se lo confesó jamás a ningún compañero" (194): to work hard now and save so as to live her future in peace. Alba's efforts and movements within the territory of the multination illustrate Braidotti's concept of the nomad and the notion of becoming woman:

> El nómade tiene un agudo sentido del territorio, pero no de su posesión.
> Como bien lo señala Haraway: uno debe situarse en algún lugar para poder hacer enunciaciones de valor general. Por consiguiente, el nomadismo no es fluidez sin fronteras, sino que consiste más bien en una aguda conciencia de no fijación de límites. Es el intenso deseo de continuar irrumpiendo, transgrediendo. (*Sujetos nómades* 77)

By way of her fleshing through of experiences and understanding of the spaces in which she has traversed, Alba has acquired knowledge that permits her to work from a position of subversion (she does work for the multinational, but it represents a means to an end). This coupled with the knowledge that she does not need Fernando nor any other man to construct and stabilize her identity are fundamental to an enhanced self-awareness, an understanding that derives from her "rhizomatic" or profound contemplation that according to Braidotti, unfolds in a "'nomadic' style" (*Patterns of Dissonance* 60). That is, the status of their relationship as the goal and endpoint of her development is called into question by the emergence of new plot intrigues that seek to expose the insufficiencies of the old. In this vein, Felski agrees with the necessity of creating alternative spaces for the construction of active female subjectivity. She states:

> The defining feature of a feminist text is a recognition and rejection of the ideological basis of the traditional script of heterosexual romance characterized by female passivity, dependence, and subordination, and an attempt to develop an alternative narrative and symbolic framework within which female identity can be located. (129)

While a negative portrayal was presented at the inception of the novel—a representation of female alienation—through a multiplicity of intrigues, the protagonist works to overcome these debilitations. Alba's unhealthy consumption of celebrity denied her the opportunity for active self-formation and independent self-fulfillment. All the while she was clinging to a relationship based on psychological dependence with a lover unable to acknowledge women other than in relation to his own emotional and sexual interests, as commodities. That is, she displaced her need to foreground her identity and distinguish herself from others based on attention from a man.

The key transformation of the text—Fernando's imprisonment providing Alba the space she needed to cultivate and nurture her self—takes the protagonist from an inert state or an imposed alienation to a qualitatively different concept of self. Within this narrative, the heroine maneuvering as other among patriarchal landscapes—techno scene, penitentiary, multinational—survives and strengthens her self. Ironically, her celebrity boyfriend suffers, and ultimately, destroys himself. Grijalba offers a narrative of opposition through the resistance and survival of Alba. The social and ideological constrictions, which traditionally have defined women's roles within the social scope, are systematically called into question. The rupture with tradition materializes by way of the inward recognition and rejection of the ideological basis of existing gender roles. Furthermore, this rupture is expressed through actively displacing the fulfillment of Alba's boyfriend's needs for hers. The shifts in physical space, from the techno scene to the multinational, are symbolically important to the evolutions manifesting within her personal relationship with herself and Fernando. In this transformation, she moves outward from the oppressive environment of the techno scene (as *she* experienced it) to the spaces of the multinational, yet another patriarchal structure, but the difference is that she relies and depends upon herself. There is a definite emphasis on autonomy as she shifts from one mode of being to a radically altered one. Through her rejection of the model of the traditional heterosexual couple as a means of self-definition, Alba establishes alternative symbolic configurations that provide a locus of meaning. The experiences she undergoes, while difficult and painful, are viewed as essential stages in her maturation process; her interactions with the world help to mold and form the parameters of her subjectivity.

External exploration both parallels and contributes to the discovery of her interior self. In this context, self-awareness is depicted as piece-meal and accumulative, a trajectory of development that takes into account various steps. The unfolding of the text is hinged on the goal of retrospective self-knowledge and understanding; as a result, the aspects of the novel garner significance in relation to the various developments. That is to say, after the imprisonment of Fernando, Alba delves into discovering her own talents and nurturing herself. This dedication led to promotions as well as a profound sense of worth attached to her job. Not that she loves it, but rather it provides a means to achieve the ultimate end. Along her journey, Alba ascends to a position of more responsibility requiring her to travel to exotic places such as England and Morocco. On one of her business trips, she worked closely with Paul, the company's top client. Embodying the complete opposite of Fernando "Paul parecía un chico responsable, educado, estaba forrado y era atentísimo con ella . . . un poco pesado para su gusto y sin demasiada chispa" (203), the attention she receives from him, stemming from professional involvement yet transforming to romantic, appeals to her as well as appears to be poetic justice. The narrative voice states: "Por una vez un hombre (aunque no le gustara, daba igual) dejaba de prestar atención a una chica perfecta para atender a una mortal con defectos. Alba lo tenía claro: Paul le caía bien" (202). Moreover, due to his affinity for her, she was given certain privileges—the charge of his account, the company's largest. Her behavior is notable; while she in no way solicited his attention, professional or romantic, she utilizes the situation to her advantage. That is not to say that she allows him to seduce her or vice versa to advance further within the multinational, but rather she dedicates herself to her work while basking in the unsolicited male attention. Her colleagues, however, are not as receptive to her promotions and even accuse her of throwing herself at Paul to secure his account. This verbal attack resonates throughout her being, in particular due to the newfound pride she attaches to it. Her brilliant response to a female coworker, however, further evidences her nomadic wandering:

> De todas formas, no deberías pensar que todo el mundo consigue las cosas como tú: tirándose a los jefes. Supongo que no te lo podrás ni imaginar, pero también hay tías que logramos ir ascendiendo poco a poco por méritos propios. Si no puedes sorportarlo y necesitas pensar que escalamos puestos con tus mismos métodos es tu problema, pero a mí no me metas en tu mismo saco porque somos muy distintas. (223)

While Alba is aware that her promotion by Paul does not stem entirely from her professional merit, she also recognizes that she does not directly nor indirectly pander for his attention as a means of ascension. The ownership of her voice highlights what Maria Lugones and Elizabeth Spelman affirm. They note that possessing a voice is "integral to leading a life rather than being led through it" and "being silenced in one's own account of one's life is a kind of amputation that signals oppressions" (Lugones and Spelman 19). Alba's past silence disabled her agency, for the alternative to articulating her own experience and her own goals in her way is to live a contrived version of her self. Nevertheless, throughout her journey, Alba gradually acquires and appropriates her own voice in accord with her desires.

That she was given the most important account in her public relations firm introduces a distinct series of intrigues into the mix. Responsible for the marketing and image of Paul's company, Fake London, Alba was required to dedicate much time and energy to the success of the project that required travel to London. Indeed, as her professional devotion to this client intensified, her identity became inextricably linked to the space of the multinational:

> Lo de la cuenta de Fake London la tenía obsesionada; después de la conversación con Sara estaba convencida de que tenía que hacer todo lo posible para que aquello saliera bien. A medida que iba investigando y metiéndose en el asunto se daba cuenta de que ese trabajo le apetecía cada vez más y además tenía la corazonada de que podía conseguir su objetivo, que no era tan difícil como había pensado. (227)

While Alba received pleasure actively creating her subjectivity vis-à-vis the consumption of elements central to the multinational, her boyfriend Fernando spins further out of control, consuming a hefty array of chemical enhancements—alcohol, marijuana, and anti-anxiety pills such as lexatin—and (ironically) being consumed by his paranoid jealousy of Alba and her movements. His state of being, far from pleasurable, provides Alba with a sense of relief and also poetic justice. The narrative voice elaborates: "Había instantes en los que se sentía feliz, satisfecha de que la justicia poética se impusiera y Fernando pudiera entender (por propia experiencia) lo que ella había sentido cuando tardaba dos días más de lo previsto en volver de una gira o si no la llamaba a la hora que había quedado. Pero su satisfacción no era plena" (228). Interestingly, Alba recognizes that their situations are ironically reversed; while she does not wish this feeling of impotence on anyone, it does lead to further 'rhizomatic' contemplation regarding her own state of affairs. For the first time she consciously noted the message her subconscious has been attempting to send her for months: "A lo mejor deberíamos dejarlo" (229). While these words—a rupture in the relationship—appeared frightful to Alba for years, to the point that she tolerated emotional negligence and abuse to not hear them from Fernando, recently they hinted at liberation:

> La ruptura era algo en lo que nunca había querido pensar seriamente. Le dolía demasiado y para evitarla, para conseguir que Fernando no llegara nunca a decir esas cinco palabras, había aguantado, aguantado y aguantado, hasta límites que ella misma, objetivamente, hubiera censurado. Pero desde hacía algún tiempo, la ruptura le empezaba a parecer una liberación y el miedo había cambiado de bando. Ahora Alba estaba aterrorizada por Fernando. (229)

The evolution of her feelings toward Fernando evidences a key transition in her self. Her porous character results complex and contradictory as she undergoes the process of sorting through mixed messages. Alba experiences sensations of female empowerment and liberation juxtaposed with dependence. This paradox stems from her participation within the culture of the techno scene; it is a culture of consumption, in her experience, that positions women as both commodities and consumers. Hence, she negotiates her presence within the space of the multinational in new and ambiguous ways, whereby the existence of her shifting consciousness is made concrete in moments of contradictory experience.

Alba's goal is change, and this requires that she take responsibility for her own life and actions. A patriarchal society expects women to be totally giving and available, downplaying their own needs, ambitions, and desires, as well as fears and guilts. In consuming the techno scene and the celebrity of her boyfriend, Alba repressed natural ambitions opting for martyrdom. With the advent of Fernando's incarceration, Alba arrives at the realization of her improper desiring. This working knowledge, in conjunction with her experiences inside and outside of the techno location, impulsed a willingness to act on behalf of her self and her respective desires. It is noteworthy that her business trip to London marks a culminating point in the potential separation between Alba and Fernando. The night before her departure, the couple made plans to dine out on Calle Barbieri, an evening that was quashed by Fernando's over indulgence in pharmacological enhancements, which left him in a chemically induced stupor. Stood up, worrisome Alba returns home to find her boyfriend, yet again, passed out. Her worry, nevertheless, quickly converted to intense anger. Nonetheless, she gathered her energies to focus on her advancement when she really wanted to provoke a heated argument with him: "¡Para qué? Si no se va a enterar de nada. Estará hasta arriba de pastillas y me va a poner más histérica . . . además pues no, mejor no porque podemos estar discutiendo hasta las tantas y hoy tengo que dormir bien, que mañana me espera un día fino. Que duerma o que haga lo que le dé la gana, a mí ya me la suda" (235). Effectively, Alba does not subordinate her interests or energies for those of Fernando. While her sense of self and perhaps that of her femininity are contradictory, it is within this mismatch that she triumphs. Weedon contends: "only a conscious awareness of the contradictory nature of subjectivity can introduce the possibility of political choice between modes of femininity in different situations and between the discourses in which they have their meaning" (87). Alba and her body, as a subject in process, are sites of potential revolution as she battles to define her femininity and social role while adding meaning to her experiences.

Within the location of the multinational, Alba's subjectivity is in the process of active formation. This is achieved via fleshing through a multiplicity of experiences and appropriating the knowledge gleaned to her advantage. An intrigue that portends further ambiguity and provokes profound questioning on Alba's part is the interest her "superjefe" (240) Paul takes in her. While flattered by the attention—something she feels unaccustomed to—she feels overtly manipulated by his interests. That is, upon arriving in London, a business trip that was to last for the weekend, she and her boss Santiago are told that due to issues with the marketing boss they will have the weekend free and begin business on Monday. While Santiago was pleased with the extra time—days he could devote to perusing the high-end shopping district—Alba felt otherwise. She ruminates: "no estaba tan entusiasmada, estaba prácticamente segura de que Paul sabía lo del cambio de día de la reunion hacía mucho tiempo y que les había obligado a ir antes para pasar unos días con ella" (241). In particular, Alba remains concerned because she, now, would have no excuse to not attend an overnight trip-hop festival with him. It is interesting to note that this situation provokes contemplation not only for Alba but also Paul. He wonders why this intelligent and attractive woman has captivated him, as she is not his usual type: "objectivamente podría tener bastante que envidiar a las decenas de pijas londinenses de metro ochenta, cincuenta y cinco kilos, pelo rubio perfecto, veintipocos años y educación exclusiva que andaban detrás de él desde que se había separado por última vez" (242–43). Parallely, for the protagonist this situation with Paul brought to mind Barbie dolls, gifts her grandmother brought her from the United States that sparked interest and caused jealousy among her friends, as in Spain they were commodities not readily available. She contemplates how she carried the doll around school allowing her friends to play with her Barbie: "A ella no le costaba ningún esfuerzo porque siempre había odiado las muñecas y la Barbie le parecía una hortera y mucho más aburrida que el Exin Castillos, que era con lo que se pasaba horas. . . . Y además se sentía muy culpable por no apreciar eso que todo el mundo envidiaba" (243). This timely reflection can be read as resistance to aligning herself with the patriarchal beauty cannon and her defiance of stereotypical gender expectations. Furthermore, while Alba understands that she is a commodity, she also notes that she does not have to completely buy into this dominant structure; rather in doing so, she stands to lose the autonomy that she has acquired since Fernando's incarceration. Perhaps most importantly, she arrives at a deeper understanding of her desires and needs:

> Se acordó de Fernando y se dio cuenta de que no le echaba de menos, que incluso estaba feliz de encontrarse fuera de casa, sin tener que aguantar los cambios de humor y la desidia de su novio. Por primera vez en muchos años se daba cuenta de que no estaba enamorada de nadie. Ya no quería a Fernando y, por muchos esfuerzos que hiciera, a Paul parecía que tampoco. (243)

While admitting to herself that she is not in love with either Fernando or Paul, she still finds herself in ambiguous terrain. Indeed she accepted a dinner invitation to the hippy-chic Momo, a restaurant frequented by celebrities such as Vanessa Paradis, Kate Moss and Jade Jagger, which placed her in a fashion quandary. Alba resolved the dilemma and decided to sport "un pantalón de seda salvaje verde y un top de espejitos y patchwork hindú" (247), as she wanted to fabricate a carefully chosen image: a hippie yet trendy look that did not portend a night of passionate sex. After crafting her image, in which she concomitantly commodifies herself as a culturally sophisticated and worldly woman, Alba meets up with Paul, only to become repulsed by his treatment of her. While she realizes that vis-à-vis consumption choices she fabricates herself as a type commodity, she did not create a sexually charged self. Hence, Alba becomes offended by Paul's presumptuous advances:

> Instantes después de salir del hotel, Paul la había rodeado por la cintura y Alba no sabía cómo reaccionar. Ese exceso de confianza la molestaba, pero tampoco le parecía lógico decirle que la soltara. Un par de veces, al cruzar una calle o sortear algún obstáculo, Alba se había zafado de la mano aprisionadora, pero a los pocos segundos volvía a estar ahí entre la cintura y la cadera, demasiado cerca del glúteo. (248)

Along her journey from passivity to active self-formation, Alba has fleshed through myriad experiences to uncover her true desires and likewise act on behalf of her needs. The episode that occurred in route to Momo serves as a further experience that awakens the protagonist due to her feelings of discomfort and dismay resulting from Paul's advances and his "mano aprisonadora" (248). While Alba does not access her voice, skirting his advances when possible, she does become angry with herself, thinking: "No, si a este paso, termino casándome con él por no decirle que no a nada, con la edad me estoy volviendo más gilipollas" (248). Reflecting upon her silence as well as the repercussions on her career if she were to break it, Alba heads down the path to reclaim that from which she has been disinherited. In the middle of dinner, Alba excuses herself and retreats to the bathroom where she has a revelation; after vomiting up her meal—a moment in which she felt a special particular clarity and an affinity with Fernando—she told herself: "*Cuando suba tengo que decirle a Paul lo que pienso, no puedo estar con tonterías. . . . Voy a dejarme de mentiras . . . la mentira siempre se vuelve en tu contra*" (252). Evidenced by her admission, in acquiring and fleshing through knowledge, Alba is able to express her awareness via self-possession. Upon revealing to Paul—who reacted quite well because he was convinced that with patience he would end up conquering her—that she had no romantic interest in him, Alba experienced an overwhelming sense of relief and tranquility, such that she slept the entire night and awoke with more energy than she had felt in years: "Era como si la hubieran desenterrado. Estaba pletórica sin motivo" (254). This moment of tranquility was interrupted by dark thoughts of Fernando; she wondered why he had not called her nor answered the telephone at home and this line of questioning temporarily displaced her peace as jealousy surged to the foreground. Nevertheless, her curiosity and fears were eased after reading the morning edition of the Spanish newspaper *El Mundo*.

> «Muere Fernando Duarte, el líder del grupo Asian Vibes. El guitarrista y cantante de una de las bandas más punteras del panorama independiente español falleció la tarde de ayer en su domicilio de Madrid. Fuentes cercanas a la familia afirman que la causa del deceso fue una sobredosis involuntaria de barbitúricos y alcohol. Agencia Efe». (254–55)

Within minutes of reading the obituary, Alba receives a telephone call from Pablo, who was concerned with her reaction to the news of Fernando's death. Yet she admits to him, "No, de verdad que estoy bien. No entiendo por qué, pero por primera vez en un montón de tiempo me siento muy bien, muy tranquila. . . . Te lo digo a ti porque a otro me daría vergüenza, pero es como si me hubiera liberado de algo, no sé, no puedo evitarlo" (255). Within hours of this admission, Alba returns to Madrid to attend the wake; seeing Fernando in his black velvet Dolce & Gabanna suit, Alba can only murmur "*¡Qué guapo está!*" (256), thinking about the favorable state of rigor mortis, an ironic reflection that she also makes at the opening of the novel. In the distance she heard Fernando's mother pray that he rest in peace, to which Alba could only reply: "«Sí, ya era hora, por fin descanso en paz»" (256).

Conclusions

As evidenced by the nomadic wanderings of the protagonist Alba, martyrdom not only transmits a negative message but also represents a perverse manner of expressing herself and gaining control of her life. The journey to self-awakening illustrates an attempt to (re)present and reassemble a female embodiment that in the past was given. While consumed by the techno scene and celebrity image of her boyfriend, Fernando, Alba keeps an ethic of silence. Her experiences within this territory unveil the contradictory reality of consumption, the results of which produce an unhealthy subject. This isolates her from her organic self and prevents her from creating an active female subjectivity. However, in her passage from one location to another—the territory of techno to that of the multinational, she does not annhilate her subjectivity but rather reconfigures it, invoking a self who is not terrified of solitude, a subject who is individual yet connected. Alba expresses an empowered figuration. Her actions are not a rebellion, but an essential to speak the truth of her self. Instead of placing her focus on controlling the environment surrounding her, she acts within and becomes part of an 'imagined community' of the multinational, that in complex and contradictory modes offers her the opportunity to actively create female subjectivity and experience a sense of autonomy.

Notes

1. A theremin is the grandfather of electronic music. Electronic instruments trace their roots to this particular instrument. Russian physicist Leon Theremin (1896–1993) invented the theremin.

2. British native Phil Russel was one of the proponents of the first People's Free Festival at Stonehenge. Writing in the aftermath of Woodstock, his goal was to establish communal gatherings whose primary focus was to validate an alternative existence fostered through spiritual activism and intimately linked to techno music.

3. There is much debate surrounding the genesis of techno music. Some theorists (Kumagai 1994) claim that it started in the early 1980s in the abandoned warehouses of Detroit, pioneered by three DJs named Magic (Juan Atkins), Reese (Kevin Saunderon), and Mayday (Derrik May). Nevertheless, others maintain that this phenomenon has roots in England.

4. Said's *Orientalism* has been critiqued by various scholars such as Gayatri Chakravorty Spivak and Homi Bhaba. These vocal critics question the oversimplification of Said's argument and his dichotomization of the subordinate East and dominant West. The aforementioned critics maintain that Said's conclusions promote a static vision of power dynamics, negating the possibility for negotiation or change.

5. For 450 years, Goa was a Portugese colony that became part of India in 1961. At the end of the 1960s, Goa experienced an influx of hippies invading its beautiful shores. These hippies, fleeing urban society, searched for a paradise inconceivable in the West, one devoid of multinational exploitation and Westernization.

6. The father of MDMA (Ecstasy is the marketed name) is Alexander Schulgin, a research chemist in the U.S. While Sofía did gift the members of Asian Vibes pure MDMA, she also made it exceedingly difficult for her daughter's boyfriend, Fernando, and the other group members to obtain cocaine. This was achieved by telling the "official" dealer of the festival that the boys did not use that type of drug, even though she knew otherwise.

No es que, realmente, pensara que Manolo, Marcos y Fernando no querían comprar cocaína y que les había librado de aquel «pesado». Ella sabía que los tres consumían casi a diario y con ese acto y su filosofía de que la acción individual y cotidiana consigue transformar el mundo, había conseguido que en aquella ocasión les resultara más difícil meterse unos tiros. (54)

7. During a personal interview, Grijalba commented that the majority of the visitors at Navalcarnero (that she observed) were women. According to the author, it was exceedingly rare for a father to visit his son in prison.

8. Fernando was released from prison earlier than expected due to the generosity of Zeus, Alba's wealthy brother. Appropriating his financial resources, Zeus made a donation to the Navalcarnero penitenciary to influence and facilitate the early release of Fernando. Unbeknownst to Alba or Fernando, this donation was made by her brother to ease the concerns and life of his sister, Alba.

9. Nevertheless, it is noteworthy to mention that while Fernando feels severe discomfort in posh, pretentious surroundings, he does come from an upper-middle class family. Yet, he has always tried to construct his identity as the complete opposite, as a rebellious counterculture rock star.

CHAPTER SIX

Los placeres de Anastasia:
Sexing It Up!

"Nadie conoce mi cuerpo mejor que yo." (124)

Cultural Context

Published in 2004, *Los placeres de Anastasia* is a collaboration between a journalist, Anna García Nuñez, and the subject, Susana Plané (stage name Anastasia). A biographical account of Susana Plané's history of sexuality, the book presents a vision of the notion of Braidotti's "nomad." Through her various experiences Susana Plané owns her body and the passionate delight that she gleans from it, experiencing libidinal pleasure as an autonomous subject.

Born in the 1980s in L'Hospitalet de Llobregat, Spain, a city outside of Barcelona, Susana was exposed to a distinct discourse—not only on a societal level but also the familial. To begin with, her family was not only exceedingly liberal, but also completely and unconditionally open-minded with respect to sexuality. On a parallel level, within the Spain of the 1990s sexual equality was the law. Nevertheless, the reality remains distinct. There was a collectivity of consciousness that had demanded equality as well as denounced discrimination. Likewise, there was a growing population of liberals (Riera 176), although much to this day remains to be done with respect to gender equality. During the 1990s, feminism in Spain was active; nevertheless, there existed a patent difference between the equality of man and woman. Riera affirms:

> Hoy la condición femenina que se vende va desde la «superwoman» a la «moderna ama de casa». Una y otra solo se diferencian porque una trabaja fuera de

casa (y además en alguna profesión cualificada) y la otra cuida básicamente de su hogar pero ya no es «la ama de casa aburrida y encerrada todo el día entre las cuatro paredes de su hogar». Ambas tienen estudios, son agradables, guapas, visten a la moda, son cariñosas, activas sexualmente, quieren y educan a sus hijos, saben ser compañeras de sus maridos, les encanta salir y se desenvuelven perfectamente en su vida social. Las dos seguirán encargándose de sus casas, aunque para las tareas más pesadas pueden contratar a una asistenta. Estos son los prototipos de mujeres que mejor representan esta «moderna» femininidad a finales del siglo XX. (177)

Riera affirms that within Spain in the 1990s there existed two categories of women, which, while being unique, shared commonalities. On the one hand there was the superwoman; that is, the career woman focused on climbing the ladder of success. The other prototype is the traditional housewife, charged primarily with the care of the children and the home. While distinct, these two factions are equally subject to the care of the home domain. His quote implicitly asserts that within Spain being woman is equivalent to being linked to the domestic sphere, a position of abjection and passivity.

According to Riera:

La emancipación de las jóvenes como personas adultas solo es posible si el proceso de transición que comporta su juventud busca el mismo objetivo que históricamente ha sido privilegio del otro 50 por 100 de la humanidad: la autonomía psicológica y económica que le permite proyectar sus capacidades en igualdad de condiciones con el otro sexo. (196)

This potential emancipation of young women of the nineties is buttressed by psychological and economic autonomy. The intersection of financial and emotional stability, consequently, allows these young women to inscribe on their bodies their equal capability with respect to the masculine economy. Since her youth, Susana has achieved this emancipation, as she is an autonomous subject freely electing, while subverting societal norms, her lifestyle. Anastasia's body is inscribed with a plethora of cultures of consumption: sex, dancing, fashion, playboy girl, porn star, and her desire to be an object looked upon. This biographical account is a testimony of a happy, uninhibited, and consumerist urban tribe.

Aside from the liberal influence of her parents, Susana was raised in the 1990s amidst an environment in which the focus was placed on the day, rather than the future. In a study of Spanish youth attitudes undertaken by Amando de Miguel in 1998, he affirms that this young milieu, in large part, followed the adage "carpe diem." He asserts: "«el futuro es tan inseguro para los jóvenes que lo mejor es vivir al día.... Destaca la significación del «presente», sea para divertirse o consumir" (257). The present time and space is that which occupies the minds of the youth culture. On a parallel level in thinking only of the present, the youth's beliefs and attitudes towards sex have become quite liberal, and indeed, the act of sexual intercourse normal outside of matrimony.

> Se destaca cada vez más como experiencia placentera. Los jóvenes de finales de este siglo incorporan esa nueva concepción de la sexualidad, que les es, por otra parte especialmente favorable. El inicio de la vida sexual activa no coincide con el comienzo del establecimiento en pareja. (258)

As Amando de Miguel elaborates, the youth culture in the 1990s has become much more permissive with respect to sexuality. Furthermore, it is not an act committed under duress, but rather one considered pleasurable by both the female and the male. This is noteworthy as historically female sexuality has been stigmatized and shrouded in shame. Maintaining a monogamous relationship, moreover, does not necessarily coincide with the decision to engage in sexual activity. Amando de Miguel's results demonstrate that "la mayoría de los jóvenes considera que está bien que los adolescentes (15 a 17 años) y los jóvenes (18 a 29 años) tengan relaciones sexuales completas sin estar casados" (258). Hence, as the survey elucidates, the institution of marriage is not only unessential, but not even a concern for the act of intercourse to occur. Furthermore, these results highlight the young age at which people are experimenting and exploring their sexuality, according to the survey, fifteen years old. Perhaps most significant, though, is the favorable reaction towards youths and young adults engaging in intercourse without commitments.

Keeping in mind the survey undertaken by Amando de Miguel and Riera's sociological study of girls and women in Spain throughout the twentieth century, it is interesting to explore the identity of Susana Plané, the protagonist of *Los placeres de Anastasia*. Stage name Anastasia Mayo, Susana Plané was conscious of and enjoyed her sexuality from the age of seven. Since that time sex has figured prominently in her choice of consumption in various ways. Through a friend, Juan, whom she meets on a sex hot line, she is introduced into the erotic, first working as a model for nude photos progressing to a star actress in pornography. While some may consider sex to be an addiction of Anastasia's, she declares with fortitude:

> Ahora soy Anastasia Mayo. Es mi nombre artístico. Hasta me han entrevistado en la tele. Mis padres, como padres de una actriz porno, también han sido

200 ~ Chapter Six

> invitados a la tele. Poco a poco, Oscar [novio de nueve años] se ha ido acostumbrando a mi nuevo trabajo. Sabe que lo hago por dinero pero también porque me gusta . . . yo ya estoy subida en la escalera del éxito. He empezado trabajando con los grandes, Max Cortés, Nacho Vidal, Rocco Siffreddi . . . y el móvil, hoy, sigue quemando . . . voy muy bien de autoestima. (122–23)

At the age of twenty-five, Anastasia won the prize "Ninfa" in the last Festival Erótico de Barcelona. She has appeared in movies such as "Serial Fucker 3," directed by Max Cortés, in "Maniacos en busca de coñitos virgenes," produced by Greg Cantauro and Ian Scott, as well as in the series "Torbe y sus Cerdilla" Volume 1 distributed by IFG. Most recently she starred in "Rocco Meats Suzie." Proud of her achievements, she considers herself an artist that performs her job for two fundamental reasons: (1) the money, and (2) the pleasure she gleans from it. Not only is she a porn actress, but also she has become renowned within Spain working with top caliber male actors, while being offered new jobs. Most importantly, she affirms that she is full of self-esteem.

This chapter is divided into three parts: "Awakening to Sexuality," "Dress Me Up, Dress Me Down!" and finally "Performance and Pornography." Each section treats the various consumption practices of the protagonist, Anastasia. Through the optic of consumption, we arrive at an understanding of how she embodies and inscribes on her body that which she elects to consume and, consequently, the neo-tribe to which she belongs. Furthermore, it will become evident that she incarnates Braidotti's notion of the feminist-female subject via her conscious manipulations of the dominant paradigm, feeling empowered all the while.

Awakening to Sexuality

> Lolita, light of my life, fire of my loins. My sin,
> my soul. Lo-lee-ta: the tip of the tongue taking a
> trip of three steps down the palate to tap, at three,
> on the teeth. Lo. Lee. Ta. (Nabokov 9)

"Con siete años ya sabía darme placer" (7). From a very tender age Susana was conscientious of her sexuality and also aware of how to please herself: "Al principio todo consistía en tocarme un poquito" (7). Through self-exploration, she became familiar with her body and the pleasures she could give to herself. While considering herself a typical child, she also felt alone due to the fact that her parents worked intensive hours. Despite the strenuous schedules of her parents, she did not become saddened, but rather on the contrary she was quite happy. This happiness stemmed from that fact that she always stood out due to her beauty: "ese gracejo que no pasaba desapercibido para nadie, y además, guapa. Me caían piropos a manta: «¡Pero qué niña más guapa! ¡Y qué bien baila!» Porque el baile como el sexo, también lo llevaba muy dentro" (7).

The discovery of her sexuality was purely casual, as she happened to find erotic magazines hidden in her grandparents' house, a place she passed the hours when her parents worked. As such, every afternoon when she would return home from school she would turn on the television to "Sesame Street" and touch herself. Watching the cartoons, her mind would conjure up images of the nude photos she saw in the hidden magazines and imitate them: "ponía mi pequeña mano en el sexo carnoso, sin vello, y la empezaba a mover. ¡Cómo me gustaba!" (8). Nevertheless, she did not experience these moments as ones of sexual nature, but rather they rooted themselves in innocence. Furthermore, these times of exploration served the purpose of relieving her of the weight of her solitude. Her afternoons of sexual experimentation alleviated her dissatisfaction of not being able to see her parents. In no moment does she place blame onto her parents for the distance imposed on the family, but rather "ese espacio vacío que tenía clavado dentro de mi lo llenaba artificialmente masturbándome" (8). In her perspective, far from being an obsession, masturbation converted into a very pleasant daily routine. This daily routine, however, did not remain an activity relegated to the proxemics of her home; in school, she would sit in the back of the classroom so as to go unnoticed by the instructor and touch herself. Anastasia's scholastic endeavors, however, were not easy for her due to her inability to concentrate and consequently her grades suffered. She recognizes the fact that she was a substandard student, but is quick to highlight her strengths as well: "me convertí en una magnífica masturbadora" (9). This quote underlines that the sexual is an affirmation. While there is normally shame tied to sexuality in childhood, Anastasia negates that feeling, rising to the full level of aesthetic satisfaction. Irigaray affirms that women, because they have been caught in a world structured by man-centered concepts, have had no way of knowing or representing themselves. But she offers as the starting point for a female self-consciousness the facts of women's bodies and women's sexual pleasure, precisely because they have been so absent or so misrepresented in male discourse. Women, she says, experience a diffuse sexuality arising, for example, from the "two lips" of the vulva, and a multiplicity of libidinal energies that cannot be expressed or understood within the identity-claiming assumptions of phallocentric discourse: "I am a unified, coherent being, and what is significant in the world reflects my male image"

(*Speculum* 7). Irigaray argues further that female sexuality explains women's problematic relationship to (masculine) logic and language:

> *Woman has sex organs just about everywhere.* She experiences pleasure almost everywhere.... The geography of her pleasure is much more diversified, more multiple in its differences, more complex, more subtle, than is imagined-in an imaginary [system] centered a bit too much on one and the same.
>
> "She" is infinitely other in herself. That is undoubtedly the reason she is called temperamental, incomprehensible, perturbed, capricious—not to mention her language in which "she" goes off in all directions and in which "he" is unable to discern the coherence of any meaning. Contradictory words seem a little crazy to the logic of reason, and inaudible for him who listens with ready-made grids, a code prepared in advance. In her statements—at least when she dares to speak out—woman retouches herself constantly. (8)

Irigaray concedes that women's discovery of their autoeroticism will not, by itself, arrive automatically or enable them to transform the existing order: "For a woman to arrive at the point where she can enjoy her pleasure as a woman, a long detour by the analysis of the various systems that oppress her is certainly necessary" (9). Irigaray herself writes essays using Marxist categories to analyze men's use and exchange of women, and in others she uses female physiology as a source of critical metaphors and counterconcepts against physics, pornography, Nietzsche's misogyny, and myth (10), rather than literally. Yet her focus on the physical bases for the difference between male and physical sexuality remains the same: women must recognize and assert their *jouissance* if they are to subvert phallocentric oppression at its deepest levels. Irigaray and Cixous go further: if women are to discover and express who they are, to bring to the surface what masculine history has repressed in them, they must begin with their sexuality. And their sexuality begins with their bodies, with their genital and libidinal difference from men. Vis-à-vis her experiences at a tender age, Anastasia experiences her own sense of *jouissance* through the realization of her female sexuality. Placing in the forefront her sexuality, Anastasia is a nomad wandering through various proxemics, partaking in new experiences that, indeed, lead her to subvert the phallocentric economy.

Released from inhibitions and conscious of her sexuality, Anastasia shared information about her masturbation rendezvous with some of her girlfriends from school. Together, they would play childhood touching games of exploration and discovery, teasing each other by saying "«¡A que te toco el culo!»" or "«¡A que te toco las tetas!»" (9). And with one of her girlfriends, she progressed even further sexually. The sharing of information and experimentation with her girlfriends proved to be relaxing, reaffirming, and regenerating for Susana because she did not feel that she was a "chica rara" (10); others, too, were experimenting with their sexuality and attaining sexual pleasure. At times she and her girlfriend would feel each other up in the territory of school bathroom and also in the space of her bedroom. While she and her friends participated in these innocent games, they were gazed upon by Susana's idols: Barbie and Ken dolls. When they finished their experimentation and her friend left, she would play with her Barbie and Ken dolls, inventing lives for them. Interestingly, Barbie, a globalized product, remained the standard of beauty that Susana hoped to attain: beautiful, elegant, slender, and very blonde. Barbie represented her idol as a youth to the point that she wanted to imitate her and possess the magic that she believed the doll to incarnate. "Yo también quiero que se note mi presencia cuando voy por la calle, que no pase desapercibida como la Barbie" (10). This quote is significant as it lends importance to the fixation on beauty, the beauty of the body, the naked human body. According to Calefato: "Barbie es cada vez más la soberana de los sueños lúdicos de las niñas" (149). Imitating the Barbie doll, indeed, was a dream of Anastasia's as she was attracted to the doll's long silky blond hair, the same hair that she herself possessed. Yet it does not stop there. Barbie stands out as: "Reina de los encuentros mundanos, experta decoradora, modelo refinada y deportista de fama: todo eso y más es Barbie" (150). In other words, Barbie was the equivalent of superwoman. Anastasia, too, excelled in the same ways due to her admiration of this doll. Nevertheless, when Susana entered her teenage years, Barbie and Ken ceased to be her idols; they fell to the wayside to be filled by other globalized icons such as Tom Cruise, Leonardo DiCaprio, Kevin Costner, and most importantly, Brad Pitt.

At the age of fourteen, the protagonist fell in love and had her first boyfriend, Sergio. This relationship, moreover, initiates her first sexual experience with a boy: "con él había revolcones y toqueteos en su casa, los fines de semana, cuando sus padres se iban a la torre. Poníamos música romántica de fondo y nos besábamos, juntábamos nuestros cuerpos, nos masturbábamos y ya está" (12). Another first with Sergio was going to the movies. They elected to see Almodóvar's *Tacones lejanos* purely due to the catchy, sexy title. Seeing this movie remained a memorable, if not unforgettable, experience for Anastasia as the movie contained many sexually explicit scenes that served to intensify her intrigue. She elaborates: "a mí se me quedó grabada la de Miguel Bosé follando con Victoria Abril en el camerino mientras el marido de ella estaba esperándola fuera" (12). The scene engraved in her memory, Miguel and Victoria in the act of intercourse while her husband waited outside, not only hints at Anastasia's fascination with sex, but also her subversion of the supposedly natural notion of the traditional woman.

Another affinity of Susana's intimately linked with the expression of her sexuality was her utter love for dancing. From a very early age she stood out as the one who would go out onto the dance floor and dance without shame, regardless of the proxemics. For instance, at family parties, she would unabashedly claim her space within the territory of dance, even going to the extreme to create a dance floor if one did not exist. Due to her suave dance moves, she received accolades from her parents as well as people that watched her. This collectivity of people: "no se cansaba de decirles [a sus padres] que tenían una niña preciosa que bailaba divinamente" (13). In her opinion, dancing came naturally such that she could dance to whatever music was playing. If not viewing cartoons, she not only watched music videos, but also imitated the artists. A North American icon that she consumed was Madonna; she blatantly admits that through watching Madonna she learned a substantial amount about dancing, music, and sexuality. She declares: "Me sabía todas sus canciones, todos sus movimientos, hasta compraba los libros que hablaban de ella" (13). According to Susana, her icon—Madonna—moved in a sensual, provocative, and wild manner that impressed her, and opened up a new space for female creativity. She was also attracted to this global icon due to her very liberal ideology regarding sexuality. Madonna, removed of inhibitions, presents a persona that eschews the thoughts, opinions, and beliefs of others. As a result of her mannerisms, style, and convictions, this global pop star was a woman with whom the protagonist could identiy. This identification stems from the coalescence of sexuality and dancing. In this line of inquiry, dancing is a manifestation of sexuality. Via the act of dancing, women may assert their subjectivity, ignoring prescriptions and norms. As such, this outlet creates an intimate connection between female conscious and sexuality.

The proxemics of the dance club is where Susana felt abundantly comfortable within her skin. Due to the manner in which she danced, where she danced, and the fact that she did not stop dancing until she left the club for the evening were all factors that contributed to her being the focus of the gaze, both masculine and feminine. Anastasia had a routine; that is, she was accustomed to dancing brazenly in the highest part of the dance floor so that everyone present could see her. The dual elements of the dance floor and its dancers provide a sense of community. Vis-à-vis dancing, these participants, including Anastasia, are able to express themselves and their sexuality while having a good time. For Anastasia, dancing in public is not only a way of attracting people and their gazes to her body, but it is perhaps the only way that she can demonstrate, in public, her limberness, her flexibility, her sense of rhythm, and her ability to gyrate. "Mi metro y medio de estatura se alargaba unos cuantos centímetros más sobre zapatos o botas de plataforma y mi culo, virginal y bien esculpido, era el faro que atraía las miradas" (15). Of interest, she denotes her derriere as a lighthouse attracting all of the looks and attention in the club. Her derriere as a metaphoric lighthouse draws the masculine gaze, bringing them to a sense of home, her sexuality. "The gaze of the spectators clearly aids in the delineation and structure of power relationships. The person who gazes looks upon a person, object, or place. In this context, the act of looking is commonly thought of as awarding more power to the person who is looking than to the person who is the object of the look" (Starken and Cartwright 100). I contend, however, that this is not the case for Susana; she is far from a passive object. She desires and commands to be looked at as it bolsters her identity and validates her sexuality. Moreover, she gleans power from the gazes of the onlookers. She elaborates: "Cuando la gente de la discoteca enloquecía con una canción, yo seguía allá arriba y, de alguna manera, los incitaba, con mis movimientos de serpiente, a que sus cuerpos brincaran aún más" (15). Vis-à-vis her serpent-like movements she inspired the onlookers to lose their inhibitions and dance with abandon. I suggest that Anastasia's dancing and specific location—from a high position—have the potential to expand understandings of female sexuality beyond the binary "good girl/bad girl" images that often saturate the media. When a woman who is assumed to be a "good girl" goes to the highest position, dancing with a pole, she is suggesting that her sexuality need not be limited to a simple binary understanding. This woman is challenging norms and subverting mainstream notions of how a woman should act and present herself. Hence, Susana defies the notion that dance, music, and sexuality are rooted in the patriarchy. Likewise, she challenged the notion of female display, as she is not reduced to mere spectacle, but rather there is a clear semiotic intention behind her image and corporeal movements. I assert that Susana's affirmation of positive and creative sexuality provides her with a sense of self-empowerment and control of her sexuality, both integral to the notion of becoming and Braidotti's concept of the nomad.

Due to her shameless joy for dancing as well as her excellent moves, Anastasia was offered a position as a dancer, earning money, at a number of clubs. From her perspective, this was the ideal job: dancing and getting paid for what she loved most. As such, she did not give it a second thought and furthermore, her parents thought it was a great idea. Interestingly, she notes that she would do what she is doing—dancing on display—for free: "Empecé bailando por las tardes y cobrando un dinerito, 5.000 pesetas por sesión, aunque yo no lo hacía por dinero, hubiera bailado gratis si me lo hubieran pedido" (15). While she felt strong about herself and her identity as well as her job, she was not exempt from the criticism of other women who would call her various pejorative names: "«eres una zorra», «una puta», «una guarra»" (15). She did not allow these labels—all associated with prostitution—to diminish her self-esteem. Rather, she brilliantly realized that women are their own worst enemies: " . . . a mí no me afectaban porque pensaba que la que estaba bailando y disfrutando con lo que hacía era yo. Les daba rabia que yo atrajera las miradas de sus amigos o novios. Era envidia, las mujeres somos así. En vez de ayudarnos entre nosotras, parece que disfrutamos jodiéndonos" (15). In the face of hypocrisy and gossip, Anastasia creates an autonomous self, rooted in her own search for happiness, while dismissing the misogynistic innuendo and slander. Thus, go-go dancing proves to be liberation for Anastasia as she grooves to the music, moves her body with grace and confidence, and captivates her audience with her power. This line of thought recalls Deleuze and Guattari's notion of becoming woman. These philosophers elaborate:

> Becoming-woman involves carrying the indeterminacy, movement, and paradox of the female stereotype past the point at which it is recuperable by the society as it presently functions, over the limit beyond which lack of definition becomes the positive power to select a trajectory (the leap from the real of possibility into the virtual—breaking away). (87)

Rather than rethinking "women's work," "ways of being/knowing," etc., as the cultural feminists of the 1980s and earlier proposed, Deleuze appropriates an alternative in the meaning of woman altogether. He argues that paradigmatic alteration is essential to yield the positive change in material conditions that answers the demand for a wider range of potential gender expressions. In order to be successful at dismantling the traditional metaphysical understanding of sexual difference, Deleuze argues that both women and men must think and traverse beyond gender. The intentional divestments of hegemonic gender intertwined within becoming-woman, it is reasoned, can potentiate the evolution of the existing social order for the better.

While Deleuze's application offers promise, I approach a crucial question Deleuze neglects to address: the difference between man and woman. Deleuze proposes that becoming-woman transpires when woman ceases to embody the tradition; she is dynamic, molecular, and in the process of evolution. Nevertheless, Deleuze overlooks a decisively important reality: the stakes and investments for men and women are not the same with respect to the project of becoming-woman. Feminists, notwithstanding, can apply those aspects of Deleuzian thought that enable our own dynamic yet materially grounded becomings. Early feminist responses to Deleuze's situation of "becoming woman" outside of empirical gender raised suspicions such as those voiced by Rosi Braidotti in her text *Nomadic Subjects*:

> Clearly, the woman occupies a troubled area in this radical critique of phallogocentrism: insofar as woman is positioned dualistically as the other of this system, she is also annexed to it. Deleuze—not uncharacteristically ignorant of the basic feminist epistemological distinction between Woman as representation and women as concrete agents of experience—ends up making distinction internal to the category of woman herself. (116)

Other feminist critics of Deleuze were concerned that becoming-woman threatens to make material conditions faced by women within contemporary culture appear to be abstract. Feminists argue that the demand for social and sexual autonomy was and still is an important aspect of feminist praxis. It appeared to these critics as if women, who have historically been condemned to the body, yet dispossessed of their bodies, were being asked by Deleuze to think of their bodies as something inorganic, less than real. Collectively, they pose the following questions and concerns: How can we deconstruct a subjectivity over which we have never enjoyed control? How can we jettison the category of sex when no sexual symmetry has ever been achieved? Although they may not have identified themselves explicitly as corporeal feminists, these critics were, nevertheless, at the forefront of a critical and ongoing dialogue between philosophy, feminism, and the body.

Sexual difference indeed is a reality and a primary and essential aspect of human subjectivity. As a go-go girl, Anastasia represents the hottest woman on the scene; she is the queen of the club. Whether in a cage or on a podium, she represents the chosen person. Most significantly, she loves to dance and dance and dance, and gets paid for it too. As a go-go girl, her choice of clothing is noteworthy. Go-go girls wear makeup and little kinky white boots or platforms, an essential material good for the protagonist. Women that belong to these neo-tribes generally take meticulous care of their hair and don little dresses or bikinis. Within this tribe, the bodies of these women may be read as texts, decoded by the masses via their continual negotiation of identity construction. The protagonist, too, elects to wear a bikini paired with her sexy high-heeled white boots. Specifically, Anastasia's choice of vestment inscribes her body charging it with a highly sexualized nature. She elaborates: "Casi todas las tardes de los fines de semana me montaban con unos amigo en un autocar que salía de Viladecans, con mi mochila llena de trapos, bikinis, botas de plataforma y adornos" (16). Prepared, she was; by way the consumption of showing off her bikini as well as her body, Anastasia articulates an identity that subverts hegemony, while being legible to the masses. Not only do her actions defy patriarchal norms, but also she receives agency and libidinal pleasure from her job. Due to her liberal background, Anastasia was not taught to associate shame with female sexuality, yet another attack on the dominant paradigm. More importantly, she did not have to hide her chosen job from friends nor family, again reinforcing her organic relationship with her body. Indeed, the protagonist was supported and aided in her endeavors by her close friends and, even more noteworthy, her family. Her parents, both in their late thirties, could not have been more proud of their daughter much to the surprise of her friends. "Mis amigas no entendían que a mis padres les parecieron bien que hiciera de go-go. . . . Yo incluso pedía a los míos que vinieran a recogerme cuando acababa la discoteca, porque al verlos me sentía más seguro" (17).

At the age of sixteen, while dancing in the club Tutan, she met her future long-term boyfriend Oscar. That particular day, she performed assuming a childlike look juxtaposed with the sultriness of a Lolita. "Aquel día llevaba un bikini muy mini. La parte de arriba, anudada al cuello, realzaba mis pechos. La braguita era un tanga y llevaba unas botas con plataforma de color blanco. El pelo, recogido en una colita, me hacía más niña y, al mismo tiempo, aun más mis ojos rasgados. Iba de Lolita" (17). Her projected look, composed of a cocktail of accoutrements, produces a hybrid: sultry, sexy, yet adorned with a youthful innocence. The look of youthfulness is significant as it places her in a traditional category; she represents a girl who has not been penetrated by a man. In this line of inquiry, it brings to mind the biblical myth of mother Mary, a virgin who conceived through Immaculate Conception. Through the style she chooses to adopt, Anastasia is by virtue associated with this notion. Yet, at the same time enter power dynamics; as a young girl, Anastasia represents one of the many male fantasies as her perceived naïveté supposedly lends power and domination to the masculine.

Essentially, Anastasia's image is juxtaposed with the basic element of the Lolita. The term Lolita was coined by the Russian author Vladimir Nabokov and remains the very title of one of his novels.[1] The word refers to an adolescent girl considered to be very seductive, especially if the girl is younger than the age of consent. In the marketing of pornography, this word, Lolita, has been used to refer to any attractive woman who has only recently reached, or is still younger than, the age of consent, or sometimes to refer to women who only appear younger than the age of consent. In this vein, the concept of Lolita relies on a childlike innocence that is not childish in the least. This hybrid look that Anastasia consumes—part child and part seductress—and the protagonist's performance subvert the unitary notion of Woman; she is multiple, molecular, and ascertains an active agency. While some may argue that Anastasia, as a go-go girl, remains pure simulacra, I assert that she is a hybrid comfortable with her sexuality and being gazed upon. Indeed, she gleans power from the ever-pursuing voyeur gaze of the crowds, and in particular that night, Oscar's gaze. Anastasia elaborates upon Oscar: "En seguida me di cuenta de que había puesto sus ojos en mí, así que no dudé en mover el culo a consciencia. Y claro, tenía a la gente bailando a mis pies, sabía que él tenía una buena visión de mi cuerpo" (17). To digress, some scholars contend that those that possess the gaze retain the power and the object looked upon remains passive spectacle. This, however, does not prove to be with case. Anastasia is the one with the power and the control. While she does exhibit and take pride in certain body parts, such as her "culo," she is by no means reduced to those parts. Indeed, working within the proxemics of the club, she is a commodity and conscious of her currency; nevertheless, in no way does she feel dehumanized nor a mere sexual object. The antipornography faction, scholars such as Catherine MacKinnon and Andrea Dworkin, disavow individual control over thought and actions, yet this remains a debased view of humanity and does not offer an escape from the binary opposition of Woman/Man.

> Typically, [Dworkin and MacKinnon] disregard the work of social psychologists for whom the relationship between attitudes and behaviour, between what we think and what we do is problematic. According to social psychologists, the relationship is . . . largely indeterminate; there is no way of specifying what the behavioral outcomes are of specific attitudes, especially when we live in a world of contradictory messages. . . .
>
> Our distinctively human capacity is to think, select, interpret and reinterpret content, to read texts on different levels and in different ways. The result is a broad spectrum of possible attitudes which loop back to shape how we read future texts. . . .
>
> Thus, when Dworkin-MacKinnon collapse the distinction between dream and deed, fantasy and act, thought and behavior, they construct a Skinnerian model of human nature which, in turn, justifies an elaborate system of social control. (Qtd. in Strossen 147)

An image that one woman perceives as misogynistic discrimination may for another woman reaffirm her desires and her equality; an image that one woman conceives of as subordinating, another may perceive as liberating, as is the case for Anastasia. Anti-pornography feminists assert that women have historically and persistently been subjugated in the realm of sexuality; nonetheless, that perspective is highly debatable. Carol Cassell elaborates: "Sex has historically been a commodity. It's a valuable source of power.... Sexual power is . . . the female commodity" (Qtd. in Strossen 151). Along the same line of thought, Nancy Friday has contended that "women have always derived power from withholding sex" (ibid). Thus, images that superficially portray a sexually subordinate female may be interpreted as going against the grain; they may be read as a protest of the inequalities and the lack of recognition of difference within the domain of sexuality. For example, while gyrating her body to the rhythmic beats, the protagonist clearly notices that she commands Oscar's undivided attention. As his gaze penetrates her, she also utilizes her gaze, as a weapon, to glean power. She confesses:

> Yo, disimuladamente, le lanzaba una miradita con estos ojos verdosos que he sacado de la mezcla del color de los ojos de mi madre y de mi padre. Los ojos, mi mirada, mi otra arma. En ese juego de ver pero no tocar yo sabía que llevabe ventaja. Era evidente que le gustaba lo que estaba viendo, y yo me apliqué para que mis movimientos fueran más insinuantes. (18)

Through the power of her gaze and the gyrations of her body, she controls, plays with, and intensely captivates Oscar. She personifies herself as sexually autonomous and in complete control of her sexual destiny. By way of choices in cultures of consumption, Anastasia expresses herself as a pure exhibitionist who celebrates the personal growth she experiences through her dancing performances.

Anastasia's commanding presence of sexuality is not only apparent within the proxemics of the dance club, but also in other locales, or while she is simply walking down the street. Even though she was in a committed relationship with Oscar, she still elected to validate herself through the men's reactions to her physical presence and corporeal movements. For her, this charade was but one of the ways in which she affirms her existence: "ya buscaba gustar a todos los demás. Era mi forma de reafirmarme como persona. Quería, más bien necesitaba, que me desearan, que se fijaran en mí, y hacía todo lo posible para atraer la atención de los chicos" (23). In consideration of Anastasia's confession, it is necessary to state that certain feminists may read her need for validation as a weakness of the passive woman. In their line of inquiry, she would be considered dependent and at the whims of a man, lacking agency and representation, always incarnating the absence. Yet, I elect to consider her actions and testimonies through a distinct optic. I contend that her behavior remains empowering to her and also allows her to reduce men to pathetic simpletons, befuddled by her beauty.

> Era muy consciente de mi físico, del morbito que les daba a los chicos y también a los hombres; no pasaba desapercibida para ellos. Los ojos masculinos se perdían entre mis piernas, en la raja de mi culo y en mi cara de niña guapa, y a la vez, aguerrida. Así se disparaba mi autoestima.
>
> Me gustaba, aún me gustaba, ir por la calle y escuchar «¡ay, que guapa!» o un simple «¡joliiiiiin!», mientras me comen con la mirada pero eso no quiere decir que esa persona sea mi tipo. No me enrollo con cualquiera, no soy una ninfómana. Pero los piropos, vengan de donde vengan, me alimentan, me dan vida. (23)

The previous quote exemplifies, yet again, the power Anastasia gleans from being gazed upon. From a different angle, that is the masculine one, she may remain a commodity and represent nothing more than spectacle for sore eyes. Yet, how she experiences being gazed upon is quite the contrary. It activates her, energizes her, gives her agency, and allows her to play power games with men, games in which she has total control because she incarnates their unfulfilled desire. She further empowers herself by stating that she is not a nymphomaniac nor does she sleep around; rather, she teases men with her beauty, a weapon that she knows how to wield. Moreover, she reiterates that she does not actively search out men for company or sexual pleasure; at the same time, this young woman asserts that if she has an interest she will hunt them down. "Pero no soy de esas que van por ahí buscando un tío para follar, no salgo a la calle desesperada. Pero si me buscan, y a mí me apetece, los cazo" (24). Anastasia reaffirms the power of her sexuality and her desire by way of the aforemention quote. She is not in need of a man, yet if she finds one pleasing she will hunt them down. The choice of words "cazo" is both noteworthy and strong, as it is a term generally associated with the masculine economy. Nevertheless, she re-appropriates the term for her own usage, elucidating her agency vis-à-vis her movements within the patriarchal paradigm. According to her negotiation and appropriation of this term, she utilizes it to describe how she approaches a man in which she is interested. Yet again, through her confessions, the reader is presented with a young woman who knows what she wants and is not afraid to achieve it. Removed from the margins, she retains total control over her female sexuality.

From a very young age, Anastasia has incarnated Braidotti's concept of a nomad. Refusing to be categorized, she is dynamic and multiple. In this vein, she contemplates her experiences in a rhizomic manner, linking her love for dance and her appreciation for her sexuality as fundamental components of her identity. These elements emerged during her adolescence and have continued to shape and confect her lifestyle. Through her words and actions, she negates the unitary concept of Woman. While she may work in and traverse territories deemed as patriarchal, she subverts the norms and experiences autonomy that offers her libidinal returns.

Dress Me Up, Dress Me Down!

The body, metaphorically speaking, is akin to a hanger that not only displays but also embodies the clothed self. At the same time, the clothed body is a vehicle that projects a multitude of representations according to individual taste, legible to the masses. In this context, body dressing disguises the body, which consequently results in the codification of the exterior, endowing it with social meaning. Wittgenstein proposes an incisive metaphor for clothing: "El lenguaje disfraza los pensamientos. Es justamente de este modo que desde la forma exterior del traje no se puede concluir en la forma del pensamiento revestido; ya que la forma exterior del traje está formada por otras finalidades que no son exactamente las de dar a conocer la forma del cuerpo" (Qtd. in *El sentido de vestir*, Calefato 13). As Wittgenstein elucidates, clothing functions as a type of syntax that encodes and inscribes the body, at the same time that it permits it to transmit messages to society at large to be read textually. Body dressing and decoration serve to create the body and construct it within the surrounding world. Consumption of fashion is not a moral issue, but rather it stands out as an aesthetic choice that defines the person. Of high significance, the value of body dressing lies not in the usage of the clothing, but in its ability to communicate to the masses. Calefato affirms:

> El valor de un objeto no consiste ni en su funcionalidad—en su valor de uso—ni tampoco en su valor de intercambio entendido en un sentido tradicional. En la época actual, que se puede definir como época de la comunicación total, el valor hay que entenderlo precisamente como valor comunicativo cuya medida está fundada, sobre todo, en la innovación y en la velocidad. (20)

In this line of inquiry, fashion is a system of signs that speak to the world about the person and this process is understood as a continuum. In electing a particular style, a person also expresses a relationship with the world and particular subcultures. At the same time, the body retains fantastic power by way of its entrance into world commodification and fetishization. Simply stated, the clothed body ceases to be just a body, rather by virtue of personal choices the body has converted into an interactive and active symbol. Calefato states:

> A través de las mascaras de la mundanalidad, el cuerpo revestido es hoy en día algo más que un cuerpo "automático," más que, por así decirlo, el cuerpo en la era de su reproducibilidad técnica. Se ha convertido en un cuerpo mutante, es decir, en un cuerpo que cambia su apariencia en virtud de valores relacionales, en virtud de una especie de categoría de la alteridad implícita en lo "mudano." Estos valores producen estilos de vida que pueden dirigir hacia elecciones estéticas, fuerzas, comportamientos, aspiraciones y proyectos que, de otro modo, no estarían "a la altura de los tiempos" sino en forma convencional y subordinada. (66)

Fashion, thus, may be considered as a system capable of guaranteeing mediation between likes, common sense, and community. It situates itself as an immediate method of communication as well as a constitution of aesthetical election. Whether the clothes are name brand or vintage, they retain meaning and extend their symbolic value much further than the simple reference of the individual. It is fair to say that aesthetics have evolved over the course of human existence and, moreover, they have become of greater importance in the confection of identity. Finkelstein elaborates:

> While techniques for styling appearances have radically altered over the centuries, they are, nonetheless, as popular in contemporary society as in any previous time; indeed, the availability of goods and services has meant that the fashioning of appearances is probably greater in the twentieth century. This suggests that the perceptual conspiracy which allows the artificial complexion and body shape to be seen as a natural representation of character, and the fashioned styles of beauty to be accepted as expressions of human sensibility, remains as convincing as ever. (3)

Fashion, dress and the body are not only both cause and effect of one's own most private experiences and preferences, intertwined together they are also the means of presenting or communicating those experiences and preferences socially, in public. Similarly, the body is not only the most intimate of personal "belongings," but also intensely political: posture, gestures, and proxemics serve to denote power relations. Rather than seeing consumption as primarily a leisure pursuit involving a choice of consumer "lifestyles" (Shields), focusing on consumption as practice also leads to an emphasis on consumption as work, accomplished by skilled social actors. While some critics have tended to dismiss the cultural significance of clothing because of the continuous reappraisal and innovation of fashion, others have pointed to the close connection between clothing and the body (Entwistle and Wilson). This is, in part, an issue of distinct research traditions. While cultural studies have tended to adopt a semiotic approach to clothing-as-sign—as displayed on the hanger or the catwalk—feminist social science has studiously explored the dressed body, to research the social significance of clothing in terms of the wearer's embodied identity, rather than how the body is experienced affectually. Hence, material culture is an exploration of consumption as social practice (and of the human and non-human networks within which those practices are enacted) and the delineation of commodity-specific cultures of consumption.

Sociology has neglected the body as Veblen and Simmel saw only wastefulness in fashion; Sweetman suggests that cultural theory has overlooked fashion (59). Body dressing serves a dual function. On the one hand, fashion and dress are meaningful phenomena, sign systems, or means of communication. Yet, if we were to only consider linguistic models, we would reduce the dressed body to purely abstract symbolic systems. On the other hand, it is of great consequence to investigate human embodiment and the significance of the body. Sweetman argues that the principal, canonical approaches to fashion and dress have, in large part, ignored their phenomenological, material or "affectual" aspects and uses. In this line of thinking, Maffesoli suggests a way of studying fashion as a social process in which corporeality is one of the ways that social being, or "sociality," is constructed. Similarly, Efrat Tseëlon extends the concern with subjectivity toying with the notion of masquerade to use in the exploration of how identities, (including gender identities), may be constructed and deconstructed through fashion, uncovering new, active, and liberated versions of femininity. In the same vein, DuGay argues that consumers are constituted as autonomous, self-regulating and self-actualizing individual actors, seeking to ascertain power and pleasure vis-à-vis their assemblage and re-assemblage of identities that they confect according to personal elections. The social is always in the process of becoming, sustained through more-or-less durable networks of connection and through various socio-technical apparatuses.

In *Los placeres de Anastasia*, the protagonist confects her identity through a concatenation of elements. In particular, the reader is witness to Anastasia's abundant consumption of fashion. By way of her personal selections, she codifies her body according to the type of clothing as well as the brand of clothing she sports. At the age of seventeen, Anastasia began to supplement her dancing income by working in her father's, Hilario, upscale furniture store called Formes & Disseny. There were months in which, if sales were good, she would earn up to 200.000 pesetas, money that was dedicated to "mi ropa, mis salidas, mis cuidados" (27). Due to her income she was permitted to purchase herself whatever she deemed necessary, and she took great pleasure in the act of shopping and coming home with a new good. By virtue of consumption, Anastasia negotiates her identity, implicitly posing questions such as "Who am I?" and "How do I want to construct my life?" Everyone wants to know the answer to these questions and, teenagers are especially curious; youths look to popular culture for clues about life. There do, however, exist scholars that demonize consumption believing that the masses are bombarded with spectacle and they are told that the answers lie in a shopping mall. They ascertain that consumption practices are based on the same message: Beauty can be bought! If you buy a certain product, your life will be wonderful. Having said this, I assert that while this may be possible for some, it is not the case for Anastasia. Via consumption of fashion she can connect with particular neo-tribes, or adopt an identity just for an evening. Our society does not so much resemble a melting pot, but rather a buffet—a bazaar in which the purveyors of goods and services spend large sums of money each year marketing the foods, clothing, objects, vacations, and events that help people express their (and others') identities (Lury). For Anastasia, consumption is provocative, intriguing, and farseeing, illuminating an important aspect of our contemporary way of life. Grosz highlights: "the very sense of the self is linked to the subject's sexual and bodily specificity" (144). Grosz provides insights into the way a libidinally invested image of the body is constructed out of culturally contingent meanings, desires, and fantasies. Her approach places at the forefront the process of the continuous reconstruction of the sexed body, which at the same time explicitly negates the existence of a "natural" body (142–43). The emphasis on reconstructing and rewriting the body has an iconoclastic ring to the Spanish public who, due to the machista society, favors a rather essentializing view of "the eternal feminine identity" and of bodily differences as ontologically given. Grosz's theoretical framework opens up a possibility to reconcile psychoanalytically centered feminist theories with cultural studies analyses and also aids in the analysis of the protagonist, Anastasia. The rapprochement between post-structuralism and cultural studies is particularly useful for a Spanish reader as it enables her to introduce culturally specific determinations into feminist readings of mass media. Combining the two approaches can be instrumental in working out a Spanish perspective and voice in feminist studies. In light of this, through her maneuverings, the protagonist comes to exemplify the nomad, fleshing through experiences and working within the patriarchy to her advantage, all the while enjoying the power she commands.

Peppered in her objects of consumption are North American icons such as the Backstreet Boys and Brad Pitt. This is evidence of the effects of globalization in the 1990s in Spain. Not only does she possess one poster of the Backstreet Boys, but also she displays four of Brad Pitt amongst a plethora of clothing. Similar to her choice in men, her style was particular: very sexy. "Todo era muy femenino, sexy, mini, nada de pijoterismo, ni de estilo «hippy»" (36). The favorite moment of this self proclaimed "fashion victim" (37) was to wear each outfit for the first time: "Si ir de compras me resultaba toda una aventura, lo mejor venía luego: el momento de estrenar lo que me acaba de comprar" (36). Anastasia gleaned power from the flattering comments made by her friends; vis-à-vis consumption, she confects an identity that is multiple, dynamic, and unique. Her friends would comment: "«¡Jolines, tía, otra vez vas de estreno! ¡No paras!»; «¡Pero si parece que vas de fiesta cada día!»" (36). The flatteries bestowed upon her by her friends recall the concept of the Barbie doll. While Anastasia may have opted to consume different North American icons, the ideology of the Barbie doll remains a salient feature of her consciousness. Just like Barbie, Anastasia's identity is, in part, confected by way of the consumption of clothing and the great care she takes of her body. The construction of her constitution is akin to that of the Barbie doll. Calefato affirms: "Concierne al juego de vestir, desvestir y revestir, del peinado, de arreglarse con maquillajes y joyas, de teñirse el pelo con apropiados colores efímeros o de conseguir que las versiones 'articuladas' lleven a cabo osados movimientos gimnásticos" (152). Hence, there are a series of rituals—dressing, redressing, attention to hair, and fixing up oneself—that correspond to Anastasia's aesthetic sense, which consequently serve to mold and shape her identity. Further calling attention to herself, this feminine, sexy fashion victim prefers to don the colors black and red as they both contrast well with her gleaming blond locks and convert her into even more palatable eye-candy.

Body dressing is about hybridization, resistance, ambivalence, boundary-crossing and a more material form of cultural politics. It may be said that the protagonist's body dressing decisions are based upon the consumption of images from international magazines such as *Cosmopolitan*, *Ragazza*, *Vale*, and most significantly, *Playboy*, a magazine that she always bought for herself. The idea of femininity as represented in these magazines is radically devalued and instrumentalized, women being reduced to anatomy, to parts of the body that provide female pleasure. There arises the difficult question as to how these representations may yield pleasure to a female public. It is interesting that in these magazines, for all the degradation women and female sexuality is submitted to, there exists a sense of agency. Though heavily incriminated for their loose morals, the women these magazines narrate are anything but passive victims. The bare-breasted images, as seen in *Playboy*, suggest not only unrestricted male desire and pleasure but also female potency and transgression. A female public can safely enjoy the latter as both images and stories apparently pose no threat to patriarchal views on femininity. At the same time, however, the latter rely on a similar mechanism for providing pleasure and adopt the same indirect and paradoxical line of empowering their female public without apparently questioning traditional values and roles. All women's magazines share one more feature: they almost exclusively disseminate images of Western women, an incidence attributed to the globalization of cultures as well as the adoption of North American values and ideals. This feature is not unrelated to the oblique strategy of producing pleasure and empowering the public. These magazines have tried to fill the void with "imported" Western images. The very foreignness of the images, rather than alienating the public, has great legitimacy and persuasive power.

Magazines for young women, for example, are, not surprisingly, packed with images of Western film stars (this recalls Anastasia's obsession with Brad Pitt) and top models. What is interesting about their fascination for young adults is that they feed ideal desires. The attitude of star worshipping that the magazines encourage thus evinces locally inflected features. Images of Claudia Schiffer, Cindy Crawford, and Naomi Campbell stand for the ideal of unattainable female desirability and at the same time reflect an image of the glamour and abundance of the West, viewed as a utopian world. Much of the pleasure in looking at these images derives from an imaginary identification with the stars, patently evident in Anastasia's persona. Magazines, not unlike soap operas, offer women, such as Anastasia, an escape into a fantasy world. The selection of images printed in the magazines, as well as the texts accompanying them, indicate a process of negotiation between the public readership and the text. The visual representations of the female body carry, simultaneously, Western significances about femininity and Spanish perceptions of this Western ideal. The very images, the bodies themselves, seem to encode and rewrite the female body. A particular question that does arise is whether the pleasure female readers derive from these pictures is that of the voyeur, identifying with a male position (Mulvey 1991), or whether these readers can also experience different types of pleasure. I contend, as illuminated through the maneuverings of Anastasia, that these images endow women with agency and power.

Images of Western stars as employed by magazines reveal a striking emphasis on sexual difference. For example, cosmetics and clothing have come to signify a model of femininity and are associated with power, sexual pleasure, and material wealth. As exemplified by the thought processes of Anastasia, indulging in these material goods may potentially be a manner of building one's self-confidence and self-esteem. By virtue of reading the magazines, the female readers are presented with the opportunity to partake in the very cultural practices that have fashioned these famous bodies. There is an implicit promise that the gap between the two worlds, which is inscribed on female bodies, could be bridged by making Spanish bodies look similar to the Western ones. Disciplining their bodies according to Western norms further implies a seemingly liberating rupture from the masculine economy. While the fashion magazines may be considered typical reading material for a young woman of Anastasia's age, she stands out as a total dissident purchasing *Playboy*, a magazine explicitly intended for and marketed to the masculine viewer. In doing so, Anastasia consciously breaks a societal taboo. She subverts even further the norms of society by watching and enjoying porn movies as well as the material in the magazine *Playboy*. This subversion of sexuality does not only occur within the realms of her home, but also when she is on the dance stage. For instance, one night in which she had to dance, she decided to don a Scottish short skirt paired with a pink camisole. The overwhelming image that comes to mind is that of the Lolita. The innocence of the color pink and the Scottish patterned mini-skirt represent the attraction to youth, while the short skirt and the camisole converted her into a seductress. Hence, the design of the clothing yielded her innocent, yet the cuts of her clothes render her seductive. The mini-skirt alone speaks volumes as it represents a realization of liberty in the face of censorship and hypocrisy. The combination of the various pieces produces a hybrid, nonessential representation of woman: the naïveté of the youth intersected with the sultriness of the femme fatale.

Insofar as her rupture with convention, Anastasia continues to re-appropriate the very notion of woman on various planes. That same evening during a very sensual song, she approached her girlfriend Eva, "una amiga con la que mutuamente nos habíamos tapado más de una infidelidad" (45), and began to seductively dance and flirt with her, "nos lanzábamos a práctica unos movimientos con roces, es decir, con un poco de «flirteo»" (45). Effectively, Anastasia's performance toys with the naturalized concepts of Man/Woman. While her intention was not to perform a lesbian show for the hungry eyes of the spectators, her actions unequivocally destabilize gender binary oppositions. Furthermore, she gleans power from this performance, as her primary intention was to captivate the attention of a gorgeous waiter at the club. Indeed, Anastasia embodies a force to be reckoned with. She is the one driving the men crazy and reducing them to pure simpletons. At the same time, the men play into her various games, she conquers them willfully, and then leaves them wanting for more. This attitude is not relegated to the terrain of the club, but proliferates throughout all dimensions of the protagonist's life. In the street, she performed for the male onlookers by virtue of the manner in which she walked. She always knew that she had two specific assets to command masculine attraction: her captivating green eyes and her strikingly sculpted "culo" (49). On an affectual level, it is interesting to explore the embodiment of Anastasia's public gait. She elegantly strolls down the street, taking short steps so as to highlight her adeptness in femininity and sensuality. She admits:

> He sido una chica coqueta, lanzada, derrochadora, y muy clara a la hora de hablar, sin pelos en la lengua. Una chica que sabía cruzar las piernas con grandes dosis de erotismo; que arqueaba una ceja como las estrellas de Hollywood; que sabía meterse un dedo en la boca y poner cara de niñita; que se mordía un poco los labios como si estuviera impaciente, o que iba a por todas y entonces los ojos escupían desafío y morbo. (49–50)

Without a doubt, Anastasia embodies the notion of Lolita. Her body exudes sexuality, as evident through the way she evocatively crosses her legs to the flirtatious manner in which she arched her eyebrow. Juxtaposed with the concept of seductress is the element of innocence as manifest through the way she playfully placed the tip of her finger in her mouth to the childish faces she would make. In sum, the importance attached to self-fashioning and subsequent embodiment cannot be emphasized enough. In this context, Radner affirms: "woman is most feminine when she is not herself, when she enacts an elaborate masquerade" (52). It is interesting that the same attitude towards self-fashioning and masquerade is parallel to what women's magazines preach to its readership. What distinguishes the model of the "Western" woman from the "traditional" one is the desire to invest time and money in the fashioning and re-assembling of her body. This process involves a transgressive position: woman becomes the subject, rather than the mere object, of her own fashioning and confection. In Radner's words, these women are "the producers rather than the products" of this procedure (149–50).

The performance of the masquerade, the possibility of reconstructing one's "look" creates a sense of freedom and autonomy that translates into libidinal pleasure. Besides the pleasure derived from narcissistic involvement with one's own body, the women willing to devote part of their time and money to the care of their body may potentially experience a sense of freedom and autonomy, as is the case for Anastasia. The decision to dedicate their energy and their selfhood to themselves and ignore the needy voice of the others, be that only for brief periods of time, is an act of "independence" which increases the women's "self-respect" and self-esteem (Svendsen 9). Thus, this masquerade produces resistance to traditional, patriarchal roles and norms, which demand the total sacrifice of their energies for the welfare of the masculine economy. Women feel empowered as desiring subjects, capable of their own re-creation, and in control not only of their bodies but also of their lives. The innovative multiple self, the new identity created by means of refashioning one's body has the potential to aid in the heightening of personal happiness as well as success in one's job and social life. Having stated this, one must also consider the fundamental motives of the magazines: to attract an audience that purchases and consumes their product. As such, there is a pressing tone in the comments on seductive images of Western stars which impulses the readers to imitate the stars and refashion themselves to be just as attractive, just as sexy (this recalls Anastasia's obsession with Madonna)—all the time assuring them that they, the readers, may attain the same looks, features, and attitudes portrayed through the glossy pages of the magazine.

While the creativity and the liberating thrust of the self-fashioning masquerade remains viable, one must be mindful of a series of factors that potentially serve to undermine its practice. First of all, it may be considered to reinforce traditional, patriarchal definitions of femininity, conceived of exclusively in terms of desirable physical appearance and viewed from the perspective of the male gaze. No matter how much women may enjoy their subject position as producers of their looks, it is possible that the goal pursued reinscribes them in traditional roles as objects of desire. Secondly, the self-fashioning creativity renders itself to normalizing pressures exerted by mass media representations. Women are compelled to reshape their looks after a given pattern, while following a given beauty technology. The aforementioned notwithstanding, even if our pleasures and desires are partially reappropriated within patriarchal scripts, the messages these images convey are still seductively subversive, covertly transgressive, and create a path for more radical feminist positions. For instance, Anastasia comments that by way of her body dressing coupled with her ability to seduce men, whether it be in bed or on the street, she retains an active position of power. While she performs within the masculine economy, she is afforded libidinal pleasure by virtue of consumption and how she embodies the objects she elects to consume. She elaborates:

> Seducía en la cama, pero también jugaba a seducir en la calle. Mis medidas no son 90, 60, 90, pero siempre me he puesto lo que he querido: tops reducidos a

la forma de sujetador, camisetas muy ajustadas, minifaldas o minivestidos, pantalones que marcaban la raja de delante y la de atrás, y zapatos con tacones de vertigo y empeines rocambolescos. El cabello lacio o con marcados rizos, rubísmo, siempre bien cepillado, era un elemento importante a la hora de coquetear con los chicos. . . . Y nunca he salido de casa buscando rollos, he ido con mucha seguridad a todas partes porque sabía que si un día no picaban, ya picarían al día siguiente. A medida que los chicos se rendían a mis encantos, la confianza en mí misma iba aumentando. (50–51)

As Anastasia succinctly describes, the power she possesses over men is impressionable to the point that she may reduce them to blathering fools. Of significance, she may be said to represent the notion of the femme fatale. The concept of the femme fatale projects a direct attack on the traditional stereotype of woman. Anastasia refuses to play the role of wife and mother that the traditional society prescribes for women. As such, she is transgressive in that she utilizes her cunning and sexual attractiveness to gain her independence and command attention regardless of the proxemics. Likewise, she exudes a unique sexuality, which she uses to define herself and manipulate men in order to gain a certain sense of autonomy from mainstream society. Her body, her clothing, her words, her actions, and her ability to hold the gaze create a highly charged sexual image that defies attempts by the men in her life to control her or return her to her proper place as a woman. Unlike the notion of the femme fatale, though, Anastasia is not destroyed or rendered passive in the end; rather she skyrockets to celebrity status, her works diffused both nationally and internationally, commanding attention and respect. Furthermore, she lingers in the masculine imagination as a sexually exciting, living character who never accepts the role that society prescribes for her. Anastasia's unique power is a consequence of her willingness and ability to express her selfhood in sexual terms. As a variation of the femme fatale, the protagonist threatens the status quo precisely because she controls her own sexuality outside of the confines of the institution of marriage. As her confessions patently demonstrate, Anastasia uses sex for pleasure and as such this emancipation commands the masculine gaze. Nevertheless, their gaze does not reduce Anastasia to simulacra, but rather it empowers her, endows her with agency, and most importantly yields libidinal returns.

Performance and Pornography

Generally speaking, 'Sex Positive' means rejecting the dominant view of sex as somehow something shameful (especially for women), and embracing any and all consensual sex practices between one, two, or more adults as healthy, and without needing apology, justification, and (for some) social contextualization. Rejecting the accumulated cultural baggage that surrounds it, and enjoying sex for what it is, however you do it, with whomever you do it. It means looking at the diversity of sexual practices . . . including homo/bisexuality, genital-to-genital, oral, anal, digital to genital/anus, S/M, B/D, the spectrum of fetishes to be found among humans, the use of sex toys, masturbation, group sex involving any or all of the above, et al. . . . as being positive and not feeling that one need be ashamed of any consensual sexual practices between adults. (Greer 1999)

There exists a mélange of elements that Anastasia consumes which serve to carefully mold and confect her identity. At the forefront, though, lies her female sexuality that has been an integral piece in the construction of her self since her early childhood years. After having danced at clubs for a number of years, Anastasia opts to take a job as a phone sex girl, fulfilling male and female fantasies by way of her voice, simulated fantasies, and articulations. Vis-à-vis this job, Anastasia happens to meet Juan, a married swinger living in Madrid. Embracing him as a friend proved to be fortuitous for Anastasia's future career—star of pornographic films—as he had intimate connections in this specific business. Prior to her entrance in this genre of film, Juan aided Anastasia in obtaining a job posing as an erotic model. She accepted this line of work for two reasons: "por el dinero y por que tenía la posibilidad de hacer algo que siempre había querido hacer. Desde que era una niña me encantaba que me fotografiaran, nunca perdía la oportunidad de salir en una foto" (88). While Anastasia explicitly states that money is a motive for accepting a position as an erotic model, this is overridden by her elation and excitement, as she has always desired to be the focus of the camera since she was a child. The fact that she is nude or semi-nude in the photographs does not bother or cause her discomfort on any level as she does not see nor feel shame about her body, her sexuality, and the pleasure that her body bestows upon her. She elaborates:

> Posar con poca ropa no me suponía ningún problema. ¡Pero si desde los 15 años bailaba así, medio desnuda! Para mí también era normal pasearme por casa ligera de ropa, con tan solo una bata roja japonesa, abierta, y sin nada debajo. Nunca me ha importado que mis padres y mi hermana me vieran así. . . . La idea de que alguien pudiera ver esas fotos realizadas por un profesional me dio un subidón." (89)

Indeed, the protagonist feels no shame, embarrassment, or unease regarding her body. Rather, she is quite the exhibitionist in both the proxemics of the public and also the private, her home. As soon as the photography shoot began, she felt as if she had evolved. She reveals: "en cuanto oí el click de la cámara me transformé" (89). The eye of the camera initiated a transformation in Anastasia. Her performance was natural, undisturbed by feelings of awkwardness or nervousness. This is due largely to the fact that she is proud of her body and owns her sexuality. By way of her sensual movements, Anastasia expresses and communicates her identity, which is foregrounded in her sexuality. Regarding her performance she declares:

> No me tuve que esforzar en quedar bien, no tuve que interpretar, porque la provocación y la sensualidad forman parte de mi forma de ser, surgen con la misma facilidad que a otros les sale una sonrisa. Me sentí como pez en el agua. El fotógrafo casi no hablaba, con solo una pocas indicaciones yo sabía lo que él quería. Y se lo daba de todo corazón, sin trampa ni cartón. Estoy convencida de que si hubiera tenido un palmito más hubiera llegado a modelo de fotografía de alto standing. (90)

As a nude model, the protagonist feels like she is in her own environment and moreover is comfortable in her skin. The protagonist does not have to act nor be told what to do or how to move, but rather she dominates the scene, wielding power through her brazen, inherent sexuality. The very sound of the flash on the camera energizes and animates her, "Oía el flash de la cámara y, automáticamente aumentaba mi deseo por gustar. Soy exhibicionista, y eso juega a mi favor. Ante la cámara siento que tengo mucho poder. Y durante la sesión gasto mucha energía porque intento sacar todo lo que hay dentro de mí, incluso más" (90). Her exhibitionist nature lends Anastasia a clear advantage, plus the fact that nude modeling proves to be an empowering experience for her to the point that she dedicated her body and soul to the job at hand.

Due to the fact Anastasia rapidly excelled as a nude model, her friend, Juan, proposed to her that she try out pornographic movies. From her perspective this sounded like a phenomenal idea, as her identity revolved around female sexuality rooted in her exhibitionist nature. Together they decided to attend the Cine Erótico de Barcelona in order to network and fish for any potential possibilities. Before perusing the film festival and attempting to retain a part in a film, the protagonist needed to have an artistic name, which would lend credence to her experience. This was an easy task for her. She immediately and decisively opted for Anastasia, the name of a popular North American singer. Not only was this North American woman's music pleasant to the protagonist, but also she was profoundly attracted to the look she sported. The singer was "rubia despampanante, sexy, con gafas cibernéticas, tops muy ajustados y muchas tetas. La solían promocionar con el ombligo al aire y pantalones muy bajos de cintura. . . . Tuve claro que ese era el nombre idóneo" (99). It is significant that what she chooses to consume, a North American music star, is how she wants to be identified and seen by the masses. In electing the name Anastasia, the protagonist, too, can assume her identity: a sexy blonde whose body dressing was relegated to tight tops revealing her chest and low-rising pants, which revealed her stomach. Anastasia strives to identify with those who espouse the same beliefs and likes as herself. This consumption of lifestyle viscerally clashes with the traditional prescription for Woman. In participating in this genre, Anastasia is fully conscious that her body manifests as a commodity, yet at the same time, she experiences active authority and power in her choices and actions. In this vein, porn does not just sell sex, but rather it places on the market a mélange of accoutrements—clothes, body parts, books, magazines, and celebrities. This also holds true for the neo-tribe that composes and constitutes the film festival. For Anastasia, participating in this culture of consumption was a very pleasant shock. "El sexo, allí se mostraba de una forma desinhibida, sin tapujos" (100). As she intimately witnessed, sex evolved from a hidden taboo to a celebration of libidinal pleasures due to the liberty associated with this neo-tribe's ideology. Within this environment, Anastasia was able to partake, as a viewer, sex that did not follow norms or prescriptions, but rather it was transgressive, subverting societal dictates.

> Cuando te lo dan y te lo enseñan todo, el sexo pierde su parte oscura, sus sombras. Cuando el cuerpo se exhibe sin antifaces, sin disimulo, como un espacio abierto apto para el disfrute, el sexo se deshace de su misterio, de su magia. Cuando te lo disparan así, a bocajarro, el sexo es solo eso, sexo. Y yo estaba encantada de ver el sexo de esa manera, desnudo, sin aditivos ni conservantes. (101)

As a voyeur, the protagonist watches the multiple sex scenes that were occurring around her. Due to the various sexually explicit presentations, the act of sex became demystified and transformed into a normal activity. In this context, these scenes portray open sexuality free from shame and victimization. Surrounded by diverse expressions of sexuality and nude bodies, the protagonist is offered a vision of power and joy in the sexual arena. Forming part of the scene, Anastasia strutted around in white stiletto heels and a very short dress that revealed the delectable and commanding curves of her body. Her thoughts reveal:

> Seguro que pensaron que era una actriz porno, motivos no les faltaban porque, además de mi forma de vestir, aquel día me appliqué en acentuar mi paso insinuante. Mis andares eran lujuriosos; mi mirada maliciosa; mi boca, una rodaja de sandía muy dulce y mis manos, rematadas con una uñas kilométricas, no paraban de zarandear mi cabellera rubia. (101)

While not yet participating in porn movies, she already plays the part vis-à-vis her choice of dress, her sensual and commanding gait, and her seductive facial expressions. It is noteworthy to consider her embodiment while in the territory of this particular neo-tribe. The protagonist played the part of a porn star; this was achieved through her choice of dress as well as her highly provocative gait. Furthermore, her face evanesced sweet temptation, while simultaneously her ultra-long fingernails flirtatiously played with her long, blonde locks. In her consumption of and participation in the festival, Anastasia was noticed and approached to participate in a porn flick. This news elated, but also paradoxically unnerved her: "Lo que realmente me preocupaba era fracasar, que me dijeran que aquello no era lo mío, que no follaba tan bien como yo pensaba, que no tenía futuro en ese campo. El porno era un mundo que solo conocía como espectadora pero no sabía nada sobre su funcionamiento" (103). Unconcerned with ethical or moral decisions, Anastasia is preoccupied that she is not as sexy or good as she believed herself to be. Moreover, she needlessly fretted to the point of worrying about her utter lack of experience in this arena.

Before the investigation delves into an exploration of Anastasia, her consumption of pornography, and resulting embodiment, it is fitting to first discuss the history of pornography and the heated feminist debate that surrounds this topic. The origin of the word pornography dates back to well over two centuries ago. A nineteenth-century art historian coined the term "pornography"; he used the word to describe erotic paintings and statues found a century earlier by archaeologists in Pompeii and Herculaneum. Both historians and scientists were stunned by the graphic depictions of sexual acts, representations of art that previously had adorned public places in these two ancient cities. Rooted in the Greek words "porne," meaning prostitute, and "grapho," signifying writing, the common dictionary definition for the word pornography is "writing or pictures intended to arouse sexual desire." Pornography has presented feminists with an intriguing and intensely oppositional debate. On one hand, critics signal the relation between pornography and violence against women, as well as its damaging yet fundamental role in major dimensions of the patriarchal economy. On the other hand, there exists the notion of the emancipatory potential of pornography as it potentially liberates female sexual inhibitions and at the same time provides affirmation of the consumption of a plethora of sexual practices. The two groups that concern this debate are anti-pornography feminists (MacKinnon and Dworkin) and feminist sex radicals (Duggan and Greer).

The first camp, anti-pornography feminists maintain that pornography reduces power, making it equivalent to the domination of men over women. It is a tenet of this ideology that domination births and manifests in gender differences; these differences are reified by the patriarchy such that the hierarchical paradigm does not stand to be questioned. These critics contend that pornography serves one and only one function: to humiliate, subordinate, and degrade women. Both of the aforementioned anti-pornography feminists believe that female sexuality is constructed at the hands of male power and that pornography exemplifies sexuality. MacKinnon perceives sexuality as being profoundly embedded in the feminine experience and defines pornography as sexually explicit material which subordinates women through pictures or words" (3). As such men have the ability to be dominant and women, the binary opposite, to be submissive. Essentially she contends that men "sexualize inequality," subsequently creating supposedly natural categories of sexuality. She elaborates:

> Sexuality . . . is not a discrete sphere of interaction or feeling or sensation or behavior in which preexisting social divisions may or may not be played out. It is a pervasive dimension of social life, . . . a dimension along which gender occurs and through which gender is socially constituted. . . . Dominance eroticized defines the imperatives of its masculinity, submission eroticized defines its femininity. . . . Sexuality itself the dynamic of the inequality of the sexes. (*Toward a Feminist Theory of State* 130)

MacKinnon's critique of pornography sustains itself by the unwritten, implicit understanding of heterosexuality as a practice. In this context, pornography serves to transmit the dominant ideology: heterosexual domination. She views the power of men as the principal element in gender hierarchy. The biological difference between the male and the female, as presented in the gender hierarchy, permits male dominance to exist in the realm of sexuality. She elaborates that there are dual dynamics occurring in pornography. "Pornography makes inequality into sex, which makes it enjoyable, and into gender, which makes it seem natural" (ibid. 3). According to MacKinnon, within the masculine economy, the hierarchal paradigm defines sexuality:

> From the testimony of the pornography, what men want is: women bound, women battered, women tortured, women humiliated, women degraded and

defiled, women killed. Or, to be fair to the soft core, women sexually accessible, have-able, there for them, wanting to be taken and used, with perhaps just a little light bondage. Each violation of women—rape, battery, prostitution, child sexual abuse, sexual harassment—is made sexuality, made sexy, fun, and liberating of women's true nature in the pornography. (ibid. 138)

Andrea Dworkin, sharing MacKinnon's theoretical perspectives, agrees that pornography represents sexuality's construction in action. Dworkin stresses that the very term, pornography, is pejorative in meaning as it was first used to describe prostitutes in the nineteenth century. She contends that the violation of women is made sexually; this critic asserts: "the major theme of pornography as a genre is male power, its nature, its magnitude, its use, its meaning. . . . Male power is the raison d'etre of pornography; the degradation of the females is the means of achieving this power" (*Pornography: Men Possessing Women* 24–25). In her perspective, gender insubordination stands out as a means by which men express their power by dominating women and maintaining female submissiveness. Moreover, Dworkin declares that male dominance is equivalent to male pleasure. Within the proxemics of pornography is where Dworkin sees male sexuality being represented (ibid. 5) which, furthermore, encompasses notions of power and agency. The critics that espouse anti-pornography contend that sexuality is a territory in which women are relegated victims of violation. In 1983, MacKinnon and Dworkin drafted a model anti-pornography law that was passed by the Minneapolis City Council. Effectively they stated that pornography "is a practice of sex discrimination" and furthermore it is the "graphic sexually explicit subordination of women through pictures and/or words" (MacKinnon and Dworkin 138). In the law they cooperatively drafted, the two anti-pornography feminists devised eight criteria to support their claim that pornography's singular function exists in its subordination of women. These eight components are:

  a. women are presented as dehumanized sexual objects, things or commodities; or
  b. women are presented as sexual objects who enjoy humiliation or pain; or
  c. women are presented as sexual objects experiencing sexual pleasure in rape, incest or other sexual assault; or
  d. women are presented as sexual objects tied up or cut up or mutilated or bruised or physically hurt; or
  e. women are presented in postures or positions of sexual submission, servility, or display; or
  f. women's body parts—including but not limited to vaginas, breasts and buttocks—are exhibited such that women are reduced to those parts; or

g. women are presented being penetrated by objects or animals; or
h. women are presented in scenarios of degradation, humiliation, injury, torture, shown as filthy or inferior, bleeding, bruised, or hurt in a context that makes these conditions sexual. (Dworkin and MacKinnon 139)

Central to the aforementioned arguments is that pornography is the oppression of women, whom are mere pawns and victims of the masculine economy. Anti-pornographic feminists believe that pornography is a doubly oppressive action against women: once when it is produced and again when it is watched. Thus, according to this particular ideology, pornography aids in the establishment of a social construct in which men are privileged aggressors subordinating and removing all power from women, while diminishing their existence to the whims of the power paradigm.

Symptomatic of MacKinnon and Dworkin's arguments is the thought process that woman is always coerced into pornography, effectively declaring that no woman may volunteer or consent to perform sexually explicit productions. At the same, the two theorists reduce relationships of power to domination and subordination, that is, a master/subject type of relation. Asserting that men are powerful and women stripped of power always relegates women to the position of victim while the male is always the authoritarian in command. This line of inquiry not only ignores but also denies the manners and modes in which some women experience power and confect subjectivity. In a sense, it may be stated that these critics' claims serve to continue the subordination and passivity of women, objectifying them by way of the Manichean ideology.

The opposite extreme of the anti-pornographic camp is that of sex radical feminists. Sex-positive feminism is a movement that arose in the 1980s as a visceral reaction to the efforts made by MacKinnon and Dworkin to restrict various mediums of sexual expression. At the root of this movement is the belief in sexual freedom, which opposes any legal or social efforts to control sexual activities between any number of consenting adults. Sex-positive feminists are against efforts initiated by the government, conservatives, and feminists that attempt to control and infringe upon the female body and female pleasure. Furthermore, sex-positive feminism values sexual gratification, freedom of expression, and all medium that are utilized as potential methods by which women may achieve sexual gratification. In contrast to the ideology of MacKinnon and Dworkin, this faction contends that pornography may offer women a way to explore and affirm their sexualities while providing information on sexual techniques, promoting sexual autonomy, and above all, encouraging female pleasure. Pornography, then, may potentially be a way for women to experience sexual alternatives, break cultural stereotypes, and empower themselves through the assertion of their female sexual subjectivity. Instead of viewing women as powerless, radical sex feminists conceptualize female power as achieved through sexual pleasure. Moreover, it is their assertion that to perceive women as powerless is to deny them agency and relegate them as pawns of the masculine hegemony.

Feminist sex radicals reject the definition of pornography as put forth by MacKinnon and Dworkin. As Duggan affirms, one of the fundamental goals of the feminist sex radicals is "to counter antiporn accounts of 'pornography' as unified (patriarchal) discourse with a singular (misogynistic) impact. Against this account, we argued that sexually explicit material called 'pornography' are full of multiple, contradictory, layered, and highly contextual meanings" (7). According to this camp, pornography has a plethora of functions. They maintain that women may be empowered by the consumption and production of pornography, despite the fact that it is a product of the masculine economy. Vis-à-vis pornography women may not only be an agent of sex, but also own their sexuality. Indeed, the consumption of pornography on the part of women is socially subversive and also equivalent to an act of patriarchal resistance. Hence, pornography may possess positive benefits:

> Pornography has served to flout conventional sexual mores, to ridicule sexual hypocrisy and to underscore the importance of sexual needs. Pornography creates many messages other than woman-hating: it advocates sexual adventure, sex outside of marriage, sex for no reason other than pleasure, casual sex, anonymous sex, group sex, voyeuristic sex, illegal sex, public sex. Some of these ideas appeal to women reading or seeing pornography, who may interpret some images as legitimating their own sense of sexual urgency or desire to be sexually aggressive. (Duggan, Hunter, and Vance 82)

Indeed, pornography may undermine society's repressive attitude toward sexuality. Via their consumption of pornography (whether they are spectators or actors) women may be considered sexual agents and empower themselves by way of the decisions they make concerning their sexuality. Women's sexuality has been repressed and stifled for centuries. Due to this, pornography may be a viable manner of feeling liberation for a woman living in a culture that treats sex with suspicion, considering it a negative and dangerous force. Thus, consuming porn may be considered to radicalize the concept of Woman, rewriting and inscribing her with power, agency, and the desire to be conscious of and enjoy her sexuality.

> A woman who is raped is a victim; a woman who enjoys pornography (even if that means enjoying a rape fantasy) is in a sense a rebel, insisting on an aspect of her sexuality that has been defined as a male preserve. Insofar as pornography glorifies male supremacy and sexual alienation, it is deeply reactionary. But in rejecting sexual repression and hypocrisy—which have inflicted even more damage on women than on men—it expresses a radical impulse. (E. Willis 464)

In this line of inquiry, pornography may be considered socially subversive as it dismantles the notion of sexual repression. Women are multiple, liberated of their bodily shame imposed by Western culture. Moreover, through their consumption of pornography, women may resist the essentialized, masculine definition of Woman. Whereas the patriarchal paradigm stigmatizes female sexuality, infusing it with shame and suspicion, the nomadic wanderings into the territory of pornography destroy supposedly natural boundaries and re-create Woman as molecular and dynamic. Working within the masculine paradigm, women who consume pornography may not reinforce existing relations of domination and subordination, but rather they may create autonomous, innovative selves, free from the prolific pressures of societal repression.

Anastasia may be exemplary of the ideology of the sex-positive feminist. Through her maneuverings within this masculine reified territory, she gleans power, agency, and allows herself to feel pleasure. It may be said that she, as nomad, wanders through the proxemics of porn, confecting a self that is buttressed by sexuality, and all the while she yields libidinal returns on her investment. She delineates in detail one of her pornographic performances: "Denís empezó a darme morreos y cachetazos en el culo, después vino la mamada y, finalmente, la penetración. Durante ese tiempo no pensé en nada porque estaba muy concentrada en lo que estaba haciendo y, sinceramente, no fingí" (107). Performing sexually in front of the camera was a natural, organic experience for Anastasia. She cogently admits that during her performances, she is focused on the present and in no moment does she have to fake the pleasure she is either giving or receiving. "Y en todo momento me dejé llevar, intentaba disfrutar pero controlando siempre que la cámara pudiera captar un buen plano mío" (107). Acting in porn flicks was not just a job for Anastasia, rather it resulted in a way by which she exercises her autonomy and appropriates her sexuality for her own benefit. This elucidates the concept of the nomad as conceptualized by Braidotti. Working and traversing within the hegemonic terrain, Anastasia devises her own rules, construes her own ideology (which is counterculture), and delights in her sexuality. She is dynamic, multiple, and defies definition. The very expressions on her face "[. . .] placer que reflejaba mi cara" (107) emphasize her empowerment in the face of patriarchal discourse. Interestingly, while man tends to incarnate the position of domination and woman one of subordination, this is not the case for Anastasia with respect to her endeavors. After her very first pornographic experience, she is afforded a different opinion about her abilities to belong to and achieve success within this specific neo-tribe. Completing her first experience within this realm, the protagonist blatantly brags about the sexual skills she possesses and her ability to perform spontaneously. "No me tuvieron que decir «ahora tienes que jugar con ello» porque yo ya sabía lo que tenía que hacer. No soy creyente, ni siquiera he hecho la primera comunión, pero ese día di dos veces gracias a Dios. Se lo merecía" (109). Ironically and rather subversively as well, she expresses her gratitude to God for both her performance and pleasure she received.

After her first experience—a three-day video shoot—Anastasia was hooked into the idea of acting in pornographic films. Not only did she want to be an actress, rather the best: "Llegué a casa, con 1.500 euros en el bolsillo, fruto de tres días de rodajes, y con una idea muy clara: llegar a ser una estrella del porno" (111). Anastasia desired to be the celebrity porn star, even selecting to consume a particular idol, Laura Angel: "[. . .] cotizada actriz checa, aunque parte de su carrera la ha desarrollado en Francia. Laura estaba pensando en retirarse y había montado su propia empresa. Era una de las grandes a nivel europeo y había conseguido un montón de premios" (111). The protagonist elects to consume as idol a beautiful woman with looks very similar to her own. Most importantly, though, she places emphasis on the financial and independent success that this woman has achieved. Disavowed of dreams of men caring for her, Anastasia focuses her energies on attaining her own stability and financial independence, which she has worked to attain since she was sixteen. Indeed, Anastasia dedicated herself to being the best, all the while receiving pleasure and gratification.

Anastasia had a clear purpose for participating within the territory of the porn industry. To begin with, she enjoyed what she did, she was good at it, and she relished the idea of trying new experiences. She declares to her boyfriend, Oscar:

> Se lo dije bien claro, sin rodeos: yo era así, y aquello, lo del porno, me apetecía hacerlo. Había sentido el mismo impulso que a las 18 años me había llevado a Madrid a experimentar algo nuevo al lado de María. ¿Por qué? Porque soy una mujer impulsiva y hago las cosas sin pensar. No había que darle más vueltas. Era solo sexo. Los sentimientos los tenía bien guardados bajo llave y tenían un rostro bien concreto, el suyo. (116)

The protagonist succinctly and decisively confesses her choice of jobs to her boyfriend. Although admitting to being impulsive, Anastasia does not express a drop of remorse nor guilt nor shame for her choice of profession. On the contrary, she explicitly expresses to her boyfriend the delight she takes in her performances, while reassuring him that it was only sex. Anastasia was capable of separating her feelings from the pleasure that she received through sex. While Anastasia, her parents, and eventually her boyfriend strongly supported her in her endeavors, she was not free from being the topic of gossip or stigmatization. In fact, her good friend was so brazen and quick to judge when she says to Anastasia: "¿Qué pensaría la gente si me vieran contigo, una actriz del porno?" (117). The protagonist, however, is cognizant of the patriarchal power structure which privileges man while shaming and marginalizing woman. She protests:

> Puro machismo. A un tío no se le machaca tanto, tiene vía libre para hacer en este campo, está más aceptado socialmente. Si es un hombre piensan que es un auténtico macho por que se folla a un montón de tías y, encima, cobra, pero si eres una mujer se les viene abajo el ideal femenino. Si encima tienes novio, a él lo ven como a un cornudo y a ti, como a una cualquiera. (117–18)

Anastasia signals the pernicious stereotyping of men and women in the porn industry. While society views a man that partakes in the pornographic realm as more virile and powerful, a woman maneuvering within the same terrain is the target of pejorative criticisms. Conscious of this supposedly "natural" paradox, the protagonist commands even more power and agency as she traverses within this space, working toward her advantage while yielding libidinal returns. Even more empowering, Anastasia knows herself and recognizes herself as an autonomous being who has chosen to defy social norms, yet is not only comfortable with this selection, but also gleans power and delectation from this via. She exclaims to her boyfriend's mother, a woman who maintains and promotes the traditional concept of Woman: "[. . .] yo, con mi vida y mi cuerpo, podía hacer lo que me diera la gana. Le dije que no pretendía que me aceptara, solo que me respetara. «No soy una zorra, ni una guarra. Con que lo acepten mis padres y mi novio tengo suficiente»" (119). Vis-à-vis her comment, Anastasia takes ownership of her body and her female subjectivity in the face of misogyny. She recognizes that the people that matter most—her parents and her boyfriend, Oscar—accept without condition her choice of lifestyle consumption. Moreover, she does not live under false pretenses, believing that society at large will accept her ideology and praxis; she only asks that she be respected.

Since her first porn video shoot, Anastasia has rocketed to success both within the proxemics of Spain and internationally. She no longer has the need to work as "dependienta" (122) as she is not lacking in the financial arena. The key to her success, she maintains, is her joy for sex that manifests through her corporeal language. She proudly admits: "Es que si yo no disfrutara haciéndolo, la cámara lo notaría, captaría a una tía fría. Y eso es una ventaja, me lo digo yo y me lo dice todo el mundo, «es que además de hacerlo bien se nota que te gusta»" (122). Anastasia patently reiterates the pleasure and power she acquires from her position in the porn industry. Furthermore, she also attributes her success to her ability to take pleasure and control of her sexuality. This, she recognizes, is not possible for everyone; many succumb to societal norms and pressures, repressing their desires and sexuality. "Soy feliz. Hasta ahora, he hecho todo lo que me he propuesto. A mucha gente le gustaría hacer realidad sus fantasias sexuales, pero no puede, y si llega a realizarlas, ha de esconderse de su familia, de su pareja, de todos" (123). Anastasia, on the other hand, has crossed boundaries, de-naturalizing the essentialized conception of Woman. She is happy with her life, her choices of consumption, and most importantly, her integrity. The protagonist proudly admits that she does not have to hide her lifestyle, as many are forced to do, as she is an active agent in the negotiation of the construction of her female subjectivity. Due to her positive attitude, joy for pleasure and gratification, as well as the sexual talents she possesses, the protagonist has climbed the ladder of success, working with the celebrities of the porn industry such as Max Cortés, Nacho Vidal, and Rocco Siffreddi. She is quick to add, with a dose of arrogance, that her phone lines are burning and the offers she is receiving continue to be more and more tempting: "[. . .] y el móvil, hoy, sigue quemando. Las propuestas son cada vez más tentadoras" (123). Highlighting the success she has had in this territory, she has even won prizes for her acting abilities in the porn industry. Further evidence of her nomadic wanderings is her realization that both a plan and precaution are of utmost important to achieving super-success. She does not merely flaunt her body as an object, but rather she creates a persona and a future rooted in forethought and preparation with respect to her chosen profession.

Conclusions

> Hoy, ante un espejo, me siento más poderosa. Voy muy bien de autoestima. Soy una Barbie morbosa que sigue levantando pasiones allá donde va. Nunca me ha gustado vivir en un mundo anodino, sin relieves, un mundo en el que no fuera capaz de tirarme a la piscina, de experimentar. Aún no me he roto ningún

pie cayendo en el abismo; no tengo cicatrices en el corazón, solo malos momentos.

Mi piel fresca, de terciopelo blanco, huele, una vez más, a hierbabuena. Intuyo el placer. Beso el espejo, me beso a mí misma, y mis piernas se aprietan entre sí con fuerza. Me gusto. (123–24)

Gazing upon her reflection in a mirror, Anastasia feels a surge of empowerment, a rise in her self-esteem, and, more significantly, is more than content with the image presented to her. Ironically she deems herself a Barbie doll; nevertheless, she does not represent the typical doll of a child, rather she incarnates a quite transgressive twist. Vis-à-vis a myriad of experiences, the protagonist learned from an early age the power and liberty associated with her female sexuality. By being conscious of her sexuality, Anastasia carefully negotiates and articulates her identity through a mélange of accoutrements: clothing, dance, the gaze, and sex. The resulting confection yields a woman that is multiple, defies patriarchy's essentialized notion of Woman, and furthermore, resists the masculine economy. Fleshing through experiences and traversing through various proxemics, the protagonist arrives at a heightened sense of self; she not only accepts her sexuality, but she likes whom she is and is capable of pleasuring herself.

Actively removing herself from the state of an object, whether dancing, modeling, or acting, Anastasia is a sexual subject wielding power and resisting the notion of the static, passive female. Through her consumption of sex-related material, Anastasia has the power to construe her female sexuality as necessarily subversive. This transformation impacts her experiences, and hence her subjectivity, thus making it possible for her to experience performing and consuming pornography in a liberating way. She is Braidotti's nomad; devoid of notions of salvation, she seeks to regenerate, foregrounding her identity in her female sexuality.

Note

1. Vladimir Nabokov was born in St. Petersburg into a wealthy, aristocratic family. His father, Vladimir Dimitrievich Nabokov, was a liberal politician, lawyer, and journalist. The household was Anglophile; Nabokov spoke Russian and English, and at the age of five he learned French. Although he published a number of novels prior to *Lolita*, it remains one of the most controversial novels of the twentieth century. The story, told from the point of view of Humbert, recounts and describes the desire of a middle-aged pedophile, Humbert Humbert, for a twelve-year-old girl. It was the publishing of this novel in 1955 that allowed Nabokov to abandon his teaching position at Cornell University and devote himself entirely to writing.

CHAPTER SEVEN

Interconnections

"It's our memory that connects us."

—Sonia Sanchez qtd. in Baumgardner and Richards, 67

Four contemporary Spanish women writers, seven female protagonists, and a myriad of cultures of consumption yielding in divergent representations of female subjectivity: Are the narrativized realities portrayed disparate images or interconnected vignettes of female identity? While the four authors have lived distinct personal narratives and have pursued dissimilar paths in many spheres, the tie that binds Lucía Etxebarria, Gabriela Bustelo, Silvia Grijalba, and Susana Plané remains their negotiation of female subjectivity through the optic of cultures of consumption. Each, in her own manner, portrays the female subject and her becoming; this process is intimately linked to her maneuverings through the consumer realm, selection of particular goods and codes, and subsequent re-appropriation of goods. Indeed the mode in which each author cultivates female subjectivity is distinct; nevertheless, each etches protagonists who negotiate meaning. By way of the various protagonists' appropriation of particular goods (tangible or abstract), they associate with a specific "imagined community." The dynamic relationships occurring among the protagonists and the consumer realm result in the construction of meaning and transmission of codes, legible to the masses. It goes beyond symbols of simply images of pleasure. Rather, through consumption each protagonist navigates a multiplicity of codes in the journey of becoming an active female subject, an agent with potential to enact change and evolve. Furthermore, in the case of some of the protagonists, there may exist liberatory potential stemming from the autonomous self-creation vis-à-vis the consumer realm.

The process of becoming for each of the protagonists is also hinged on the continuous interrogation of the hegemonic system and conventional gender roles. Again through divergent means, each protagonist, by way of the construction of her subjectivity through the specific accoutrements of the culture of consumption, questions her identity and that of Woman within the traditional patriarchal model. Cognizant of the power structure, each moves through spaces (those with which they associate) confecting their identity according to will, yet conscious of how their position relates to that of the power paradigm. The commonality amongst these women is their utilization of experiences and fleshing through of memories to enact change and arise to a higher understanding of their selfhood. In this sense, according to the postulations of Braidotti and her theory of nomadic subjectivity, the protagonists arrive to embody the feminist female subject who has abandoned longing for salvation, and instead has focused on regeneration either through subversion of the power structure or working within it to her advantage. Either way, these various portrayals evidence the dynamic multiplicity of female subjectivity.

Due to personal narratives, experiences with global economies, and their notions of female identity, Plané, Grijalba, Bustelo, and Etxebarria may have, perhaps, been influenced to examine female subjectivity in conjunction with cultures of consumption within contemporary Spain from various platforms. What remains clear, though, is their dialogue with the international via the inclusion of global brands, locales, markets, cultural trends, and use of the English language in their narrative. Silvia Grijalba, for instance, explores the movement of the female subject, Alba, within the techno scene as well as the multinational. She traces the evolutions in the identity of Alba as she passes from one territory to the other, obviously intimately linked also to the position of her boyfriend, Fernando. It is interesting to note that these two territories are ones in which Grijalba herself has profound knowledge: the capitalist empire from her work at the newspaper *El Mundo* and the musical landscape through her direct and indirect participation in that area (playing, DJing, and reporting). The identity of the protagonist is closely related to her surroundings and that which she consumes within the two territories; in the techno scene—drugs, music, the celebrity of her boyfriend, unhealthy obsession—and in the multinational, she experiences more power (linked to the demise of Fernando) and consumes higher-end labels while maintaining hybridization via her indie look. Most importantly, though, is that as she traverses the two areas, both patriarchal in nature, she gains a deeper understanding of herself and her own needs. This translates into the construction of an active subjectivity and awareness of self, despite the constraints inherent to the power system. Alba nomadically wanders, utilizing her memory and experiences as guide, and arrives at a position of peaceful understanding: she rejects the notion of a savior and begins her own process of rejuvenation. Grijalba's portrayal of female subjectivity opens the possibility for the redefinition of Woman.

In the same vein, García together with Plané recount Susana's life, beginning with her adolescence and continuing through the present. What is significant is that from a very young age, Susana is not only conscious of her sexuality, but also she foregrounds her very identity in her sexuality. From dancer to phone sex girl to porn queen, Anastasia has always commanded the attention of the male gaze. While some may argue that she is merely an object to be looked upon, Anastasia proves that to be false. By virtue of her exhibitionist nature, the protagonist gleans power, control, and most importantly, libidinal pleasure. She maneuvers through a patriarchal dominated economy and is aware of the structure and its "inherent," unwritten rules. Yet, she freely admits that she knows how to play the game, a declaration that exposes her ability to work within the masculine paradigm to her advantage. Traversing through various proxemics (all of them defined by the patriarchy) and fleshing through various experiences, the protagonist arrives at the knowledge that she enjoys her body and her self. Relinquished of the shame attached to female sexuality, Anastasia is free to explore and negotiate her subjectivity according to desire. Her identity, nevertheless, is composed of various accoutrements that play up her sexuality. Indeed, it is by way of this economy that she achieves liberation and a libidinal return on her investment. As such, she incarnates the feminist-female subject as construed by Braidotti.

Likewise, Bustelo traces the construction of female subjectivity through the locus of consumption. Unlike the cultures of consumption depicted in Grijalba's novel, Bustelo examines the space of the underground life of the movida madrileña juxtaposed by the consumption of drugs, music, high-end goods, dancing, and the gaze. Similar to Grijalba, Bustelo explores the relationship among female identity and consumption, as well as the process of becoming achieved via contemplation yielding a more heightened awareness of self (Braidotti). Dissimilar to Grijalba, Bustelo toys with the conventional conception of Woman—that of the femme fatale—to interrogate and subvert the hegemonic prescriptions for gender norms. Within the underground scene of the movida nightlife, Vania flits among various locales, voluntarily playing into the game of stalker, her identity manifesting in a chameleon-like manner. Nearly always highly sexually charged, Vania moves among the 'authentic' spaces of the bars, displays herself (knowing she is a commodity) for the gaze, and feels empowered. Indeed she participates in the game, yet her narrative does not call for nor need a male, but rather she objectifies the masculine by way of the power she ascertains through the image she appropriates and projects. Entangled by the "mania persecutoria," vulnerable videotapes, two-way mirrors, and the knowledge that she is under constant surveillance, Vania does not render passive; she actively creates her selfhood and fluctuates from positions of "mirada" to that of "mirona." Working from a position of power, Vania uses her gaze to unveil the stalkers and as such erases the constraints and subdues their power. The novel playfully toys with the creation of female identity in a world constructed and ruled by hegemonic norms. Likewise, it unveils the plethora of consumer goods and their relationship in the construction of female subjectivity. Vania enters into the game through partaking in the consumer realm. These participations evidence nomadic wanderings that engage Vania to question and manipulate the symbolic to her advantage while freely creating her selfhood; as such, she embodies the feminist female subject and a distinct potential for the redefinition of Woman.

Etxebarria's narrative presents diverse portraits of the three Gaena sisters and their construction of identity contingent upon consumption of territory and the respective accoutrements. While distinct in identity, the commonality among the Gaena siblings is their quest for knowledge, for an understanding and acceptance of who they are. This is arrived upon by way of their individual contemplations of experiences, fleshing through history, their understanding of the power paradigm, as well as an understanding of themselves. Divergent in representation, the youngest, Cristina, incarnates counterculture and interrogates hegemonic norms while at the same time working within the system to her benefit. Moving from the realm of the multinational to the bar scene, Cristina elected to have more control over her time and body space. Despite her knowledge, she was denied access due to despotic practices, furthermore, within this territory, her body felt inorganic, artificially programmed and constricted for the benefit of those in the upper echelons of the company. While recognizing the patriarchal nature of the bar, she is cognizant that her body—as bartender—is the focus, on display for the consuming eyes; yet, ironically she condescends their hungry looks while benefiting from the financial gain. Questioning all dominant power structures, Cristina understands herself and the power that she possesses. She engages in nomadic thinking by way of her "rhizomatic" contemplation of self and surroundings as well as active self-formation via the space of counterculture. In distinct contrast to her sister, Rosa is programmed, digitalized, and coded according to the tenets of capitalism and advancing technologies. She, too, initiates nomadic contemplation by way of her interrogation of gender roles, which stems from being female in a male dominated economy. Colonized to believe that she had to deny all emotion and feeling, but rather control and program her selfhood according to logic and rationalism (masculine associated qualities) to achieve success and to just be. Working through memories and experiences, she allows herself to explore her emotions. She is cyborg: constructed in part by technology but also human, allowed to feel at harmony with her emotive self. The oldest sister, Ana, also presents a representation that deviates from the other two; she is the housewife incarnate. Ana fabricates her life patch-working together the elite brands and odd chores she must complete around the domestic sphere, as that was what she had learned from her mother and society. Maintaining her house of elaborate immaculate quality, as if it were uninhabited, represented a ritual significance; just in the same way, she constructed her self around the consumption of very expensive and international goods. Yet there were fault lines. Ana could not be the perfect mother, housewife, and just be. After periods of ingesting chemical cocktails—one to wake her up and another to help her sleep—profound sadness, and utter despair, Ana begins her own quest for identity. Abandoning all that she knew, she journeys towards regeneration of self, a healthy one based upon her own active self-construction. It is important to note that the consumption of high-end goods is not the factor that caused her demise and passivity, rather the internalization of unrealistic expectations that she herself did not know if she really desired or desired because of what she had been taught by social and familiar discourse. In sum, all three articulate their identity via their consumption of object and symbols; their identities are in flux and evidence the multiplicity of the female subject.

In conclusion, female identity has been grounded in theories postulated during the Enlightenment, elaborating that Man is rational and active and Woman, his opposite, is passive and a lack. The identity of Woman has been essentialized by the masculine dominated economy to signify an inferior being. Whether it manifest as mother, wife, or daughter, She was always the other. This study, however, dismisses theories grounded in Enlightenment thought and rethinks the notion of Woman. Through the analysis of the various protagonists, the concept of Woman has become radicalized: She is no longer an essence, but rather She represents a multiplicity of becomings, of female subjectivities. This research has not proposed the destruction or overturning of the hegemonic system, but rather proposes manners in which the female subject may negotiate an active subjectivity, either subverting the system or working within it to her advantage. In the postmodern era, the concept of becoming or constructing subjectivity is intimately linked to cultures of consumption, by which each of the protagonists has negotiated meaning and actively forged a female subject. Some of the protagonists even experienced a libidinal return via their personal interactions with specific cultures of consumption and their playing with various accoutrements associated. Each of the protagonists represents an individual with a unique history and narrative; nevertheless, there exists a commonality among these women. While wandering different paths, each embarked upon a journey that led them to interrogate their individual selfhood as well as their surroundings. Likewise, by way of their contemplation and fleshing through of experiences, the protagonists, as nomad or cyborg, work with the knowledge and traverse spaces with more profound insight into their selfhood and the desire to redefine the notion of female subjectivity, rejecting essence and grounded identity. As unveiled in the literature under discussion and exposed in the vast and intensive political, social, and economic changes transpiring in present day Spain, there exists transformations in the contingencies of female identity; likewise, these distinct media (literature, sociological surveys, inauguration of new political cycle) demonstrate the need for a redefinition in the concept of female subjectivity, a transgression, a radicalization of Woman. To close, this inquiry cites the scholar Sargisson whose thoughts succinctly predicate the rethinking of Woman, not through destruction, but rather by way of the creation of new spatial constructs in which to engage in the negotiation and articulation of the female subject. Sargisson affirms:

> Not only does the present need to be critiqued but its status, and that of women within it, need to be questioned. Transgression of social codes, of the concept of order, and of generic conventions all comprise elements of a practice, which I have called radical and transgressive utopianism, that seeks to subvert and exploit the ways in which our perceptions of reality (and the concepts that enable us to make sense of reality) are constructed. By dislocating the present, we can, I suggest, create new conceptual space which allows challenges to the present to be made, and permits the desire for change to become manifest and "meaningful." (225)

After having read the investigation in its whole, another thought to consider is: what is the significance of this investigation with respect to current

Spanish reality? Indeed, there are interconnections that are grounded in the potential for the redefinition of the female subject in contemporary Spain. Of primary significance is the change in the political cycle. On March 14, 2004, just days after a terrorist attack at the central train depot Atocha in downtown Madrid, the results of the elections defied the predictions. The Spanish Socialist Workers Party (PSOE), led by José Luis Rodríguez Zapatero, garnered a majority of seats in the Congress of Deputies. Their win represented a tremendous defeat for the governing People's Party (PP), led into the campaign by Mariano Rajoy and supported by the governing Prime Minister José María Aznar. This abrupt paradigm transformation signals that a new stage has begun, evidenced by Zapatero's announcement of his intention to form a minority PSOE government without a coalition. The results of the elections are remarkable as they demonstrate a prominent increase in electoral participation, especially among the youth, who concentrated their support behind the PSOE leader Zapatero. The electoral outcome also implies a desire among the Spanish society to end authoritarianism and stringent right-wing politics, while opening the potential to recognize the plurality into which Spain has bloomed. The stunning political transformation, ending nearly a decade of the conservative regime at the helm, promises the possibility of real change that undoubtedly will reverberate in the conception of female identity. Indeed there are visible signs of this change, as well as the evolution in women's identity within the past decade within the proxemics of government, multinational, and music, to name a few. The realm of music (producers and musicians) was constructed and dominated by the masculine, and when there appeared a female musician, she was the exception, not the norm. This, however, is changing as more women participate. According to Aguilera, in Spain,

> Las chicas le han entrado al rock de forma masiva y por los canales más marginales. La presencia femenina es especialmente destacada en el escaparate de la música independiente. Desde los sellos pequeños llegan mozas que cantan en inglés o español las variantes del rock y del pop. Abanderadas de este movimiento fueron las hermanas Llanos, núcleo duro del grupo Dover, que creció hasta el punto de ser fichado por una multinacional. (www.elmundo.es/larevista/num177/textos/gentes2.html/)

Explicit in Aguilera's investigation is not only significant female participation in the music world, but also the success female groups attain. On a political level, one only need mention María Teresa Fernández de la Vega, the very first female vice president and minister to the president. Prior to this position, in 1996, she triumphed (along with the first victory of the Partido Popular) as the delegate of Jaén. Her achievements provide motivation and serve to dismantle barriers imposed upon the woman. Women have also effectuated meaningful progress in the business world. According to surveys undertaken by the Instituto de la Mujer, in the third trimester of 2004, 421,900 Spanish women directed large companies and 138,500 Spanish women maintained direction of small businesses with less then ten employees (Encuesta de Población Activa, INE). While these statistics may seem inferior to masculine involvement, nevertheless, they indicate an alteration in ideology and the continued advancements on behalf of the Spanish woman. Taking into consideration these few examples, indeed, the political shift that transpired in March 2004 incarnates the potential to yield many more modifications in the construction of female subjectivity.

While at a paradigm level the political change holds many promises for the recognition of enhanced freedom, this transformation has also reflected at the individual level. During a personal interview with Silvia Grijalba, I posed the question: ¿Cómo es la situación femenina actual en España? In her opinion, this question was of much significance for the construction of female subjectivity in light of the displacement of the PP regime by PSOE. Grijalba responded:

> Pues . . . esta pregunta viene en un momento que para España es bastante favorable porque el nuevo gobierno de Zapatero . . . la mayoría de las ministras son mujeres. Entonces esto está muy bien nunca había ocurrido. La vicepresidenta del gobierno es mujer . . . la mujer se va mejorando. Yo creo que sí se va mejorando. Lo que pasa es que todavía queda muchísimo por luchar. . . . En España tenemos que recordar que tenemos una tradición machista de siglos y siglos. (Personal Interview 2004)

Her comments and observations regarding the propitious political changes are of significance as they highlight the possibilities that are opening for women, ones that offer potential for multiplicity in subjectivity and reject essence. Yet, at the same time Grijalba points to the work that exists for the emancipation of female subjectivity in Spain, a country steeped in a machista tradition.

Similar to the political sphere, on both social and economic levels there also exist many interconnections. As evidenced previously by Ingelhart's investigation of contemporary Spanish social values and also elucidated in Amando de Miguel's sociological research, Spanish society continues to experience many changes that are reflected in the transformation of their social values. As affirmed by both of the aforementioned scholars, the attitude of the Spaniards is becoming more secular as well as much more tolerant. This, in consideration of the economic growth that has occurred in Spain within the last two decades, points towards the need for a re-examination of the identity of woman. Given the inception of the current political cycle in combination with the evolving social values and increasing globalization of Spain, it would be fertile future investigation to explore how the political, economic, and social transformations that are presently occurring (and will continue) serve to further destabilize the natural notion of Woman and open up the future possibility for female plurality.

Bibliography

Aguilera, Ricardo. *El Mundo: La Revista.* www.elmundo.es/larevista/num177/textos/gentes2.html/.

Anderson, Benedict. *Imagined Communities: Reflections on the Origin and Spread of Nationalism.* London: Verso, 1991.

Baudrillard, Jean. *The Consumer Society: Myths and Structures.* London: Sage, 1970.

———. *The Mirror of Production.* St. Louis: Telos Press, 1975.

———. *In the Shadow of the Silent Majorities or the End of the Social and Other Essays.* Trans.

———. *Simulacra and Simulation.* Trans. Sheila Faria Glaser. Ann Arbor: University of Michigan Press, 1994.

Paul Foss, P. Patton, and J. Johnson. New York: Semiotext(e), 1983.

Bauman, Zygmunt. *Postmodern Ethics.* Oxford: Blackwell, 1993.

Baumgardner, Jennifer and Amy Richards. *Manifesta: Young Women, Feminism, and the Future.* New York: Farrar, Straus and Giroux, 2000.

Bedoya, Juan G. "Encuesta Mundial de Valores." www.elpais.com/?d-date=20040630.

Bell, Daniel. *The Coming of Post-Industrial Society: A Venture in Social Forecasting.* New York: Basic, 1973.

Berger, John. *Ways of Seeing.* London: BBC and Penguin, 1972.

Bertens, Hans. *The Idea of the Postmodern.* London: Routledge, 1995.

Best, Steven and D. Kellner. *The Postmodern Turn.* New York: Guilford Press, 1997.

Bey, Hakim. *The Temporary Autonomous Zone, Ontological Anarchy, Poetic Terrorism.* Brooklyn: Autonomedia, 1991.

———. *Hakim Bey.* http://www.hermetic.com/bey/index.html.

Bocock, Robert. *Consumption.* New York: Routledge, 1993.

Bordo, Susan. *Unbearable Weight: Feminism, Western Culture, and the Body.* Berkeley: University of California Press, 1992.
Bourdieu, Pierre. *Distinction: A Social Critique of the Judgment of Taste.* Trans. Richard Nice. Cambridge: Harvard University, 1984.
Bovenschen, Silvia. "Is There a Feminine Aesthetic?" *New German Critique* 10, (1977): 111–37.
Bowlby, Rachel. "The Feminine Female." *Social Text* 7 (1983): 54–68.
———. *Just Looking: Consumer Culture in Dreiser, Gissing, and Zola.* New York: Methuen, 1985.
Braidotti, Rosi. "The Politics of Ontological Difference." *Between Feminism and Psychoanalysis.* Ed. Teresa Brennan. London: Routledge, 1989. Pp. 89–105.
———. *Patterns of Dissonance.* Cambridge: Polity, 1991.
———. *Nomadic Subjects: Embodiment and Sexual Difference in Contemporary Feminist Theory.* New York: Columbia University Press, 1994.
Brooks, Peter. *Body Works: Objects of Desire in Modern Narrative.* Cambridge: Harvard University, 1993.
Bustelo, Gabriela. *Veo, veo.* Barcelona: Editorial Anagrama, 1996.
———. Personal Interview, June 23, 2003.
———. Personal Interview, June 2, 2004.
Butler, Judith. *Bodies That Matter.* New York: Routledge, 1993.
———. *Gender Trouble.* New York: Routledge, 1999.
Calefato, Patrizia. *El sentido del vestir.* Valencia: Instituto de Estudios de Moda y Comunicación, 2002.
Campbell, Colin. *The Romantic Ethic and the Spirit of Modern Consumerism.* Oxford: Blackwell, 1987.
Carroll, Lewis. *Through the Looking Glass.* New York: Signet, 1960.
Cassell, Carol. *Swept Away: Why Women Fear Their Own Sexuality.* New York: Simon & Schuster, 1984.
Chambers, I. *Migrancy, Culture, Identity.* London: Routledge, 1994.
Cixous, Hélène. "The Laugh of Medusa." Trans. K. Cohen. *Signs* 1 (1976): 875–93.
Collin, Matthew. *Altered State: The Story of Ecstasy Culture and Acid House.* London: Serpent's Tail, 1998.
Cortina, Adela. *Por una ética del consumo.* Madrid: Santillana Ediciones Generales, 2002.
Costa, Pere-Oriol, J. Manuel Pérez Tornero, and Fabio Tropea. *Tribus urbanas: El ansia de identidad juvenil: Entre el culto de la imagen y la autoafirmación a través de la violencia.* Barcelona: Paidós, 1996.
De Lauretis, Teresa. "Feminist Studies/Critical Studies: Issues, Terms and Contexts" *Feminist Studies/Critical Studies.* Ed. T. de Lauretis. London: Macmillan, 1986. Pp. 1–20.
———. "Desire in Narrative." *Alice Doesn't: Feminism, Semiotics, Cinema.* Bloomington: Indiana University Press, 1987. Pp. 204–12.
Debord, Guy. *The Society of the Spectacle.* New York: Zone Books, 1994.

Deleuze, Gilles and Félix Guattari. *A Thousand Plateaus: Capitalism and Schizophrenia*. Minneapolis: University of Minnesota Press, 1987.
Derrida, J. and C. V. McDonald. "Choreographies." *Diacritics* 12 (1982): 70–86.
Donskis, Leonidas. *Identity and Freedom: Mapping Nationalism and Social Criticism in Twentieth Century Lithuania*. London: Routledge, 2002.
DuGay, P. *Consumption and Identity at Work*. London: Sage, 1996.
Duggan, Lisa. *Sex Wars: Sexual Dissent and Political Culture*. New York: Routledge, 1995.
Duggan, Lisa, N. Hunter, and C. Vance. "False Promises." FACT Book Committee, *Caught Looking*. New York: Caught Looking, 1986. Pp. 239–41.
Dunn, Robert G. *Identity Crises: A Social Critique of Postmodernity*. Minneapolis: University of Minnesota Press, 1998.
Dworkin, Andrea. *Pornography: Men Possessing Women*. New York: Putnam Books, 1981.
Dworkin Andrea and Catherine MacKinnon. *Pornography and Civil Rights: A New Day for Women's Equality*. Minneapolis: Organizing Against Pornography, 1988. Pp. 138–42.
Dyer, Richard. "In Defence of Disco." *On Record*. Ed. S. Frith and A. Goodwin. London: Pantheon, 1990. Pp. 151–60.
"Encuentros digitales." *El Mundo*. 17 Septiembre 2002. http://www.el-mundo.es/encuentros/invitados/2002/09/508/.
Entwistle, Joan and E. Wilson. *Body Dressing*. London: Berg Publishers, 2001.
Etxebarria, Lucía. *Amor, curiosidad, prozac y dudas*. Barcelona: Plaza & Janes, 1997.
———. *El mundo es así para Lucía Etxebarria*. <http://teleline.terra.es/personal/luciaetx/mundo.htm>.
Ewen, S. and E. Ewen. *Channels of Desire: Mass Images and the Shaping of American Consciousness*. New York: McGraw-Hill, 1982.
Falcón, Lidia. *Los nuevos mitos del feminismo*. Madrid: Vindicación feminista, 2000.
Falk, Pasi. *The Consuming Body*. London: Sage, 1994.
Featherstone, Mike. *Consumer Culture and Postmodernism*. London: Sage, 1991.
———. "The Body in Consumer Culture." *The Body: Social Process and Cultural Theory*. Ed. M. Featherstone, M. Hepworth, and B. Turner. London: Sage, 1991. Pp. 377–89.
Felski, Rita. *Beyond Feminist Aesthetics: Feminine Literature and Social Change*. Cambridge: Harvard University Press, 1989.
———. *Doing Time*. New York: New York University Press, 2000.
Figueras, Josefina. *Moda española: Una historia de sueños y realidades*. Madrid: Ediciones Internacionales Universitarias, 2003.
Finkelstein, Joanne. *The Fashioned Self*. London: Polity Press, 1991.
Fiske, John. *Understanding Popular Culture*. Boston: Unwin Hyman, 1989.
Foucault, Michel. "Technologies of the Self." *Technologies of the Self*. Ed. L. H. Martin and P. H. Hutton. London: Tavistock, 1988.

———. *Power/Knowledge: Selected Interviews and Other Writings, 1972–1977.* Ed. and Trans. C. Gordon. New York: Pantheon Books, c1980.

———. *Discipline and Punishment: The Birth of the Prison.* Trans. A. Sheridan. New York: Vintage Books, 1979.

Frank, Thomas. *The Conquest of Cool: Business Culture, Counterculture, and the Rise of Hip Consumerism.* Chicago: University of Chicago Press, 1997.

———. "The Rebel Consumer." *Commodify Your Dissent.* Ed. T. Frank and M. Weiland. New York: Norton, 1997. Pp. 29–78.

Friedan, Betty. *Feminine Mystique.* New York: Dell Publishing, 1984.

Friedman, J. *Cultural Identity and Global Process.* London: Sage, 1996.

Fuat Firat, A. and N. Dholakia. *Consuming People: From Political Economy to Theaters of Consumption.* London: Routledge, 1998.

Fundación FOESSA. *Informe sociológico sobre la situación social en España.* Madrid: Euroamérica, 1976.

Gallego, María T. *Mujer, falange y franquismo.* Madrid: Taurus, 1983.

Gallero, José Luis. *Sólo se vive una vez: Esplendor y ruina de la movida madrileña.* Madrid: Ardora, 1991.

Gamson, Joshua. *Claims to Fame: Celebrity in Contemporary America.* Berkeley: University of California Press, 1994.

García Nuñez, Anna. *Los placeres de Anastasia.* Barcelona: Aleph, 2004.

Goffman, E. *Behavior in Public Places: Notes on the Social Organization of Gatherings.* New York: Macmillan, 1967.

Golombisky, Kimberly. "Ladies' Home Erotica: Reading the Seams between Homemaking and House Beautiful." *Journal of Magazine and New Media Research* (Spring 1999). http://www.bsu.edu/web/aejmcmagazine/journal/archive/spring-1999/articles.html.

Gottdiener, Mark, ed. *New Forms of Consumption.* Lanham, MD: Rowman & Littlefield, 2000.

Graham, Helen. "Women and Social Change." *Spanish Cultural Studies.* Ed. H. Graham and J. Labayni. New York: Oxford University Press, 1995. Pp. 99–115.

Graham, Helen and Jo Labanyi, eds. *Spanish Cultural Studies.* New York: Oxford University Press, 1995.

Greer, Germaine. *The Whole Woman.* New York: A. Knopf, 1999.

Gregson, N. and L. Crewe. "Beyond the High Street and the Mall: Car Boot Fairs and the New Geographies of Consumption in the 1990s." *Area* 26:3, 1999. Pp. 261–67.

Grijalba, Silvia. *Alivio rápido.* Barcelona: Plaza y Janés, 2002.

———. Personal Interview. May 21, 2004.

Grosz, Elizabeth. *Volatile Bodies: Toward a Corporeal Feminism.* Bloomington, IN: Indiana University Press, 1994.

Haraway, Donna. "A Cyborg Manifesto: Science, Technology and Socialist-Feminism in the Late Twentieth Century." *The Cybercultures Reader.* Ed. D. Bell and B. Kennedy. London: Routledge, 2000. Pp. 283–90.

Harris, Daniel. *The Aesthetics of Consumerism.* New York: Da Capo Press, 2001.

Hassan, Ihab. "Desire and Dissention in the Postmodern Age." *Kenyon Review* 5 (1983): 1–18.
Held, D., A. McGrew, D. Goldblatt, and J. Perraton. *Global Transformations: Politics, Economics and Culture*. Cambridge: Polity Press, 1999.
Hoagland, Sara Lucia. *Lesbian Ethics: Toward New Value*. Chicago: Institute of Lesbian Studies, 1988.
Huxley, Aldous. *Island*. New York: Harper, 1962
Instituto de la Mujer. *El largo camino hacia la igualdad: Feminismo en España 1975–1995*. Ministerio de Asunto Sociales, 1995.
———. *Encuesta de Población Activa*. INE, 2002.
Irigaray, Luce. *This Sex Which is Not One*. Trans. Catherine Porter. Ithaca: Cornell University Press, 1977.
———. *Speculum of the Other Woman*. Trans. Gillian C. Gil. Ithaca: Cornell University Press, 1985.
———. "Women on the Market." *This Sex Which is Not One*. Trans. Catherine Porter. Ithaca: Cornell University, 1985. Pp. 170–91.
Izquierdo, José María. *Narradores españoles novísimos de los años noventa*. http://www.hf.uco.no/kri/spansk/emne/spa1301/textos/sem/ultimanarrativaespizquierdo.pdf.
Jameson, Frederic. *Postmodernism, or The Cultural Logic of Late Capitalism*. Durham: Duke University Press, 1991.
Kaplan, E. A. *Women and Film: Both Sides of the Camera*. New York: Methuen, 1983.
Kellner, Douglas. *Media Culture*. London: Routledge, 1995.
Kumagai, H. "Raving Unity: Exploration of the Raving Community." *Sociology* (1994): 303–31.
Langman, Lauren. "Neon Cages: Shopping for Subjectivity." *Lifestyle Shopping*. Ed. Rob Shields. London: Routledge, 1992. Pp. 40–82.
Larumbe, María Angeles. *Una inmensa nimoría: Influencia y feminismo en la Transición*. Zaragoza: Prensas Universitarias de Zaragoza, 2002.
Leitch, Vincent B. "Costly Compensations: Postmodern Fashion, Politics, and Identity." *Modern Fiction Studies* 42 (Spring 1996): 111–28.
López, Francisca. "Sujeto femenino en contextos de modernidad tardía." *NUI Maynooth Papers in Spanish, Portuguese and Latin American Studies* 7 (2003): 1–23.
Lugones, Maria and E. Spelman. "Have We Got a Theory for You! Feminine Theory, Cultural Imperialism and the Demand for the Woman's Voice." *Women and Values: Readings in Recent Feminist Philosophy*. Ed. M. Pearsall. CA: Wadsworth Press, 1986. Pp. 19–31.
Lurie, Alison. *El lenguaje de la moda*. Barcelona: Paidós Contestos, 1994.
Lury, Celia. *Consumer Culture*. New Brunswick: Rutgers University Press, 1996.
MacKinnon, Catherine. "Sexual Politics of the First Amendment." *Feminism Unmodified*. Cambridge: Harvard University Press, 1987. Pp. 207–13.
———. *Toward a Feminist Theory of State*. Cambridge: Harvard University Press, 1989.
Maffesoli, Michel. *The Time of the Tribes: The Decline of Individualism in Mass Society*. London: Sage Publications, 1995.

Magda, Rosa María Rodríguez. *Feminismo fin de siglo: La seducción de la diferencia*. Barcelona: Icaria, 1994.

Malbon, Ben. "*The Club*: Clubbing: Consumption, Identity and the Spatial Practices of Every-Night Life." *Cool Places: Geographies of Youth Cultures*. Ed. Tracey Skelton and G. Valentine. London: Routledge, 1998. Pp. 266–85.

Mandel, Ernest. *Late Capitalism*. Trans. Joris De Bress. London: Versos, 1999.

Marx, Karl and F. Engels. *Communist Manifesto*. Trans. Sam Moore. Harmondsworth: Penguin, 1967.

———. *Collected Works: Vol. VI*. Trans. Jack Cohen. New York: International Publishers, 1976.

Mauss, Marcel. "Techniques of the Body." *Sociology and Anthropology*. Ed. Levi Strauss. Paris: University of Paris, 1968. Pp. 98–123.

McCracken, Grant. *Culture and Consumption: New Approaches to the Symbolic Character of Consumer Goods and Activities*. Bloomington: Indiana University Press, 1988.

McRobbie, Angela, ed. *Postmodernism and Popular Culture*. London: Routledge, 1994.

———. "Shut up and Dance: Changing Modes of Youth Feminity." *Postmodernism and Popular Culture*. London: Routledge, 1994. Pp. 155–76.

———. *Back to Reality? Social Experience and Cultural Studies*. Manchester: Manchester University Press, 1997.

Miguel, Amando de. *Dos generaciones de jóvenes 1960–1998*. Madrid: Instituto de la Juventud, 2000.

Miller, Daniel, ed. *Acknowledging Consumption: A Review of New Studies*. London: Routledge, 1995.

———. "Introduction: Anthropology, Modernity and Consumption." *Worlds Apart: Modernity Through the Prism of the Local*. Ed. D. Miller. London: Routledge, 1995. Pp. 134–89.

Montrelay, Michele. "Inquiry into Femininity." *m/f* 1 (1978): 83–101.

Mulvey, Laura. "Visual Pleasure and Narrative Cinema." *Visual and Other Pleasures*. Bloomington: Indiana University Press, 1989. Pp. 14–26.

———. *Visual and Other Pleasures: Language, Discourse and Society*. New Hampshire: Macmillan, 1991.

Nabokov, Vladimir. *Lolita*. New York: Vintage Books, 1955.

Nixon, Sean. "Have You Got the Look? Masculinities and Shopping Spectacle." *Lifestyle Shopping*. Ed. Rob Shields. London: Routledge, 1992. Pp. 149–69.

Online Etymology Dictionary. Maintained by Douglas Harper. 17 May 2005. http://etymonline.com.

Oswald, Laura. "The Place and Space of Consumption in a Material World." *Design Issues* 12 (1996): 48–62.

Página homenaje a Sara Montiel. <http://pagina.de/saritisima>.

Pini, Maria. "*Women and the Early British Rave Scene.*" *Back to Reality? Social Experience and Cultural Studies*. Ed. A. McRobbie. Manchester: Manchester University Press, 1997.

Radner, Hilary. "Roaming the City: Proper Women in Improper Places: A Few Thoughts on the Role of Fashion Photography in Feminine Culture." *Spaces of Culture: City/Nation/World*. Ed. Mike Featherstone and Scott M. Lash. London: Sage Press, 1999. Pp. 86–100.

Radway, Janice. *Reading the Romance: Women, Patriarchy, and Popular Literature*. Chapel Hill: University of North Carolina Press, 1984.

Real Academia Española. *Diccionario de la Lengua Española: Vigésima Segunda Edición*. Real Academia Española, 2001.

Requena Santos, Félix, coord. *Sociedad, cultura y desarrollo: Apuntes para un análisis comparado entre España y los Estados Unidos*. Málaga: Universidad de Málaga, 1999.

Riera, J. M. and E. Valenciano. *Las mujeres de los 90: El largo trayecto de las jóvenes hacia su emancipación*. Madrid: Ediciones Morata, 1993.

Riquer i Permanyer, Borja. "Adapting to Social Change." *Spanish Cultural Studies*. Ed. H. Graham and J. Labayni. Oxford: Oxford University Press, 1995. Pp. 259–82.

Rivera, María-Milagros. *Mujeres en relación: Feminismo 1970–2000*. Barcelona: Icaria, 2003.

Rivière, Margarita. *Lo cursi y el poder de la moda*. Madrid: Espasa Calpe, 1992.

Rojek, Chris. *Celebrity*. London: Reaktion Books, 2001.

Ross, Andrew. *No Respect: Intellectuals and Popular Culture*. Routledge: New York, 1989.

Said, Edward. *Orientalism*. New York: Vintage Books, 1979.

Sargisson, Lucy. *Contemporary Feminist Utopianism*. London: Routledge, 1996.

Saunders, N. *Ecstasy and the Dance Culture*. Exeter: BPC Wheatons, 1995.

Scanlon, G. M. *La polémica feminista en la España contemporánea (1968–1974)*. Madrid: Akal, 1986.

Schroeder, Jonathan. "Consuming Representation: A Visual Approach to Consumer Research." *Representing Consumers: Voices, Views, and Visions*. Ed. B. Stern. London: Routledge, 1998. Pp. 193–230.

Segarra, Marta and A. Carabí, eds. *Feminismo y crítica literaria*. Barcelona: Icaria, 2000.

Sendón de León, Victoria. *Marcar las diferencias: Discursos feministas ante un nuevo siglo*. Barcelona: Icaria, 2002.

Shields, Rob. "Spaces for the Subject of Consumption." *Lifestyle Shopping*. Ed. Rob Shields. London: Routledge, 1992. Pp. 1–21.

Silverman, Kaja. "Masochism and Subjectivity." *Framework* 12 (1980): 2–9.

Skeggs, Beverley. "A Good Time for Women Only." *Deconstructing Madonna*. Ed. Fran Lloyd. London: Batsford, 1993. Pp. 271–81.

Sklair, L. *Globalization: Capitalism and Its Alternatives*. Oxford: Oxford University Press, 2002.

Sontag, Susan. "Notes on Camp." *Against Interpretation and Other Essays*. New York: Anchor Books, 1990. Pp. 275–92.

Spelman, Elizabeth. "Woman as Body: Ancient and Contemporary Views." *Feminist Studies* 8.1 (1982): 109–31.

Spink, J. *Leisure and the Environment*. Oxford: Butterworth-Heinemann, 1994.
Stella S. P. "'Rebels without a cause': Male Youth in Italy around 1960." *History Workshop Journal* 38 (1994): 157–78.
Stoltzfus, Ben. *Lacan and Literature: Purloined Pretexts*. New York: State University of New York, 1996.
Storey, John. *Cultural Consumption and Everyday life*. London: Arnold. 1999.
Strathern, Marilyn. *Partial Connections*. Lanham, MD: Rowman & Littlefield, 1991.
Strossen, Nadine. *Defending Pornography: Free Speech, Sex, and the Fight for Women's Rights*. New York: Scribner, 1995.
Sturken, Marita and Lisa Cartwright. *Practices of Looking: An Introduction to Visual Culture*. Oxford: Oxford University Press, 2001.
Suleiman, Susan. *Subversive Intent: Gender, Politics, and the Avant-Garde*. Cambridge: Harvard University Press, 1990.
Svendsen, Mette Nordahl. "The Post-Communist Body: Beauty and Aerobics in Romania." *The Anthropology of East Europe Review* 14(1) (1996): 12–14.
Synnott, Anthony. *The Body Social: Symbolism, Self, and Society*. New York: Routledge, 1993.
Sweetman, Paul. "Shop-Window Dummies? Fashion, the Body, and Emergent Socialities." *Body Dressing*. Eds. J. Entwistle and E. Wilson. Oxford: Berg, 2001.
The Internet Classics Archive: Of the Epidemics, by Hippocrates. Trans. Francis Adams. Maintained by Daniel C. Stevenson, Web Atomics. May 17, 2005. http://classics.mit.edu/Hippocrates/epidemics.1.i.html.
Tucker, Robert C., ed. *The Marx-Engels Reader*. 2nd ed. New York: Norton, 1978.
Turner, Graeme, F. Bonner, and P. D. Marshall, eds. *Fame Games: The Production of Celebrity in Australia*. Cambridge: Cambridge University Press, 2000.
Twitchell, James B. *Lead Us Into Temptation: The Triumph of American Materialism*. New York: Columbia University Press, 1999.
Valiente Fernández, Celia. *El feminismo de estado en España: 1983–1994*. Madrid: El Instituto de la Mujer, 1994.
Van Zoonen, Liesbet. *Feminist Media Studies*. London: Sage, 1994.
VVAA. "«Hablar la Mujer»." *Cuadernos para el diálogo*. Madrid: 1986.
Weedon, Chris. *Feminist Practice and Poststructuralist Theory*. Cambridge: Blackwell, 1987.
Williams, P., P. Hubbard, D. Clark, and N. Berkeley. "Consumption, Exclusion and Emotion: The Social Geographies of Shopping." *Social and Cultural Geography* 2: 203–20.
Willis, Ellen. "Feminism, Moralism, and Pornography." *Powers of Desire: The Politics of Sexuality*. Ed. Ann Snitow, C. Stansell, and S. Thompson. New York: Monthly Review, 1983. Pp. 82–88.
Willis, P. *Profane Culture*. London: Routledge, 1978.
Wilson, Elizabeth. *The Contradictions of Culture: Cities, Culture, Women*. London: Sage, 2001.
Young, Iris Marion. *Throwing Like a Girl and Other Essays in Feminist Philosophy and Social Theory*. Bloomington: Indiana University Press, 1990.

Index

Aguilera, Ricardo, 241
Alivio rápido, 153–96
Amor, curiosidad, prozac y dudas, 67–114
Anderson, Benedict, 7, 15, 23, 52–55, 62–64. *See also* imagined communities
anti-pornography, 209–10, 226–28

Barbie, 192, 203, 216
Baudrillard, Jean, 15, 41–43, 45, 60, 125, 183; cult of celebrity, 163
Bauman, Zygmunt, 36, 132
Baumgardner, Jennifer, 29, 235
Bell, Daniel, 5
Berger, John, 130–31, 146
Bertens, Hans, 5, 26, 138
Best, Steven, 39
Bey, Hakim, 79
Bocock, Robert, 14, 35–37, 60, 169
body dressing. *See* fashion
Bordo, Susan, 50–51, 108
Bourdieau, Pierre, 101
Bovenschen, Silvia, 142
Bowlby, Rachel, 45, 70, 78–79
Braidotti, Rosi, 2–3, 14, 24–30, 45, 68–69, 75–76, 79, 81, 86, 88, 100,110, 129, 133–34, 138, 149, 186–87, 197, 200, 205, 207, 211, 230, 234, 236–37; countermemory, 27; nomad, 2–3, 14, 17, 27–30, 39, 45, 52, 55, 68–70, 76, 79, 110, 129, 132, 138, 140, 150, 156, 174, 186–87, 197, 202, 205, 211, 217; rhizomatic, 187, 190, 212, 239; working through, 27–28
Bustelo, Gabriela, 1–2, 18, 21, 24, 115–20, 122–24, 127, 131, 134, 137, 144, 149, 236–37
Butler, Judith, 97, 118, 141–42, 144

Calefato, Patrizia, 84, 126–27, 203, 212–13, 216
camp, 127–28, 130, 144
celebrity, 161–62
Chambers, I., 140
Cixous, Hélène, 111, 185
Collin, Matthew, 157–59
consumption, 35–55; active, 39; Middle Ages, 38; origin, 10; Spain, 45–49
Cortina, Adela, 38, 44, 48, 54

Costa, Pere-Oriol, 82–84
cyborg, 3, 16–17, 90–93, 98, 155, 178, 239–40

dancing, 3, 79, 134, 136, 138–40, 149, 159, 176–79, 198, 204–6, 216, 214, 234, 237
de Lauretis, Teresa, 88, 146
Deleuze, Gilles, 206–7
Derrida, Jacques, 134
Donskis, Leonidas, 158
drugs, 3, 16, 18, 68, 79, 81, 85–86, 109, 118, 121, 132, 134, 136, 139–40, 150, 158–60, 162, 164, 171–72, 176–78, 181, 236–37
Duggan, Lisa, 229
Dunn, Richard, 117
Dworkin, Andrea, 129, 209, 226–29. See also anti-pornography

ecstasy. See MDMA
Entwistle, Joan, 214
Etxebarria, Lucía, 1, 2, 15–16, 21, 24, 67–68, 70, 72, 89, 99, 110, 112, 115, 235–36, 238
Ewen, Elizabeth, 12, 44
Ewen, Stuart, 12, 44

Falcón, Lidia, 33
fashion, 3, 18, 45, 49–50, 53–54, 68, 71, 75, 80, 82, 84–86, 94, 100, 106, 118, 121, 126–29, 144, 150, 172–73, 183, 193, 198, 212–16, 218–20. See also camp; masquerade
Featherstone, Mike, 37
Felski, Rita, 112
feminismo de la diferencia, 34–35
feminismo de la igualdad, 34–35
femme fatale, 72, 141–42, 144, 173, 218, 221, 237
Figueras, Josefina, 93
Finkelstein, Joanne, 213

Foucault, Michel, 9, 53, 80, 135
Francoism, 2, 46; aperturismo, 47–48; Opus Dei, 49; regime, 31–32
Frank, Thomas, 8
Friedan, Betty, 109
Friedman, J., 156–57
Freud, Sigmund, 25, 124, 145–46

Gamson, Joshua, 166
gaze, 12, 19, 84, 118, 121, 123, 126, 131–33, 140–43, 145–50, 152, 165, 171, 203–5, 209–11, 220–21, 234, 237–38
Goffman, E., 132, 137
go-go girl, 207–8
Golombisky, Kimberly, 107
Gottdiener, Mark, 41, 44, 52
Graham, Helen, 30
Greer, Germaine, 222
Grijalba, Silvia, 1–2, 19, 21, 24, 153–56, 159, 175–76, 180–81, 186, 188, 235–37, 242; *El mundo*, 153; *Imágenes alteradas*, 153
Grosz, Elizabeth, 215
Guattari, Félix, 206

Haraway, Donna, 3, 16–17, 24, 90–93, 98, 100, 155, 178, 187. See also cyborg
Harris, Daniel, 95, 127
Hippocrates, 9
home, 103–5, 107

image. See gaze
imagined communities, 7, 14–15, 23, 36, 52–55, 69, 80, 111
Inglehart, Ronald, 3–4
Irigaray, Luce, 24–26, 28, 75, 149, 168, 171, 174, 201–2

Jameson, Frederic, 5
Jardine, Alice, 28

Kellner, Douglas, 166
Kumagai, H., 158, 179

Lacan, 25, 123–24, 145–46
la movida, 18, 118–19, 121–22, 131–33, 237–38
Langman, Lauren, 104
Larumbe, María Angeles, 33
Lilith, 110–11
Lolita, 200, 208–9, 218–19
López, Francisca, 69, 71, 73, 109
Los placeres de Anastasia, 197–234
Lugones, María, 189
Lurie, Alison, 125
Lury, Celia, 37–38, 146

MacKinnon, Catherine, 209, 226–29
Madonna, 129–30, 204, 220
Maffesoli, Michel, 23, 53–55, 80–81. See also neo-tribes
Malbon, Ben, 122, 132, 134, 136–37, 139
Mandel, Ernest, 6
Marx, Karl, 5, 15, 27, 39–42
masquerade, 126, 131, 141–42, 144, 214, 219–20
Mauss, Marcel, 134
McRobbie, Angela, 49–51
MDMA, 175–76
Miguel, Amando de, 49, 198–99, 242
Miller, Dennis, 156–57
Montrelay, Michele, 142
Mouffe, Chantal, 26
Mulvey, Laura, 145–46, 217

Nabokov, Vladimir, 208. See also Lolita
Navarro, 49
neo-tribes, 15, 23, 53–55, 69, 80, 155

Oswald, Laura, 124

Peeping Tom, 149
performance. See masquerade

Pini, 178–79
Plané, Susana, 1, 2, 21, 24, 197, 199, 235–37
Planeta X, 16, 71, 73, 75, 78–79, 83, 85–86, 93, 96
pornography, 3, 29, 146, 199, 202, 208, 225–30, 234; origin, 225. See also anti-pornography; sex-positive
PP (People's Party), 241
Primo de Rivera, Pilar, 31
PSOE (Spanish Socialist Workers Party), 241
Purcell, Henry, 94, 99, 109

Radway, Janice, 105–6; ideological seams, 105
rave, 75–76, 78–81, 83, 86, 178; techno/rave, 157, 160, 165, 174, 176, 179
Riera, J. M., 31–33, 197–99
Riquer i Permanyer, Borja de, 45–48, 116
Rojek, Chris, 161–63, 167
Russel, Phil, 157

Said, Edward, 159–60
Sargisson, Lucy, 110, 240
Saunders, N., 176
Scanlon, G. M., 31
Sección femenina, 31
Sendón de León, Victoria, 35, 89–90
sex-positive, 221–22, 228–30
Silverman, Kaja, 124
Sklair, L., 11
Spain: Catholic Church, 49; Second Republic, 31; Transition, 33. See also consumption; Francoism
Spanish Feminist Movement, 34
Spelman, Elizabeth, 189
Storey, John, 13

Suleiman, Susan, 134
Sweetman, Paul, 94

techno, 157–60, 178–80;
  commodification, 161. *See also*
  Collin, Matthew
techno-colonization, 96, 98
technology, 3–4, 16–17, 46–48, 63, 73,
  82–83, 90, 92, 93, 95, 99, 116, 122,
  136; music, 158–59, 179
third wave feminism, 24

tuberculosis, 9–10
Twitchell, James, 7, 12–13, 40, 43,
  55

Van Zoonen, Liesbet, 146
Veo, veo, 115–52

Weedon, Chris, 191
Willis, P., 172

Zapatero, José Luis Rodríguez, 241

About the Author

Candice L. Bosse received her PhD in Hispanic Cultural Studies from Michigan State University in 2005. Currently she is visiting assistant professor of Spanish at Bowdoin College in Brunswick, Maine.